Snacks & Canapés

by
THE EDITORS OF TIME-LIFE BOOKS

TIME-LIFE BOOKS·AMSTERDAM

TIME-LIFE BOOKS
EUROPEAN EDITOR: Kit van Tulleken; *Design Director:* Ed Skyner; *Assistant European Editor:* Gillian Moore; *Chief of Research:* Vanessa Kramer; *Chief Sub-Editor:* Ilse Gray

THE GOOD COOK
The original version of this book was created in Alexandria, Virginia for Time-Life Books Inc. under the title *Snacks & Sandwiches.*

U.S. Editorial Staff for *Snacks & Sandwiches: Series Editor:* Gerry Schremp; *Assistant Editor:* Ellen Phillips; *Designer:* Ellen Robling; *Chief Researcher:* Juanita James Wilson; *Picture Editor:* Adrian Allen; *Text Editor:* Robert Menaker; *Staff Writer:* Carol Dana; *Researchers:* Pamela Gould (principal), Cécile Ablack, Christine Bowie Dove, Patricia Kim, Ann Ready, Maria Zacharias; *Assistant Designer:* Peg Hosier Schreiber; *Art Assistant:* Robert K. Herndon; *Editorial Assistant:* Audrey P. Keir; *Special Contributors:* Susan Feller, Randy Houk, Mark Kauffman (text)

European Editorial Staff for *Snacks & Canapés: Series Editor:* Ellen Galford; *Series Co-ordinator:* Liz Timothy; *Text Editors:* Josephine Christian, Jane Havell; *Anthology Editor:* Markie Benet; *Staff Writers:* Sally Crawford, Thom Henvey, Margot Levy; *Researcher:* Suad McCoy (senior); *Designer:* Michael Morey; *Sub-Editors:* Charles Boyle, Kate Cann, Kathy Eason, Sally Rowland; *Anthology Researcher:* Deborah Litton; *Anthology Assistants:* Debra Dick, Stephanie Lee; *Design Assistant:* Sally Curnock; *Proofreader:* Judith Heaton; *Editorial Assistant:* Molly Sutherland

EDITORIAL PRODUCTION FOR THE SERIES
Chief: Ellen Brush; *Quality Control:* Douglas Whitworth; *Traffic Co-ordinators:* Linda Mallett, Helen Whitehorn; *Picture Co-ordinators:* Sarah Dawson, Philip Garner; *Art Department:* Julia West; *Editorial Department:* Theresa John, Lesley Kinahan, Debra Lelliott, Sylvia Wilson

ISBN 0 7054 0607 5

TIME-LIFE is a trademark of Time Incorporated U.S.A.

Cover: An assortment of snacks arranged on a serving dish makes a vividly colourful presentation. Round the edge are squares of flavoured, stacked omelettes; above these are rolled smoked salmon sandwiches and slices from a whole loaf stuffed with steak tartare. The platter is crowned by melon balls wrapped in slices of raw ham and speared with cocktail sticks for serving.

THE CHIEF CONSULTANT:
Richard Olney, an American, has lived and worked since 1951 in France, where he is a highly regarded authority on food and wine. He is the author of *The French Menu Cookbook* and the award-winning *Simple French Food,* and has contributed to numerous gastronomic magazines in France and the United States, including the influential journals *Cuisine et Vins de France* and *La Revue du Vin de France.* He has directed cooking courses in France and the United States and is a member of several distinguished gastronomic and oenological societies, including *L'Académie Internationale du Vin, La Confrérie des Chevaliers du Tastevin* and *La Commanderie du Bontemps de Médoc et des Graves.*

SPECIAL CONSULTANTS:
Pat Alburey, whose experience includes preparing foods for photography and teaching cookery, is responsible for many of the photographic sequences in this volume.
Richard Sax was for two years Chef-Director of the test kitchens for *The International Review of Food and Wine.* Trained in New York and in Paris, he has run a restaurant in America and written articles for a number of publications.

THE PHOTOGRAPHERS:
John Elliott, based in London, trained at the Regent Street Polytechnic. He has extensive experience in photographing a wide range of subjects for advertising and magazine assignments. His special interest is food photography.
Aldo Tutino, a native of Italy, has worked in Milan, New York City and Washington, DC. He has won awards for his photographs from the New York Advertising Club.

THE INTERNATIONAL CONSULTANTS:
Great Britain: *Jane Grigson* was born in Gloucester and brought up in the north of England. She is a graduate of Cambridge University. Her first book on food, *Charcuterie and French Pork Cookery,* was published in 1967; since then, she has published a number of cookery books, including *Good Things, English Food* and *Jane Grigson's Fruit Book.* She became cookery correspondent for the colour magazine of the London *Observer* in 1968. *Alan Davidson* is the author of *Fish and Fish Dishes of Laos, Mediterranean Seafood* and *North Atlantic Seafood.* He is the founder of Prospect Books, which specializes in scholarly publications on food and cookery. **France:** *Michel Lemonnier* was born in Normandy. He began contributing to the magazine *Cuisine et Vins de France* in 1960, and also writes for several other important French food and wine periodicals. The co-founder and vice-president of the society *Les Amitiés Gastronomiques Internationales,* he is a frequent lecturer on wine and a member of most of the vinicultural confraternities and academies in France. **Germany:** *Jochen Kuchenbecker* trained as a chef, but worked for 10 years as a food photographer in many European countries before opening his own restaurant in Hamburg. *Anne Brakemeier,* who also lives in Hamburg, has published articles on food and cooking in many German periodicals. She is the co-author of several cookery books. **Italy:** *Massimo Alberini* divides his time between Milan and Venice. He is a well-known food writer and journalist, with a particular interest in culinary history. Among his books are *4000 Anni a Tavola, 100 Ricette Storiche* and *La Tavola all'Italiana.* **The Netherlands:** *Hugh Jans,* a resident of Amsterdam, has been translating cookery books and articles for more than 25 years. He has also published books of his own, including *Bistro Koken, Vrij Nederlands Kookboek* and *Sla, Slaatjes, Snacks,* and his recipes are published in many Dutch magazines. **The United States:** *Carol Cutler,* who lives in Washington, DC, is the author of a number of cookery books, including the award-winning *The Six-Minute Soufflé and Other Culinary Delights. Julie Dannenbaum* has directed a cooking school in Philadelphia, Pa., for many years and is the author of several cookery books and numerous magazine articles. *Judith Olney* received her culinary training in England and France and has written several cookery books. *Robert Shoffner* has been wine and food editor of the *Washingtonian* magazine since 1975.

Valuable help was given in the preparation of this volume by the following members of Time-Life Books: *Maria Vincenza Aloisi, Joséphine du Brusle* (Paris); *Elisabeth Kraemer* (Bonn); *Ann Natanson, Mimi Murphy* (Rome); *Bona Schmid* (Milan); *Carolyn T. Chubet, Miriam Hsia, Christina Lieberman* (New York).

CONTENTS

Convivial Fare

As is so often the case in culinary matters, the French have the best term for snacks: *amuse-gueule*—that which amuses the palate. The implication is that sustenance takes second place; these are treats to be eaten not as part of a meal but purely for pleasure.

Almost any food can conceivably serve in this role, but some dishes seem especially designed for it. Food that can be held comfortably in the hand is ideal. Bread, serving as a container or platform for fillings, is the basis for a range of snacks from robust sandwiches to the daintiest of canapés. Other snacks may employ hollowed-out vegetables or tender pastry as containers. Small savoury morsels—cubes of meat, for example, or tiny sausages—are most easily served on cocktail sticks.

This book explores the whole range of snack-making. Pages 6-9 introduce two invaluable ingredients: a selection of colourings and flavourings for mixing with butter, and a pair of versatile sauces that can be coloured and flavoured to taste. Four chapters dealing with various sorts of snacks and canapés follow.

The first chapter focuses on a miscellany of simple foods suitable for parties: home-cooked nuts and crisps; a choice of dips and spreads; and savoury morsels such as meat chunks glazed in a rich sauce. The next chapter shows you how to make a variety of assemblies. Natural containers—such as hard-boiled eggs and hollowed vegetables—can be imaginatively filled and decorated; omelettes can be stuffed and flavoured. Pliable ingredients, such as spinach leaves or slices of smoked salmon, can be wrapped round stuffings to make delicious titbits.

A chapter concerned with snacks based on bread and pastry teaches how to make a basic bread dough and four different types of pastry dough. It then explores different ways to use dough: how to shape and fold pastry packages; how to handle fragile phyllo pastry, and how to prepare and cook pastry cases—with or without fillings. The chapter ends by demonstrating how to make the classic Neapolitan snack, pizza.

The final chapter is devoted to sandwiches and canapés—perhaps the most popular of all snack food. The sandwich derives its name from an 18th-century Earl of Sandwich who ate his meat between two slices of bread in order not to be obliged to leave the gaming table. But the basic formula of bread, butter and filling can be varied to produce snacks as different as the refreshing English cucumber sandwiches and the sustaining American double-deckers. The chapter includes delicate rolled sandwiches, colourful combinations of different breads and even constructions using whole loaves. Baked, fried and grilled sandwiches are shown, as well as four pages of ideas for making Scandinavian open sandwiches with a variety of ingredients. The chapter ends with detailed instructions on how to make and decorate delicious small canapés for more formal occasions.

Once you have mastered the principles of producing these snacks, you will be able to improvise countless arrangements and combinations to suit your own fancy. As inspiration, the second half of the book offers an anthology of 252 recipes, selected from the cookery books of 28 countries around the world.

Matching food and drink

Sausages wrapped in crisp pastry, light cucumber sandwiches and small, crusty pastry cones filled with spicy stuffing are delightful treats best appreciated when shared with friends. Like all snacks, they lend themselves to sociable eating—and drinking. In fact, it is often the drinks that determine the atmosphere of the gathering and the food appropriate to it.

Beer, for instance, calls for hearty snacks that complement its robust taste: grilled cheese sandwiches, pizza and spicy sausages. The subtle flavour of tea, by contrast, is traditionally set off by buttery sandwiches with a mild filling, such as cucumber. Delicate, ornamental canapés can be served with a variety of light wines—champagne is the perfect accompaniment.

When the beverage is assertively alcoholic and the group of friends is large, snacks usually increase in number and variety. Cocktail parties—or their equivalent—exist in almost every country. In Spain, for instance, as many as 30 different snacks may be presented to accompany chilled dry sherry and wine. Served late in the evening, the snacks are known as *tapas*, or "lids", after the bread slices that were once laid on top of wine glasses to discourage flies. Greeks serve a similar variety of light foods—known as *meze*—with ouzo, an anise-flavoured aperitif. In Denmark, arrays of open sandwiches—*smørrebrød*—accompany chilled lager or aquavit; the Russian version is called *zakuski*, and is, not surprisingly, served with a choice of vodkas.

The making of snacks

As a rule, snacks are founded on simple ingredients and cooking techniques. It is the cook's imaginative, light-hearted approach to the preparation and presentation of ingredients that turns the food into a culinary diversion, whether the occasion is a party for a hundred people, a gathering of a few good friends, or tea for two. Freshly salted, toasted almonds and crisps are easy to make; when more filling snacks are called for, a pizza or a club sandwich can provide a meal in itself. And you need only take a little extra trouble to transform such simple ingredients as toast, butter and sliced meat into the most elegant of canapés. Remember that, with many of these creations, you have the opportunity to delight the eye as well as to satisfy and amuse the palate.

Varying the Character of Butter

Butter is an indispensable element in the assembly of snacks and canapés. Used on its own, it adds richness and seals bread against sogginess. Made into a compound butter by the addition of herbs, vegetables, meat, fish or cheese (*recipes, page 167*), it transforms bread, crackers or raw vegetables into snacks of distinction.

For the best flavour, butter should always be fresh and unsalted, and if it is to be blended with another ingredient it must be soft. Warming cold butter would melt it; instead, it should be left to stand at room temperature. If time is short, cold butter can be beaten with a rolling pin to make it pliable. If you like, cream the butter with a wooden spoon or an electric beater to make it soft and fluffy.

Almost any food can be used to flavour butter, but it must first be chopped finely, puréed or pounded. The mixture may be pressed through a fine sieve to smooth it and thoroughly amalgamate all the elements. Once sieved, it can be beaten again, to fluff up the butter and mix the ingredients even more thoroughly.

You can blend butter with a single ingredient, such as anchovies or saffron dissolved in a little hot water, or experiment with more elaborate combinations, such as the pungent mixture of anchovies, black olives, capers and other flavourings known as *tapenade* (*right*). Use a processor, as here, or a mortar and pestle to purée the ingredients.

Fresh herbs, spinach and watercress produce delicately flavoured pale green butters; you can use them alone or, for a more distinctive flavour, combine them with anchovies, garlic, capers, gherkins, shallots, hard-boiled egg yolks and oil to create Montpellier butter (*opposite page, above*). Strongly flavoured blue cheeses, such as Roquefort or Stilton, marry well with butter (*opposite page, below left*). Puréed sweet red peppers will contribute their characteristic flavour and colour to a butter (*opposite page, below right*).

Compound butters may be applied in many different ways—you can use them simply as a spread on bread or crackers, as a filling for vegetable containers (*page 38*) or as a decoration for small pastry cases (*page 58*) or canapés (*pages 80-86*).

Tapenade Butter: Piquancy from Olives and Anchovies

1 **Boning anchovies.** Soak salt anchovies in cold water for a few minutes to soften them and reduce their saltiness. Split each anchovy lengthwise and pull away the backbone (*above*). Rinse the fillets; dry them on paper towels.

2 **Making a purée.** Using a small knife and your fingers, remove the stones from wrinkled black olives. Place the olives and anchovies in a food processor with capers, mustard, lemon juice, brandy and pepper; purée thoroughly.

3 **Adding oil.** Dribble olive oil into the purée, while continuing to process the paste. Check the consistency and the flavour: the paste should be moist but not runny. Transfer it to a jar and cover with a layer of oil; it will keep for several months.

4 **Blending tapenade and butter.** With a pestle, pound softened butter and a spoonful of *tapenade* in a mortar. Blend thoroughly. Taste the mixture; add more *tapenade* if you want a stronger flavour.

5 **Sieving.** With a plastic scraper, press a spoonful of the mixture through a fine-meshed drum sieve. Scrape the spread from the underside of the sieve into a bowl. Discard any debris caught in the mesh before sieving the next spoonful.

6 **Completing the spread.** If you like, fluff up the sieved butter with a fork—it should be smooth and creamy. The butter can be covered with plastic film and stored in the refrigerator for four to five days.

Montpellier Butter: a Vibrant Amalgamation

1 **Blanching vegetable leaves.** Wash and stem spinach, watercress, parsley and tarragon. Blanch the leaves in a pan of boiling salted water for 2 minutes. Drain, rinse under the cold tap and squeeze them dry. Put the leaves aside.

2 **Combining flavourings.** Peel shallots; chop them finely. Parboil, drain and squeeze them dry. Place soaked and filleted anchovies, chopped gherkins, capers, garlic and a little coarse salt in a mortar; add the shallots (*above*).

3 **Pounding the ingredients.** Pound the flavourings with a pestle; add the leaves and pound again. Add hard-boiled egg yolks (*above*), pounding them well, and softened butter. Pound again to blend all the ingredients thoroughly.

4 **Sieving.** With a plastic scraper, press the mixture through a drum sieve, a spoonful at a time. Scrape the butter from the underside of the sieve into a bowl and discard any fibres left in the mesh.

5 **Incorporating oil.** Whisk the butter. Cut V-shaped openings on opposite sides of a cork and dribble olive oil into the butter, whisking continuously.

6 **Finishing the butter.** Add more olive oil until the texture is smooth and glossy. If the butter is not required immediately, cover the bowl and refrigerate it. Whisk the mixture again before using it.

A Tangy Blend of Cheese and Butter

Pounding cheese and butter. Place soft, strong-flavoured blue cheese—here, Roquefort—in a mortar with softened butter. Pound with a pestle to blend thoroughly; press the mixture through a drum sieve with a plastic scraper. Place the sieved paste in a bowl and whisk with a metal whisk until fluffy.

Capturing the Essence of Red Peppers

Peeling sweet red peppers. Roast peppers in a hot oven or grill them on all sides until the skins blister. Cover them with a damp towel—this creates steam to help loosen the skins. When they are cool enough to handle, peel them with your fingers (*above, left*). Twist off the stems; remove seeds and pith. Push the flesh through a sieve with a pestle; add it to softened butter and sieve the spread.

Versatile Sauces

Thickened sauces that contain oil are among the cook's most useful aids in the manufacture of snacks and canapés: they can serve as dips, spreads, garnishes and fillings for assemblies.

The most familiar oil-based sauce is mayonnaise (*right; recipe, page 167*), a smooth emulsion of oil and egg yolks, flavoured with vinegar or lemon juice. Instead of egg yolks, an emulsified sauce may rely for its thickening on the flesh of cooked potatoes, mashed to a purée with garlic (*right, below; recipe, page 89*).

The rules for forming the emulsion are the same for both sauces. If the ingredients are chilled they will not combine easily. Oil, egg yolks and flavourings should be at room temperature. Potatoes should be freshly cooked and still warm. For both the sauces, the oil must be added very gradually to the thickening agents; otherwise, they will not absorb it.

For the mayonnaise, allow up to 17.5 cl (6 fl oz) of oil to each egg yolk. If the yolks and oil do not emulsify, but separate or "break", you can restore the sauce by beating a fresh yolk in a clean bowl and then, very gradually, whisking in the separated sauce. Mayonnaise lends itself to a variety of additional flavourings. Puréed garlic or mustard mixed with egg yolks will add pungency. For a milder effect, add chopped herbs or spring onions.

For the potato and garlic sauce, choose one of the waxy varieties of potato—their sticky and slightly elastic flesh creates a surer emulsion with the oil than floury potatoes. The puréed potatoes and garlic will absorb up to their own volume of oil. Lemon juice or vinegar and seasonings offset the oil's richness. You can vary the flavour of the sauce by adding ground pine-nuts or walnuts to the potatoes.

Both these sauces, once prepared, can be coloured as well as flavoured with vegetable juices or purées. Thick purées can be made from tomatoes (*right, centre*) or sweet red peppers. To make a colouring of green or gold, prepare raw spinach juice (*opposite page, centre*) or dissolve saffron in a little warm water.

A Smooth Emulsion of Oil and Egg Yolks

1 **Separating eggs.** Over a small bowl, break each egg on to the closed fingers of one hand; let the white drain through your fingers. Put the yolks in a mixing bowl steadied on a dampened towel.

2 **Whisking yolks.** Squeeze fresh lemon juice. Add salt to the yolks and whisk them until they are smooth and have become paler in colour. Pour the lemon juice into the bowl, whisking briskly.

A Rosy Red from Tomatoes

1 **Making a tomato purée.** Strain canned tomatoes and sieve them into a pan. Over a medium heat, stir the purée until it thickens; reduce the heat and stir until the purée has reduced to a thick paste.

2 **Colouring sauce.** Allow the purée to cool to prevent it from curdling the sauce. A spoonful at a time, stir it into the sauce—here, mayonnaise—to achieve the intensity of colour you want.

A Potato Thickening for a Garlicky Sauce

1 **Preparing potatoes and garlic.** In a mortar, pound garlic cloves and coarse salt. Boil potatoes until tender; drain and peel them. Add them to the mortar while they are still warm (*above*).

2 **Puréeing the mixture.** With a pestle, crush the potatoes and mix them with the garlic paste. Pound the mixture until it is smooth and elastic (*above*).

3 **Adding oil.** Begin to add the oil slowly, drop by drop (*above, left*), whisking constantly. When the sauce begins to thicken, let the oil flow in a continuous thread (*above, centre*). Increase the flow of oil gradually to a steady stream, continuing to whisk as the mayonnaise thickens further (*above, right*).

4 **Finishing the sauce.** The mayonnaise is ready when it is thick enough to form soft peaks. Store the sauce, covered, in a cool place for up to three days.

A Strong Green from Spinach

1 **Pounding spinach.** Stem, rinse and dry spinach leaves. Pound the leaves to a pulp in a mortar. Over a small bowl, set a large square of double-thickness muslin. Transfer the spinach to the muslin.

2 **Extracting juice.** Bring opposite edges of the muslin together and fold the ends to enclose the spinach. Grasp both ends of the package and twist them in opposite directions to squeeze out the juice.

3 **Colouring sauce.** To colour mayonnaise a delicate green, add the spinach juice a spoonful at a time; stir in each spoonful of the juice before adding more until the mayonnaise is the shade you want.

3 **Stirring in oil.** Add oil drop by drop, stirring the mixture all the time with the pestle (*above*). If the mixture becomes unmanageably thick, add a few drops of lemon juice. Beat the sauce vigorously.

4 **Adding lemon juice.** Continue to add oil until the potato mixture is glossy. To flavour the sauce, add freshly squeezed lemon juice (*above*).

5 **Finishing the sauce.** Use the pestle to mix in the lemon juice; taste and add more juice if necessary. Cover the sauce and serve it within a few hours.

1
Simple Party Food
A Repertoire of Festive Treats

The first serving is taken from a decorated mound of cheese spread shaped like a cake. It is composed of a variety of hard, semi-soft and soft cheeses that have been grated or mashed to a paste and blended with fresh white cheese and softened butter. The mixture, flavoured with brandy, has been garnished with chopped nuts and finely chopped parsley.

One of the most important requirements for a successful party is a generous supply of snacks that are easy to prepare and effortless to consume. Such foods should not compel guests to perform balancing acts with plates and cutlery in a crowded room; they are, for the most part, finger food—salted nuts that are picked up by the handful, creamy dips scooped up with raw vegetables, small biscuits spread with savoury pastes and chunks of meat or seafood skewered with cocktail sticks.

The snacks best suited to this purpose are usually based on a single ingredient. Some are items that are more commonly purchased than made at home—but you will be surprised to discover how easy it is to prepare salted nuts (*page 12*), crisps in a variety of unusual shapes (*page 14*) and spicy miniature sausages (*page 16*), all of which are superior in every way to their ready-made commercial counterparts.

A single distinctively flavoured ingredient—such as cheese, cooked meat or seafood—that has been mashed to a paste or reduced to a purée, will provide the basis for a dip or a spread (*pages 18-23*). The only difference between the two is in their consistency: the basic mixture can either be diluted with cream to yield a thick but pourable dip, or it can be blended with butter to form a more substantial spread. Dips and spreads, such as the buttery chicken liver spread shown on page 20 and the rose-pink crayfish dip shown on page 22, are good ways to extend a small quantity of highly flavoured ingredients. These mixtures are also an excellent means of using up leftovers: the impressive-looking cheese mound shown opposite and on page 18, for example, can be made from any odds and ends of cheese that you have on hand.

Somewhat more elaborate in execution are bite-sized morsels of meat, poultry or seafood, swathed in a rich glaze derived from the liquid they were cooked in (*pages 24-27*). This is a particularly attractive way of presenting an assortment of delicacies—small cubes of sautéed veal, pieces of squid flavoured with brandy, prawn tails quickly cooked with shallots and white wine—all conveniently speared with cocktail sticks and liable to disappear from their serving plate with gratifying speed.

Salted Nuts: Sociable Staples

The crisp texture and flavour of freshly cooked nuts makes them one of the most popular of all snack foods. Any type of nut that is easily shelled and skinned can be prepared at home: cashew nuts, hazelnuts, walnuts and Brazil nuts, for example, as well as the peanuts and almonds that are shown here.

The preliminary shelling of most types of nuts is a simple task quickly carried out by hand or with a nutcracker. Once the nuts have been shelled, the kernels are blanched. To loosen their fibrous skins, parboil them or soak them for half an hour in hot water. You can then peel the skin off each nut with your fingers or, for quicker results, roll the nuts gently between two towels to rub off their skins.

After skinning, the nuts are ready to be cooked—either by sautéing in hot oil (*right; recipe, page 105*), or, more slowly, by roasting in a low oven (*right, below; recipe, page 105*). To bring out the nuts' own flavour, choose a light, flavourless oil for frying, such as groundnut oil. Alternatively, you can impart a distinctive taste to the nuts by cooking them in an oil that has an assertive flavour of its own, such as olive or almond oil. If you are roasting the nuts, butter or oil the baking sheet very lightly, or sprinkle a tiny amount of oil over the nuts: the oven's heat will draw out the nuts' natural oils.

The traditional seasoning for nuts is salt. You can dissolve a little salt in the water used to soak or parboil the nuts, and, if you like, flavour them with garlic at the same time (*Step 2, right, above*). For a more pronounced effect, the nuts can be sprinkled with coarse salt directly after cooking, while they are still warm, then left for about 5 hours to absorb it.

To be enjoyed at their best, the nuts should be eaten as soon as possible after they are prepared, but they can be kept for up to two weeks in airtight containers.

Coating Peanuts with a Golden Sheen

1 **Shelling peanuts.** Using your fingers, squeeze the shells to split them along their ridged seams (*above*). Prise open the shells and extract the kernels. Put the kernels in a bowl and discard the shells.

2 **Softening the skins.** Pour into the bowl enough boiling water to cover the peanut kernels. Lightly crush a couple of garlic cloves and add them to the water. Add a teaspoon of fine salt. Cover the bowl with a lid; let the kernels soak for 30 minutes. Drain them in a colander (*above*).

Enhancing the Flavour of Almonds

1 **Parboiling almonds.** Bring a pan of water to the boil. Put almonds into the pan. Let the water come back to the boil; remove the pan from the heat. Strain the nuts and turn them out on to a towel.

2 **Rubbing off the skins.** Spread a second towel over the nuts. Using the palms of your hands, rub the nuts between the towels. When most of the skins have separated from the kernels, pick out the skinned kernels and place them on a buttered baking sheet (*above*). Rub the remaining nuts between your thumb and forefinger to remove the skins.

3 **Removing the skins.** Lay a towel on the work surface and spread the kernels on it. Cover the kernels with a second towel. Using the palms of your hands, gently roll the kernels between the towels (*above*): in a short time most of the kernels will have shed their skins. Remove any skins that remain by rubbing the nuts between your thumb and forefinger.

4 **Frying peanuts.** Pour oil into a frying pan to a depth of about 1 cm (½ inch). Heat the oil gently; do not let it smoke. Sauté the nuts in the oil in small batches, stirring them occasionally, until they take on a golden colour (*above*)—about 5 minutes. With a slotted spoon, remove the nuts from the pan and drain them on absorbent paper. Let them cool for a few minutes, then pour them into a bowl for serving (*inset*).□

3 **Roasting the almonds.** Preheat the oven to 150°C (300°F or Mark 2). Roast the nuts in the oven for about 45 minutes; shake the tray once or twice during cooking so that the nuts roast evenly. Lay a sheet of greaseproof paper on the work surface and sprinkle it with a generous amount of coarse salt. Pour the roasted almonds on to the greaseproof paper (*above*).

4 **Salting the almonds.** Twist the corners of the greaseproof paper together to enclose the nuts. Shake the parcel to distribute the salt evenly; leave the nuts for about 5 hours to absorb salt. Unwrap the parcel. A handful at a time, shake the nuts gently, allowing excess salt to fall through your fingers (*above*). Serve them lightly sprinkled with cayenne pepper (*inset*).□

Making Your Own Crisps

Crisps are a perennial favourite at parties, and those prepared at home are far superior to their commercially produced counterparts. They may be made from either potatoes (*right*) or the more unusual green plantain, a member of the banana family (*right, below*). Cut to an unvarying thickness, both the potatoes and green plantains will become evenly golden and crunchy when deep fried for a minute or two in very hot oil.

Potatoes, once peeled, should be immersed in cold water to prevent them from discolouring through exposure to air. Then they may be cut into a variety of shapes. Here, they are passed through a rotary shredder to form shoestrings (*Step 1, right*), but they could also be pared into curls with a vegetable peeler, or sliced into paper-thin sheets, either plain or waffled, on a mandoline.

After they are cut, potatoes should be rinsed in cold water to remove some of their surface starch, and then thoroughly dried to eliminate any droplets of moisture that would splutter on contact with the hot oil. Shoestrings can simply be rolled in a towel and squeezed free of moisture; thin rounds or curls should be gently patted dry with a towel to prevent them from breaking.

Plantains are best sliced into thin rounds. The fruit has a thick, tough peel that is removed by slitting the skin with a knife, then lifting up sections of peel one by one with the handle of a spoon—use a stainless steel one, since other metals will discolour the flesh. The plantain exudes a gummy starch; it will be easier to peel and cut if the spoon handle and the knife used for slicing are lightly coated with oil to prevent them from sticking. Keep the rounds in salted water, which gives them a finer flavour and prevents discoloration until all the fruit is sliced. Dry the slices by patting them between two towels.

You can use any unblended vegetable oil for deep frying; groundnut oil is a good choice because of its mild flavour. After frying, both potatoes and green plantains should be drained of excess oil. Unlike the potatoes, the plantains will not remain crisp for very long after frying, so they should be consumed as soon as possible.

Crunchy Potato Shoestrings

1 **Preparing the potatoes.** Peel potatoes and put them in a bowl of water to prevent discoloration. Cut the peeled potatoes into pieces that will fit into the bowl of a rotary shredder. Pass the pieces through the shredder to make potato shoestrings (*above*). Put all the shoestrings into a bowl of cold water.

2 **Drying the shoestrings.** Drain the potato shoestrings in a sieve, then spread the drained shoestrings down the middle section of a towel, leaving space on both sides of the towel uncovered. Fold the uncovered sections of the towel over the potato shoestrings. Roll the towel tightly to squeeze out moisture (*above*).

Golden Wafers of Plantain

1 **Removing the peel.** With a stainless steel knife, top and tail plantains. Taking care not to pierce the flesh inside, slit the skin of each plantain lengthwise into quarters. Then slit the skin crosswise into sections about 5 cm (2 inches) long. Dip the handle of a spoon into oil, then use it to lift off the slit peel piece by piece (*above*).

2 **Slicing the plantain.** Smear a light film of oil over each peeled plantain and on the blade of a steel knife. Slice each plantain into paper-thin rounds; alternatively, use the slicing face of a stainless steel grater, or a mandoline. Put the slices into a bowl of well-salted water—1 tablespoon of salt per litre (1¾ pints) of water.

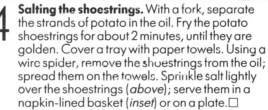

3 **Frying the shoestrings.** Pour enough oil to fill two-thirds of a frying pan. Heat the oil to a temperature of 190°C (375°F). Test the temperature with a thermometer, or drop a small piece of potato into the pan—if it sizzles immediately, the oil is hot enough to use. Immerse the shoestrings in batches in the hot oil (*above*).

4 **Salting the shoestrings.** With a fork, separate the strands of potato in the oil. Fry the potato shoestrings for about 2 minutes, until they are golden. Cover a tray with paper towels. Using a wire spider, remove the shoestrings from the oil; spread them on the towels. Sprinkle salt lightly over the shoestrings (*above*); serve them in a napkin-lined basket (*inset*) or on a plate.□

3 **Drying the slices.** Spread a towel on a work surface. With both hands, scoop the plantain slices out of the bowl of water and distribute them on the towel. Use a second towel to pat them dry.

4 **Frying the plantain.** Heat oil in a frying pan. Put the slices into the hot oil in batches. Allow the slices to cook for 1 to 2 minutes until they are crisp and golden; they cook very quickly and should be watched constantly. With a wire spider, lift the crisp slices out of the pan and place them on a tray lined with a towel to drain (*above*). Serve the slices immediately—in a basket (*inset*) or on a large plate.□

Transforming Minced Meat into Spicy Snacks

Tiny Sausages Crisply Browned

The versatility of minced meat makes it an ideal ingredient for substantial savoury snacks. Beef, lamb or pork can be cooked and served as tiny meat balls or used to fill bread or pastry cases, or sausage casings (*right*). Beef can be seasoned with herbs and flavourings and served raw (*opposite page, below*).

If the meat is used to make sausages, combine it with pork fat to keep it moist and to add flavour, allowing about half as much fat as lean meat. Beef to be served raw must be very fresh, lean and tender; it must be trimmed of every scrap of fat or connective tissue before it is chopped.

There are three methods of chopping meat. For the best results, chop it by hand, using two heavy chef's knives of equal size and weight (*Step 1, opposite page*). For quickness and convenience, however, you can use a meat grinder (*Step 2, right*) or a food processor. These give a drier result and should only be used if the meat is to be mixed with fat and cooked. Beef to be eaten raw must be chopped by hand, since this method will keep its fibres intact and retain all its natural juiciness.

The meat for sausage fillings can be chopped to an even fineness or, to create an interesting texture, some of the meat can be chopped coarsely and some finely. If you like, flavour the mixture with fresh or dried herbs, crushed garlic, spices, or a little wine or brandy. Meat to be served raw should be chopped evenly and finely and is best balanced by piquant flavourings such as the chopped anchovy fillets, gherkins, capers and shallots used here.

For the sausages, use natural casings, such as lamb's intestines or pig's small intestines. These are preserved in brine or dry-salted; they have to be soaked and cleaned before use. If your meat grinder is fitted with a sausage-making attachment, you will be able to fill the casings speedily. But you can also press the mixture into the casings through a funnel or through the nozzle of a piping bag.

For the freshest flavour, beef to be eaten raw should be chopped and seasoned just before serving; however, it may be kept, covered, for up to half an hour in a refrigerator. To serve the beef, shape it into tiny balls or use it on canapés or in sandwiches (*recipe, page 160*).

1 Soaking casings. Rinse sausage casings—here, lamb's casings are used—then put them to soak in cold water (*above*), adding 2 to 3 tablespoons of vinegar for every litre (1¾ pints) of water to remove any odour. When they are soft—after about 30 minutes—hold each casing with one end open under a tap and rinse it thoroughly with cold water.

2 Mincing meat. Weigh out the meat: two parts lean to one part fat. Trim off all connective tissue from the lean meat with a sharp knife; cut both lean and fat into small cubes. Pass all the meat through the medium blade of a meat grinder (*above*). Put the minced meat in a bowl and mix in seasonings—in this case, salt, pepper and mixed dried herbs.

6 Baking the sausages. Prick each sausage with a trussing needle or fine skewer; lay the joined links on an oiled baking sheet. Sprinkle them with oil and bake them in a preheated 180°C (350°F or Mark 4) oven for about 30 minutes, turning them occasionally. Lift them on to a chopping board (*inset, above*); cut the links with a knife. Serve the sausages hot, speared with cocktail sticks.□

3 **Attaching the casing.** Fit a sausage-making attachment to the meat grinder. Slide about 1 metre (1 yard) of casing over the nozzle (*above*), leaving 5 cm (2 inches) loose at the end. Alternatively, to fill the casings by hand, ease the casing over the neck of a narrow funnel or the nozzle of a piping bag.

4 **Filling the casings.** If you are using a sausage-making attachment, place the mixture in the bowl of the grinder. Turn the handle so that the stuffing gradually fills the casing, guide the casing off the nozzle as it fills (*above*). Alternatively, use a pestle to push the mixture through the neck of the funnel into the sausage casing, or squeeze the piping bag.

5 **Forming links.** When the casing is filled, detach it from the nozzle or funnel and knot both ends. Roll the sausage on a table to spread the filling evenly. At intervals of about 4 cm (1½ inches), twist the casing through one full turn to form individual sausages. Twist the successive links in opposite directions so that the casing does not become untwisted.

Juicy Raw Steak Shaped into Balls

1 **Mincing beef.** Trim all fat and gristle from lean beef—here, rump steak. Cut the beef into small dice. Using two heavy, sharp knives of matched weight and size, begin to chop the meat slowly. When the meat clings together in a mass, increase the chopping speed; use a rhythmic action and let the knives fall alternately. Continue until the beef is finely minced.

2 **Adding seasoning.** Soak and fillet salt anchovies (*page 6*); chop them finely. Finely chop gherkins, capers, shallots and parsley; put them in a bowl with the minced beef. Add pepper, a little salt, a few drops of olive oil and egg yolks—use about two egg yolks to every 500 g (1 lb) of meat. Combine all the meat and seasonings thoroughly with your hands.

3 **Shaping balls.** Taste the mixture and add more seasoning if necessary. Taking a teaspoonful at a time, roll the meat between the palms of your hands into small balls (*above*). Place them on a tray as you work; transfer the finished balls to a dish for serving.□

New Incarnations for Cheeses

Fresh white cheeses, such as curd cheese and cream cheese, are excellent bases for dips and spreads. To make a thick but liquid dip, they can be diluted with cream (*right*); to achieve the firmer consistency of a spread, they can be blended with other cheeses and butter (*below*).

For the dip shown here, cream cheese and *ricotta* are whisked together with cream to make them light and fluffy. To offset the mildness of these ingredients, you can mix in flavourings: cayenne pepper, salt and pepper, and finely chopped fresh herbs are added in this case, but you could also use caraway seeds, chopped spring onions, or a splash of sherry or of brandy (*recipes, pages 93-95*). The dip can be scooped up with crisps, crackers or sticks of fresh vegetables.

To create a spread, you can combine white cheeses with any other cheese you have to hand. Hard cheeses such as Cheddar and Emmenthal, blue cheeses such as Stilton and Gorgonzola, and soft cheeses such as Brie and Camembert—even if past their prime—can all be incorporated.

The cheeses for a spread must first be made malleable enough to blend into a paste. Soft cheeses can be mashed with a fork; hard ones should be grated with a hand grater or in a food processor. Some soft cheeses harden with age and may require grating. The prepared cheeses are then bound with fresh white cheese and softened butter and, in this case, they are flavoured with black pepper and brandy.

Cheese spreads may be packed into earthenware pots and served from them. Or, for a striking presentation, spreads that include a high proportion of butter can be moulded into cake-like mounds of any size—the butter ensures that the mixture will hold its shape when chilled.

Coatings of grated, ground or chopped ingredients will give the mounds a handsome surface and you can create a formal design with the aid of paper templates (*Steps 4 and 5*). The large mound that is shown here, is covered with alternating triangles of chopped nuts and parsley, but you could also use other chopped herbs, cracked black peppercorns or paprika.

A Fluffy Dip Flecked with Herbs

1 **Adding cream to cheese.** Mix together cream cheese and curd cheese—*ricotta* is used here. Pour in a little double cream (*above*) and whisk well. Season with salt, pepper and a little cayenne pepper. Add more cream, whisking again, until the mixture is moist and light but still firm enough to hold its shape.

A Sculpted Mound Fancifully Garnished

1 **Assembling the cheeses.** Pare the rind from hard and soft cheeses; cut away any mould. Mash soft cheese with a fork (*above*); grate hard pieces with a hand grater or in a food processor. Mix the mashed or grated cheese with some fresh cheese—in this case, *ricotta*, cream cheese and Saint-Marcellin.

2 **Kneading.** Add softened butter to the cheeses—allow one part butter for every four or five parts cheese depending on how much fresh cheese is used. Grind black pepper over the mixture, add a little cayenne pepper and pour in a splash of brandy. Knead the mixture thoroughly by hand into a firm paste (*above*).

3 **Forming the mound.** Spoon some paste on to a round wooden board, mashing it down to the edges. Distribute more paste evenly, pressing it down with a spoon to fill any gaps. With an oiled spatula or rounded knife, smooth the top and sides to create a cake-like shape. Refrigerate for at least 2 hours or until firm.

2 Flavouring with herbs. Wash fresh herbs such as parsley, tarragon, chervil and chives; dry them thoroughly. Chop the herbs and sprinkle them into the cheese mixture (*above*). Whisk again, adding more herbs and seasoning to taste.

3 Serving the dip. Spoon the dip on to a shallow dish. Prepare vegetables—peel carrots and cucumbers; trim and string celery hearts. Cut them into finger-length sticks; soak in iced water for 30 minutes to crisp them; drain, and place them in the dip. □

4 Covering with paper templates. Cut a circle of greaseproof paper the size of the board and fold it into eighths. Cut the paper into eight pieces along the folds and cover four alternate areas of the top of the mound. Cut paper rectangles the height of the cake to fit round the sides below the uncovered top surfaces.

5 Making the design. Chop parsley finely with a sharp knife. Sprinkle it thickly over the uncovered areas of the surface and the sides of the cake, pressing it gently and repeatedly to make it adhere. Lift off the paper carefully, leaving the exposed areas of the cake ready for a decoration of a contrasting colour and texture.

6 Completing the design. Chop roasted nuts coarsely—almonds are used here; walnuts or hazelnuts are also suitable. Spread the nuts evenly over the exposed surfaces, pressing them down with a small knife. If you like, serve the mound surrounded with triangles of toast. □

Savoury Spreads from Pounded Meats

Many sorts of meat, fish, seafood and game can be blended with butter into smooth spreads to be served with bread, crackers or toast. Butter is a neutral medium that binds the spreads; it enhances but does not obscure the distinctive flavour of the main ingredient.

Any meats used for a spread must be very tender. Long poaching is necessary to soften the ox tongue in the demonstration on the right (*recipe, page 98*). By contrast, the chicken livers in the demonstration below, right (*recipe, page 96*), need only quick sautéing. They must not be overcooked, lest they become bitter in flavour and granular in texture.

To make it spreadable, the flesh must be broken down into small particles. Depending on its texture, it may be mashed, minced, pounded with a pestle in a mortar, or—for ease and speed—puréed in an electric processor. It is best to work with a small quantity at a time, to ensure that the substance is thoroughly reduced to the desired consistency.

After puréeing, the main ingredient is blended with softened butter. This too can be done in a processor, working with small batches to ensure that the butter is evenly distributed. Then, for a particularly fine texture, press the spread through a sieve (*Step 4, opposite page, below*).

Spreads that are prepared days—or weeks—in advance of serving should be made with butter that has been clarified (*Step 2, above*). The clarifying process removes milk solids and helps the butter to keep longer. Additional clarified butter, poured over the surface of the finished spread, will form a seal that protects it from the air: spreads sealed in this manner can be kept, unopened, in the refrigerator. Potted shellfish should be served within three or four days, but meats such as potted tongue can be stored for a few weeks. Once the seal is broken, the contents should be eaten promptly.

A Robust Paste of Potted Tongue

1 Cooking a tongue. Wash a pickled ox tongue; cut away any ragged ends and cartilage. In a large pan, cover the ox tongue with cold water; bring to the boil and skim off scum. Simmer at 80°C (176°F), partly covered, for 8 hours or until the tongue is tender when pierced with a needle. Let it cool in the liquid; lift it out and peel away the skin (*above*).

2 Clarifying butter. Melt butter over a very low heat; remove it from the heat and let the white solids settle. Wring out muslin in warm water; drape it over a sieve resting on a bowl. Pour the butter carefully into the muslin (*above*); discard any solids that cling to the cloth. If the clarified butter hardens, make it liquid again by placing the bowl in a pan of hot water.

A Creamy Spread of Chicken Livers

1 Trimming the livers. Choose the palest pink chicken livers available. With a small sharp knife, remove all connective tissue and green bile stains, as these would impart a bitter taste. Cover the livers with milk and place them in the refrigerator overnight; they will become paler in colour and more subtle in flavour.

2 Sautéing. Drain off the milk and dry the livers on paper towels. Sauté them in a little olive oil over a high heat for 3 minutes, turning them with a wooden spatula (*above*). The livers should be golden-brown outside but pink inside. Remove the livers from the sauté pan and drain them in a sieve.

3 **Blending the paste.** Dice the tongue. Place a few spoonfuls of tongue in a food processor; ladle in some clarified butter (*above*). Blend thoroughly, season with pepper and ground mace, and transfer the paste to a mixing bowl. A little at a time, purée the rest of the tongue and butter. Beat the mixture thoroughly; pack it into an earthenware pot.

4 **Sealing the surface.** Refrigerate the pot for 2 to 3 hours to harden the butter; test by shaking the pot gently—when firm, the mixture will not wobble. Ladle on a thin layer of melted clarified butter, about 3 mm ($\frac{1}{8}$ inch) thick (*above*). Refrigerate again to set the surface.

5 **Serving the spread.** Cover the potted tongue with plastic film until you are ready to serve it. To serve, spoon out the paste, mashing the butter from the top into the spread. Accompany it with toast, crackers or, as here, thin slices of rye bread and gherkins.□

3 **Marinating in port.** Place the livers in a shallow dish and season them with salt and pepper. Pour port over the livers, cover the dish and leave the livers to marinate for at least 6 hours at room temperature or, preferably, overnight in the refrigerator. Remove the livers from the marinade; drain them in a sieve.

4 **Puréeing and sieving.** With a pestle and mortar, or using a food processor, purée the livers in batches and blend them with softened butter. A spoonful at a time, push the mixture through a fine drum sieve with a scraper (*above*). Discard any debris caught in the mesh before sieving the next spoonful.

5 **Serving.** Transfer the sieved purée to an earthenware pot, tapping the sides of the pot after each addition to settle the contents. Cover the pot with plastic film and refrigerate it for 2 hours to harden the mixture. To serve, spoon out the spread and accompany it with warm biscuits or, as here, slices of hot toast.□

Extracting the Succulence of Crayfish

Poached crustaceans can make delicious shellfish dips. The succulent inner parts, reduced to a smooth purée, will form the body of a dip, while the tails, kept intact and shelled, provide a garnish.

Crayfish, used here, are a particularly appropriate choice—their tails are soft and fleshy, and their bodies will yield a generous amount of purée. But you could also make a dip from large prawns or even from very small shrimps. With small species, use a large number of the creatures—tails and all—to make the purée; keep a few specimens whole to peel and serve as the garnish.

To ensure absolute freshness, crustaceans should be purchased live. Here, the crayfish are killed instantly by immersion in a rapidly boiling court-bouillon—a mixture of water, white wine, aromatic vegetables and herbs (*recipe, page 166*). A few minutes' poaching in this liquid will cook the crayfish and endow them with additional flavour.

To produce a purée, the cooked crayfish are freed of their tails; their bodies are passed—shells and all—through a meat grinder. This treatment is the most effective way to break down the shell structure and extract the soft material within it. Alternatively, you could pound the carcasses in a mortar and pass them through a food mill. But in either case, the purée must be passed through a fine sieve to remove all fragments of shell.

Cream and lemon juice, blended with this purée, will thin it and transform it into a delicately flavoured dip. The reserved crayfish tails, speared with toothpicks, will serve to scoop up the mixture. Supplement them, if you like, with crisp raw vegetables: sticks of celery, strips of fennel, wedges of courgette or—as here—chunks of peeled and seeded cucumber.

1 Poaching crayfish. Put sliced onions and carrots in a pan with celery, crushed garlic and herbs. Add cold water and salt, bring to the boil and simmer for 15 minutes. Add white wine, cook for 10 minutes; add peppercorns and simmer for 5 minutes more. Drop in live crayfish; cover and cook at a light boil for 8 minutes. Let them cool, then lift them out.

2 Separating the tails. One at time, grasp each crayfish by the neck and break off its tail (*above*); the tail will come away easily from the rest of the body. Peel off the shell from the tails exposing the soft tail meat; reserve both shell and flesh.

5 Sieving the purée. Set a fine-meshed drum sieve over a plate. With a plastic scraper, push the coarse crayfish purée through the sieve, one spoonful at a time (*above*). After sieving each spoonful, scrape all crushed shell from the surface of the mesh and discard it. Scrape off any purée that clings to the underside of the sieve; add it to the plate.

6 Whisking the dip. With a wire whisk, gradually blend double cream and a little lemon juice into the crayfish purée; use as much cream as the mixture can absorb to form a dip that is thick but pourable. Flavour the mixture to taste with salt, pepper and a little cayenne pepper. Taste, and add more lemon juice if a dip of sharper flavour is desired.

3 **Reserving the tails.** As you detach and peel the crayfish tails, place the tail meat in a small bowl. Cover the tails with a little of their cooking liquid to keep them moist, and set them aside to use as a garnish for the final presentation. Place the shells from the tails and the crayfish carcasses in a larger bowl.

4 **Mincing the crayfish carcasses.** Put the carcasses, including all of the shells, through a grinder, using the large-holed disc to grind everything into a coarse purée. As you work, press the carcasses down into the grinder with a wooden pestle or with the flat of your hand (*above*), being careful to keep your fingers well clear.

7 **Serving.** Pour the mixture into a shallow bowl. Peel cucumbers and halve them; remove the seeds by running your finger down each half. Split each half; cut it into 1 cm (½ inch) lengths. Salt the pieces generously, leave them for half an hour, then pat them dry with a cloth. Spear the cucumber and the crayfish tails with toothpicks; place them in the dip.□

Morsels of Meat and Seafood Richly Glazed

Small pieces of meat, poultry or seafood, rapidly sautéed and then simmered in stock or wine, make rich and substantial party food. Coated with a glaze derived from their own reduced cooking liquid, the succulent morsels can be skewered with cocktail sticks for serving.

A great many foods lend themselves to this treatment. Although the appropriate cooking times and cooking liquids may vary, the method of assembling all such preparations is essentially the same as that shown here for glazed cubes of veal.

The meat, meticulously trimmed of fat and connective tissue, is cubed and then quickly sautéed; onions and a bouquet garni are added to the pan for aromatic support. A little wine poured into the pan will dissolve the rich deposits formed by the sauté—a process known as deglazing. These deglazed juices, supplemented by more wine or, as here, by a jellied veal stock (*box, opposite page; recipe, page* 165) are used to simmer the meat until it is just tender. Once the meat is cooked, this liquid will form the sauce.

If you plan to use stock as the cooking liquid, be sure to prepare it at least a day in advance—veal stock will require several hours' gentle and undisturbed cooking to draw out all the flavour from the meat. When the stock has set into jelly, the layer of fat that has risen to the top is easily lifted off with a metal spoon; any remaining particles of fat can be dabbed away with a damp paper towel.

To make the sauce, the pan juices are cooked over high heat until they have reduced and thickened; while the sauce cooks, it should be skimmed repeatedly to cleanse it of any fat that rises to the surface. Once the liquid has been reduced, it can be used either on its own or enriched with other elements, such as cream or a tomato purée (*page 8*), to vary the flavour and create a more abundant sauce.

Choose a cooking liquid that will complement the flavour of the main ingredient. The sauced morsels illustrated on pages 26-27 indicate a few of the many possibilities—sautéed chicken wings covered with a white wine sauce that has been finished with cream; shelled prawn tails quickly cooked with shallots, white wine and dried herbs; cubed monkfish fillets coated with a wine sauce blended with tomato purée and cream; small pieces of squid cooked in their own copious juices and flavoured with brandy, dried oregano and cayenne pepper.

These glazed morsels can be served as they are, or they can be finished with a seasoning element that also doubles as a simple garnish. The veal cubes shown here are sprinkled with a fragrant mixture of parsley, garlic and the grated rind of orange and lemon; the preparations illustrated overleaf are finished with a scattering of fresh herbs—such as parsley, tarragon and chervil—that complement the flavours of the main ingredient.

3 Deglazing the pan. Add a bouquet garni to the pan—parsley sprigs, the green part of leek, celery, bay leaf and a sprig of thyme. Pour in enough dry white wine to cover the base of the pan (*above*); use a wooden spoon to scrape up the rich pan deposits. Add jellied veal stock (*box, opposite page*) so that the cubes of meat are barely covered.

4 Starting the sauce. Over a low heat, simmer the meat, covered, until it is tender—about 40 minutes. Remove the bouquet garni and discard it. Using a slotted spoon, transfer the meat to a plate. Transfer the cooking liquid to a small pan (*above*). To keep the veal moist and warm, return it to the hot sauté pan and cover it with the lid.

5 Cleansing the sauce. Bring the cooking liquid to the boil. To cleanse it of fat, reduce the heat and move the pan half off the heat. When a skin forms on the cooler side of the liquid, draw the skin aside with a spoon (*above*), lift it off and discard it. Continue to boil the cleansed sauce to reduce it to a coating consistency.

1 Cubing the meat. With a small, sharp knife, pare away and discard fat and membrane from a piece of meat—here, two 2.5 cm (1 inch) thick slices of veal from the rump. Slice the meat lengthwise into 2.5 cm strips; cut across the strips to make cubes. Toss the meat cubes with a little salt to season them.

2 Searing in oil. In a heavy saucepan, just large enough to hold the cubes in a single layer, heat a thin coating of oil. Over a high heat, sauté the meat for a few minutes, shaking the pan and turning the pieces with a wooden spoon to sear all the surfaces. Reduce the heat; add finely chopped onion (*above*); cook, stirring, for a few minutes, until the onion is soft.

A Basic Veal Stock

Straining stock. Cover veal knuckle, chicken wing tips and feet with cold water; bring to the boil. Repeatedly skim off scum, adding cold water to stop the boil. Add salt, vegetables and herbs. Simmer, partially covered, for at least 5 hours. Strain through a colander lined with damp muslin; when cool, refrigerate overnight, then spoon off fat.

6 Preparing a garnish. Finely chop parsley and a garlic clove. Grate the rind of an orange, taking care not to cut into the white pith. Grate the rind of a lemon in the same way (*above*); add it to the mixture. Lightly toss the mixture with your fingers.

7 Dressing the meat. Transfer the reduced sauce to the pan with the meat. Over a low heat, warm up the meat and sauce. To coat the meat thoroughly with sauce, gently turn the pieces in the sauce with a spoon and shake the pan vigorously. Remove the pan from the heat and add a handful of the garnish (*above*).

8 Serving the morsels. Using a spoon, transfer the hot meat to a serving dish. Season the meat with freshly ground pepper and the remainder of the garnish. To serve, spear each piece through the middle with a cocktail stick.□

A White Wine Stew for Chicken

Finishing a sauce with cream. Cleave chicken wings in two; cut off the tips (*left*). Sauté the pieces for 10 minutes. Add finely chopped onion; sauté for 5 minutes. Add white wine to barely cover and a bouquet garni. Simmer the chicken, covered, for 25 minutes, or until tender. Discard the bouquet; remove the chicken and pour the sauce into a small pan. Return the chicken to the sauté pan and keep it warm. Cleanse and reduce the sauce. Add cream, reduce the sauce to a coating consistency, then pour it over the chicken. Reheat the pieces. Garnish with chopped tarragon.☐

A Wine and Herb Glaze for Prawns

Seasoning with parsley and garlic. To shell prawns, split open the underside of the tail section and remove the flesh (*left*); leave the tail tip attached. Sauté the prawns with finely chopped shallots for 2 minutes, or until the prawns turn pink. Reduce the heat and pour in dry white wine and dried herbs. Cook, covered, for 5 minutes, shaking the pan occasionally. Remove the prawns; keep them warm. Reduce the sauce to a coating consistency. Prepare a garnish of finely chopped garlic and parsley; season the sauce with a handful of the mixture. Reheat the prawns in the sauce; serve them with the rest of the garnish.☐

Monkfish Cooked in a Tomato Sauce

Garnishing with chervil sprigs. Fillet a skinned monkfish tail. Cut the fillets into 2 cm (¾ inch) cubes (*left*). Sauté the cubes until they are firm and opaque, about 3 to 4 minutes. Reduce the heat, add finely chopped shallots and sauté for 1 to 2 minutes. Pour in tomato purée (*page 8*), white wine and dried herbs. Cover the pan; cook the fish until tender—about 10 minutes. Remove the fish; keep it warm. Reduce the sauce; add cream and reduce the sauce to a coating consistency. Reheat the fish in the sauce. Garnish with chopped parsley, chives, tarragon and chervil; top with chervil sprigs.□

Squid Pieces Flamed in Brandy

Colouring a sauce with tomato purée. Ask the fishmonger to clean squid; leave the tentacles whole. Cut the bodies crosswise into 2.5 cm (1 inch) pieces (*left*). Sauté the squid briefly, keeping the heat high so that the liquid exuded by the squid is quickly evaporated. Reduce the heat and add finely chopped onions. Pour a splash of brandy over the squid; set it alight. Add tomato purée (*page 8*), dried oregano and cayenne pepper. Cover the pan; cook the squid for 30 to 40 minutes, until tender. Remove the squid; reduce the sauce. Reheat the squid in the sauce. Garnish with chopped chives.□

2
Assemblies
Interplays of Colour and Flavour

By assembling two or more ingredients you can create bite-sized morsels that are among the most versatile of party foods. The elements in an assembly can be combined in a number of different ways. They may be stacked, rolled, stuffed or wrapped, and the finished product may be a neat parcel, a hollowed-out case holding a filling, or a variegated construction of several layers. Most of the assemblies that are demonstrated in this chapter require very little preparation, but they should always be carefully planned so that soft and crisp textures, bold and pastel colours, strong and delicate flavours, are well balanced.

One of the simplest assemblies is a stuffed hard-boiled egg; its halved white serves as a container, while its yolk, mashed and mixed with other ingredients, provides the filling (*page 30*). Beaten eggs are also a good foundation for assemblies; a thin omelette can be rolled round a stuffing and steamed, while thicker omelettes, binding a number of colourful flavourings, can be stacked and baked (*page 32*).

Any ingredient that is pliable enough to roll round a fairly firm filling can be used for a wrapping. These wrappers may include vegetables such as parboiled spinach leaves or broad strips of roasted and peeled sweet peppers; thin slices of cured, roasted or even raw meat; or fish, such as smoked salmon or filleted anchovies (*pages 34-36*).

Some foods make natural containers that are especially useful for moist fillings (*pages 37-39*). Branches of celery hearts, halved seeded cucumbers and small tomatoes that have been hollowed out, for example, could be stuffed with a flavoured butter or with the caper and anchovy mixture known as *tapenade* (*page 6*), or with a mayonnaise or other emulsion (*page 8*). And, although they are inedible themselves, the shells of molluscs and crustaceans also provide convenient vessels for fillings made from their own cooked flesh.

Because their actual construction is relatively simple, these assemblies lend themselves to preparation in large quantities. For best results, prepare the individual ingredients an hour or two in advance, and bring them together to form the assembly just before serving.

Speared with cocktail sticks, a selection of wrapped delicacies makes a bright display. The concentric circles here include spinach leaves enfolding mussels, slices of smoked salmon rolled round marinated cucumber, bands of roasted sweet red pepper round cheese, strips of raw beef enclosing anchovies and olives, and ribbons of raw ham round melon balls.

Stuffed Eggs: Simple and Satisfying

One of the simplest assemblies is a stuffed hard-boiled egg. The white of the halved egg provides a convenient natural container. The yolks, mashed to a paste and combined with flavourings, serve as the basis for a wide range of fillings that can simply be piled into the whites (*right*) or, for a more elaborate effect, piped through a piping bag (*box, opposite page*).

The best egg for hard boiling is several days old. A new-laid egg is impossible to peel smoothly, because its white adheres firmly to the shell membrane. You can test the age of the egg by dropping it into a pan of cold water. A new-laid egg will sink to the bottom and lie flat; an egg that is several days old will tilt because of an air pocket that has formed at its round end.

Hard boiling should be done gently. A good method is to start the eggs in cold water and simmer them at low heat. Allow no more than 10 minutes' simmering for size 2 eggs, 9 minutes for sizes 3 and 4, and 7 minutes for smaller sizes, timing from when the water starts to bubble. Plunge the eggs into cold water as soon as the cooking time is up. Otherwise, they will continue to cook in their shells. The whites will become rubbery and the surface of the yolks will turn blackish-green.

The eggs can be cooked in advance, but it is best to shell them just before they are halved. The eggs can be split lengthwise or across the middle; if cut crosswise, a thin sliver should be sliced off the bottom of each half so that it will stand upright.

To prepare the stuffing, the mashed yolks are moistened, usually with butter or mayonnaise, and combined with other ingredients that add flavour and colour. You can simply blend the yolks with a compound butter, such as a herb butter or a sweet red pepper butter (*page 7*), and top them with a sprinkling of paprika, finely chopped chervil or other fresh herbs.

For a rustic filling, you can blend the yolks with a mixture of ingredients—here, chopped capers, black olives, parsley and seasonings are combined with the yolks and blended thoroughly with olive oil. Intertwined strips of anchovies and sweet red peppers are used as a garnish. Or, using a piping bag, you can introduce two decorative stuffings of different colours into a single egg.

1 Preparing the ingredients. Place the eggs in a pan and cover them with cold water. Bring the water to a simmer over a medium heat and cook the eggs for no longer than 10 minutes from the moment the water starts to bubble. Plunge the eggs into cold water to stop the cooking and leave them to cool. Remove the eggs from the water, crack the shells with the back of a teaspoon and peel them. Slice them in half and put the yolks in a bowl. Stone black olives and chop them finely (*above*); chop capers and parsley.

5 Decorating the eggs. Hold a strip of red pepper and a strip of anchovy side by side between your fingers and thumbs; twist them gently into a spiral (*above*). Lay the garnish along the length of each stuffed egg. Arrange the eggs on a napkin-lined platter (*right*). □

2 **Making the filling.** With a fork, mash the egg yolks and mix in the chopped olives, capers and parsley. Season to taste with salt, pepper and mustard. Add enough oil to make the filling smooth and moist.

3 **Filling the shells.** With a teaspoon, fill the whites of the eggs with the yolk mixture. Shape the filling into a mound with the hollow of the spoon (*above*), packing it in lightly and smoothing over the surface.

4 **Preparing the garnish.** Soak, fillet and rinse anchovies (*page 6*). Lay the fillets on a towel to dry. Roast and peel sweet red peppers (*page 7*); halve them, remove the seeds and pith, and slice them into strips (*above*). Cut each anchovy fillet into strips roughly the same width as the peppers and then cut all the strips into approximately 5 cm (2 inch) lengths.

Fancy Twists for Filling

1 **Preparing a piping bag.** Make a smooth filling—here, the yolks of hard-boiled eggs are mixed with mayonnaise (*page 8*) and a little cayenne pepper. With your fingertip, push a nozzle that has a serrated tip—here, a 5 mm (¼ inch) nozzle—through the opening of a piping bag. Squeeze the bag round the base of the nozzle to force it into place (*above*).

2 **Filling the bag.** Fold back the top half of the bag like a cuff. Holding the nozzle, spoon in the filling until the bag is half full (*above*). Turn up the fold, hold the bag firmly at the top and, with your other hand, gently squeeze the filling down towards the nozzle to press out the air. When the filling is compact, twist the top of the piping bag to close it.

3 **Piping the filling.** Keeping your thumb over the twisted closure, press the bag with your fingers to force out the filling; support the bag with your other hand (*above*). Move the nozzle to pipe a pattern. A spiral mound, formed by lifting the bag as you pipe, is shown here.

Colourful Effects with Flavoured Omelettes

Omelettes serve as the basis of many light and colourful assemblages. The mild flavour of the eggs combines well with a wide variety of ingredients and the omelettes can be made as thick or as thin as you like. Thin, flexible omelettes will wrap like pancakes round fillings; when steamed and sliced, the assemblies reveal an attractive spiral pattern (*right*). Thick omelettes, variously flavoured and coloured, can be stacked and baked together to form a layered cake that yields brightly striped sticks (*below; recipe, page 117*).

The basic technique of making omelettes is simple. Because both of these omelettes are served at room temperature, the lightly beaten eggs should be cooked in olive oil instead of butter, which would impart an unpleasant, granular texture to the eggs when cold.

So that the omelettes will adhere to a filling or each other, they are cooked on one side only. The thin omelettes will set almost at once; to keep them flexible, they are removed from the pan as soon as they curl at the edges. The thicker omelettes

are tranferred from the pan to a baking sheet when they are set but still moist on top. For both omelettes, the final cooking process—steaming or baking—completes the setting of the eggs.

The stuffing for the rolled omelettes should be bound with beaten egg, which will set during cooking, firming the mixture so it holds its shape when sliced. Instead of the minced pork shown here, you could use finely chopped chicken or veal.

The stacked omelettes can incorporate any combination of vegetables you like. The flavourings here are puréed tomatoes mixed with roasted pepper strips, lightly sautéed mushrooms, and parboiled and chopped spinach. But you could vary the effect with stoned and chopped black olives or sautéed, shredded courgettes.

To make an omelette firm enough for stacking, the amount of beaten egg in each layer should be adjusted according to the consistency of the flavouring. A very liquid filling, such as tomatoes, needs a generous amount of egg; a bulky filling, such as spinach, needs less egg to bind it.

Egg Rolls with a Spicy Filling

1 **Making thin omelettes.** Beat the eggs lightly; add salt. Brush a pan with oil; heat it until a drop of egg sizzles on contact. Ladle in a thin layer of egg, tilting the pan to spread it evenly. Cook the omelette on one side over medium heat until the edges begin to curl—about 1 minute. Transfer it to a plate. Make more thin omelettes and stack them on the plate.

Omelettes Stacked to Yield Rainbow Stripes

1 **Assembling the ingredients.** Sieve tomatoes and simmer the resulting purée until thick, about 30 minutes (*page 8*). Sauté a finely chopped onion in olive oil until soft; add the tomato purée and strips of roasted red peppers (*page 7*). Add salt, pepper and cayenne pepper; cook for 5 minutes. Parboil spinach, squeeze and chop it, and sauté it briefly in olive oil with chopped garlic; season it with salt, pepper and nutmeg. Slice button mushrooms thinly, toss them quickly in hot oil; add salt and pepper. Beat the eggs lightly (*above*), seasoning them with salt and pepper.

2 **Cooking the omelettes.** Beat some of the egg mixture into each of the three flavouring elements. Heat 3 mm ($\frac{1}{8}$ inch) of olive oil in a 20 cm (8 inch) pan. When the oil is very hot, pour in the egg and spinach mixture. Reduce the heat, stir lightly with the back of a fork—without scraping the bottom of the pan—and cover. After a few minutes, while the top surface is still moist, slide the omelette on to a baking sheet. Make the mushroom omelette the same way (*above*).

2 **Rolling up the filling.** Mix finely minced pork with a little cornflour, soy sauce, dry sherry, salt and pepper. Beat an egg and add it to the mixture. Spoon some of the filling on to each omelette, then spread it almost to the edges with the back of a spoon. Roll up the omelette (*above*). Brush the exposed edge with a little beaten egg to seal the roll.

3 **Steaming the rolls.** Place the omelettes, flaps downwards, on a heatproof plate. Set a metal rack or trivet inside a deep pan and pour boiling water into the pan to just below the rack. Place the plate of omelettes on the rack, cover the pan, and let the water simmer for 20 minutes to cook the filling and set the omelettes.

4 **Slicing and serving.** Remove the pan of steamed omelettes from the heat; leave them until cool enough to handle. Cut the rolls diagonally into slices about 1 cm (½ inch) thick and arrange them on a platter. Serve them tepid or at room temperature, decorated—if you like—with parsley. □

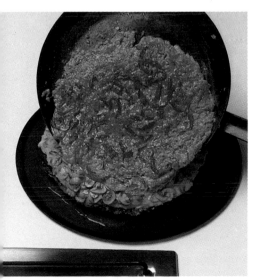

3 **Stacking.** When the mushroom omelette is cooked, slide it out of the pan on top of the spinach omelette. Repeat the process with the tomato omelette (*above*) and sprinkle grated cheese—in this case, Parmesan—over the stack. Bake it at 180°C (350°F or Mark 4) for 30 minutes to set the stack and lightly brown the top.

4 **Slicing the stack.** Remove the stacked omelettes from the oven; leave them to rest for 10 minutes. Loosen the base of the stack with a spatula. Let the omelettes cool. Slice the stack into strips, and then crosswise into 2.5 cm (1 inch) squares; halve the squares to form individual bite-sized pieces for serving.

5 **Serving the omelettes.** Place the slices of stacked omelettes on a plate, laying them on their sides to reveal their bands of contrasting colour. Serve the slices tepid or at room temperature. □

Good Things in Small Packages

A straightforward but intriguing way of combining two ingredients is by simply wrapping one element round another to form small snacks that are easy to eat by hand. Almost any food flexible enough to roll can serve as a wrapper—slices of raw or cooked meat, for example, or slices of salmon, anchovy fillets and vegetables.

The wrapper must be strong enough to cover a filling without shredding. For this reason, foods such as smoked salmon and raw ham, that are normally sliced paper-thin, must be sliced slightly thicker than usual if they are to be used successfully as wrappers. Raw beef, however, needs to be sliced as thinly as possible to make it flexible; if it is firmed in the freezer it will be easier to carve. You can also use roast beef, lamb or pork; to produce slices that are thin enough to act as a wrapping, the roast must be cold when it is carved.

Among vegetables, sweet peppers are a useful wrapping material. To make them flexible, the peppers must be roasted, peeled and seeded (*page 7*). They can then be cut into strips, rolled round a filling and skewered with cocktail sticks. Other vegetable wrappings include spinach and chard leaves, which can be made pliable by immersion in boiling water, then dried and folded round a filling.

If you like, you can spread the inside of the wrapper with butter before you use it to enclose a filling. The butter will help to hold the contents in place, supplementing the sticks that secure the assemblies.

Fillings for these edible wrappers can be almost any food that taste or fancy can conceive, as long as the food is firm and dry enough not to leak from its covering. The combinations shown here and on the next two pages represent only a few filling possibilities: smoked salmon with marinated cucumber (*below*); raw ham cloaking melon balls (*right*); strips of raw beef enveloping anchovies and olives (*opposite page, below*); and spinach leaves holding shelled, steamed mussels (*page 36; recipe, page 167*). Strips of roasted sweet pepper combine well with small cubes of soft cheese such as Taleggio, Port-Salut or Saint-Nectaire.

Although the combinations that are shown on these pages are intended to be served cold, it is also possible to serve hot assemblies. Unsmoked streaky bacon, for example, provides an excellent covering for stoned dates or for stoned and stuffed prunes (*recipes, page 112*). The assemblies should be secured with cocktail sticks, then baked or grilled until the fat runs and the bacon begins to crisp.

Most wrapped snacks take very little time to prepare. For best results, those snacks that are to be served cold should be assembled no more than an hour or two before they are needed, then chilled in the refrigerator until they are presented to your guests. Hot assemblies should be served as soon as they are cooked.

Cucumber Cloaked in Smoked Salmon

Forming smoked salmon rolls. Peel, halve and seed cucumbers; cut them into thick cross-sections. Place the pieces in a bowl, sprinkle on lemon juice, salt and chopped chives; set aside. Trim slices of smoked salmon; sprinkle them with chopped dill. Drain and dry the cucumbers. Spread the salmon with very soft butter (*left*); cut the slices into strips. Roll each piece of cucumber in a strip of salmon; chill to harden the butter. Spear the rolls with cocktail sticks; here, they are garnished with finely chopped dill. □

A Classic Partnership of Melon and Ham

Wrapping raw ham round melon. Trim the fat from the side of slices of raw ham—here, Parma ham; the meat should not be sliced too thinly. Cut each slice into two or three strips. Split a ripe melon—in this case, a cantaloup. Scrape out the seeds and cut out balls with a melon scoop (*left*). Place a melon ball at one end of each strip of ham and roll it up. Secure each roll with a cocktail stick and arrange the wraps on a napkin-lined platter (*above*). □

A Raw Beef Wrapper for Olives and Anchovies

Slicing raw beef. Trim all superficial fat and connective tissue from beef fillet. Wrap the meat in plastic film; half-freeze it until firm. Soak, fillet and drain salt anchovies (*page 6, Step 1*). Remove the stones from black olives. Using a very sharp knife, cut the beef into paper-thin slices, then into strips (*left*). Place an anchovy fillet on each strip of beef and an olive at one end. Roll up the strips of beef and secure them with cocktail sticks; if you like, place the rolls on a bed of shredded lettuce (*above*). □

A Spinach Envelope for Shellfish

1 **Opening mussels.** Soak live mussels in salted water, scrub them; discard any not tightly closed, or with cracked shells. Pull off their fibrous beards; put them in a pan with chopped onion, crushed garlic, herbs and white wine. Place the pan, covered, over a high heat; shake it until the mussels open. Drain the mussels in a colander over a bowl (*above*); reserve the liquid.

2 **Preparing spinach.** Carefully remove the stems from large spinach leaves. Wash the leaves, put them in a pan and cover with boiling salted water (*above*). Set the pan over a high heat for a few seconds, until the leaves turn bright green. Drain the leaves; run cold water over them. Spread out the leaves on a towel; lay another towel on top and pat them dry.

3 **Wrapping the mussels.** Remove the mussels from their shells; put them in a bowl and cover them with a little of their cooking liquid. Spread each spinach leaf with flavoured butter—Montpellier butter (*page 7*) is used here. Lay a mussel at one end of each leaf; roll it up, tucking in the sides (*above*). Chill the rolls. Spear them with cocktail sticks; garnish, if you like, with trimmed radishes.□

Taking Advantage of Natural Containers

Many foods supply sturdy and attractive containers for other ingredients. For instance, crustacean and mollusc shells, while inedible themselves, offer an easy way of transforming moist seafood mixtures into convenient finger food. In the demonstration on the right, the back shells of crayfish are filled with a purée made from the soft parts of their bodies, blended with butter and thickened with breadcrumbs; the tails of the crayfish provide a garnish and one fine specimen, kept intact, surmounts the display. Mussels can be treated in a similar way: once they are steamed open, their flesh can be chopped and combined with herbs and mayonnaise, then spooned back into the shells for serving (*page 39, above*).

Raw vegetables also make colourful containers for different fillings, and the containers are themselves edible. In the demonstrations on pages 38-39, celery hearts are filled with a spread made from blue cheese; scooped-out cucumbers are stuffed with a paste of black olives, capers and anchovies; and hollowed-out tomatoes contain a potato and garlic sauce.

Vegetables that release their moisture easily must be relieved of as much liquid as possible, to prevent their juices from seeping into the fillings and making them watery. Tomatoes should be salted to draw out excess moisture; after about half an hour, they should be inverted to drain out the water that has collected inside them. However, cucumbers, when salted, become too limp to serve as containers. Instead, they should be patted dry and refrigerated after filling to crisp them.

All of the assemblies shown on these pages will be at their best if they are prepared shortly before being served. If there is any interval between preparation and serving, keep the assemblies in the refrigerator, covered with plastic film.

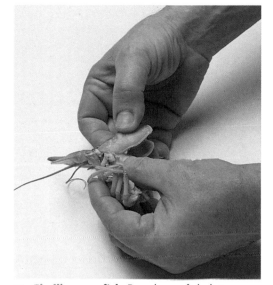

1 Shelling crayfish. Poach crayfish; let them cool in their cooking liquid. Shell the tails (*page 22, Steps 1 to 3*); reserve the tail meat, covered with the poaching liquid. Hold the back shell between your finger and thumb, and detach the underside of the body (*above*). Wash and dry the shells; trim the antennae with scissors. Reserve the back shells.

2 Filling the shells. Make a purée from all other parts of the crayfish (*page 22, Steps 4 and 5*). Season it with lemon juice, salt, pepper and cayenne pepper. Blend in softened butter and add some fresh breadcrumbs to thicken it. Using a piping bag (*page 31*), fill the crayfish shells with the purée; chill them to firm the butter. Drain the reserved tail meat.

3 Serving. Place a crayfish tail on top of each filled shell and arrange the shells on a napkin-lined platter. Garnish with chopped herbs, such as dill. If you like, keep the best-looking crayfish whole after poaching; gently pull the tail up into an arc over the body, and bend the claws back so that the tips of the pincers pierce the tail fins. Lay the crayfish in the centre of the platter. □

Cheese-Filled Celery Stems

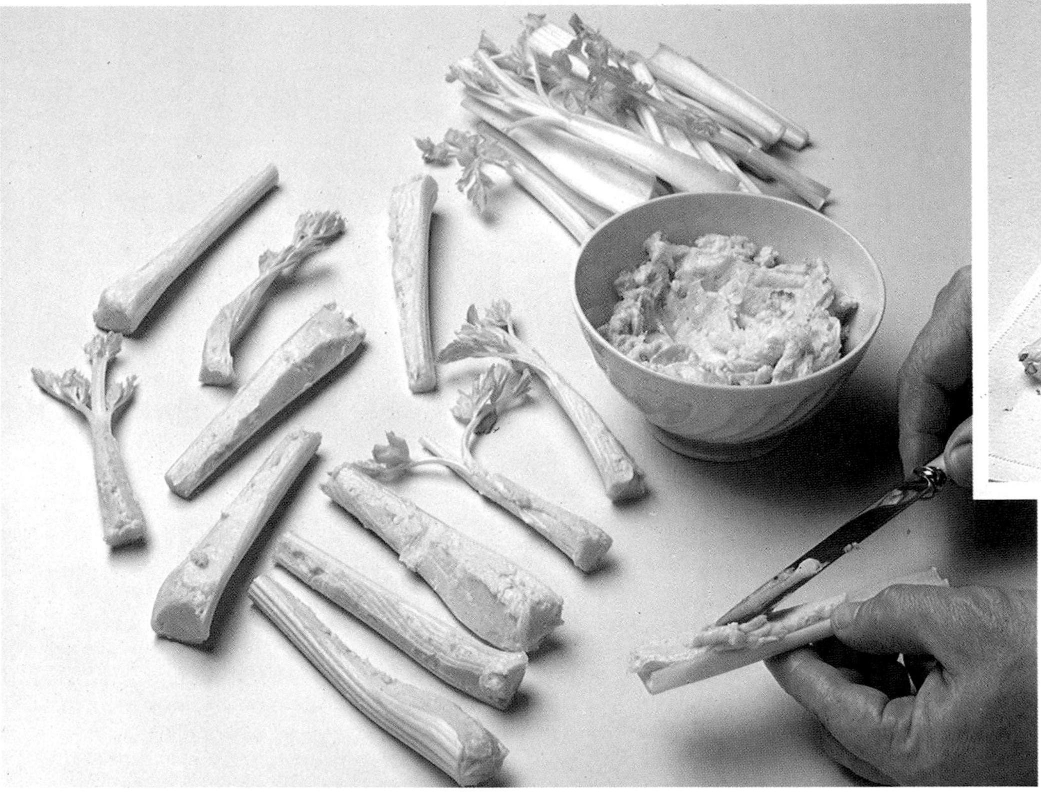

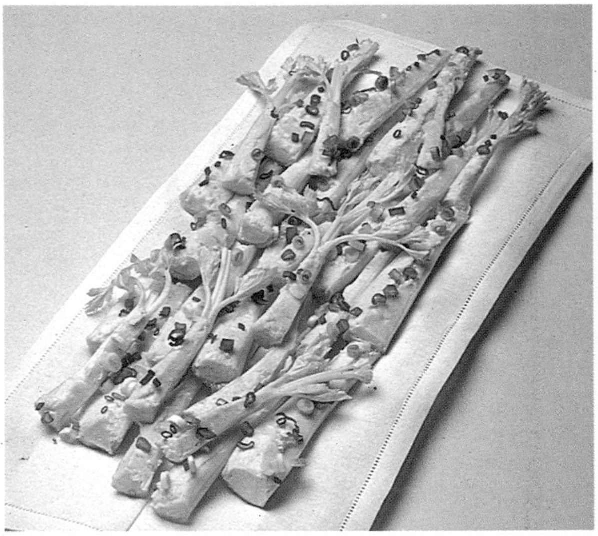

Filling celery hearts. Mash a crumbly blue cheese, such as Roquefort, and blend it with softened butter (*page 7*). Using a knife with a rounded blade, spread the cheese mixture into the hollows of sticks from the hearts of celery (*left*). Arrange the filled celery sticks on a napkin-lined platter; here, they are garnished with chopped spring onions (*above*).□

Cucumber Boats Packed with Tapenade

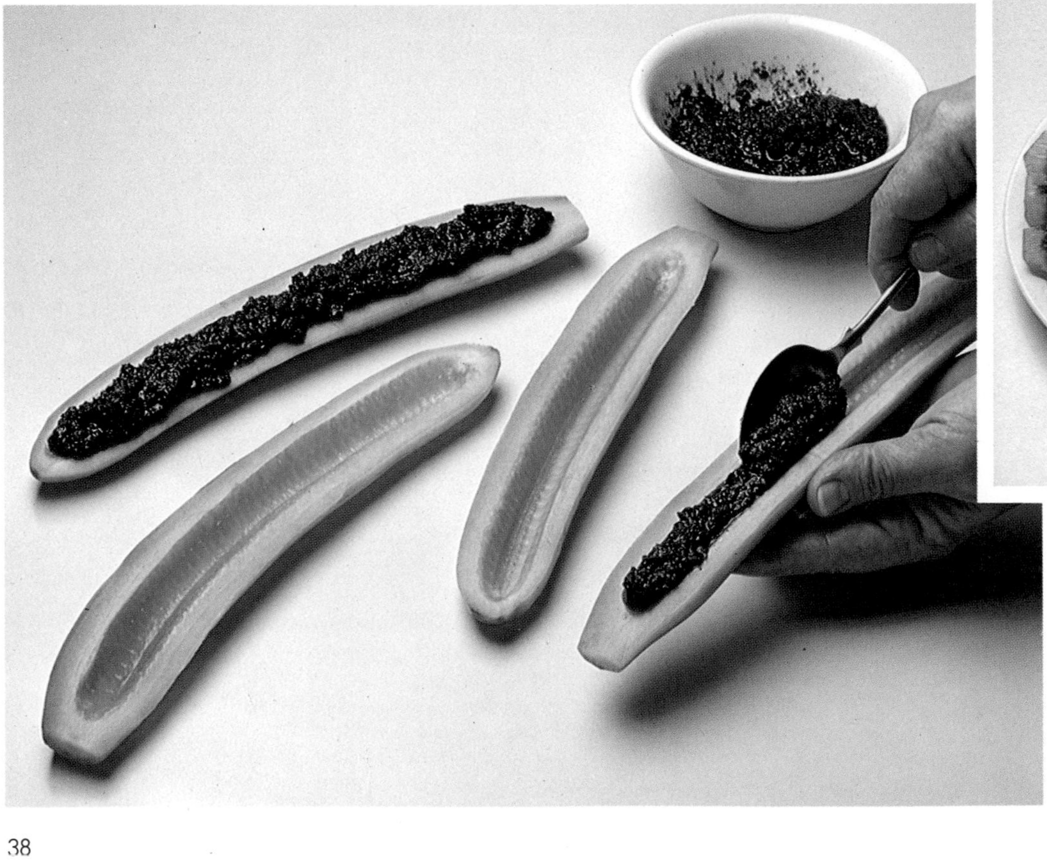

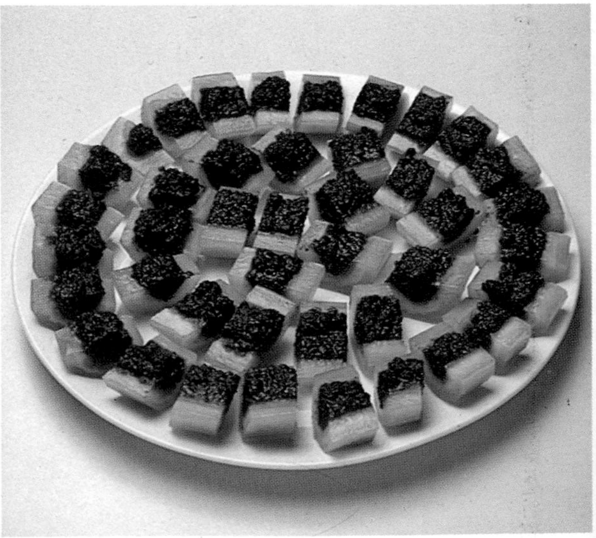

Making cucumber boats. Peel cucumbers, split them lengthwise and scoop out the seeds by running your index finger down the length of each half. Prepare a filling—in this case, a paste of black olives, capers and anchovies (*page 6, Steps 1 to 3*). Pat the cucumbers dry. Spoon the paste into the cucumber halves (*left*), then refrigerate them for 1 hour so that they will be crisp and easy to slice. With a sharp knife, cut the cucumber into pieces about 3 cm ($1\frac{1}{4}$ inches) wide and arrange them on a platter (*above*).□

Shell-Served Mussels in Mayonnaise

Filling mussel shells. Clean mussels and steam them open (*page 36*), wash and reserve the best-looking shell halves. Chop the flesh of the mussels and combine it with mayonnaise (*page 8*), chopped parsley and gherkins. Season with pepper and a little cayenne pepper. Spoon the filling on to the shells (*left*). Arrange the filled shells on a platter; garnish them, if you like, with more chopped parsley (*above*).□

Scooped-Out Tomatoes with a Garlic-Scented Sauce

Filling tomatoes. Slice off the stem end of tiny, firm tomatoes. With a teaspoon, scoop out the seeds and pulp. Sprinkle the insides of the tomatoes with salt; after about 30 minutes, invert them on a towel to drain. Cut a thin slice off their bases so they will stand firmly. Prepare a filling—here, a potato and garlic sauce (*page 8*) mixed with chopped parsley. Spoon the filling into the tomatoes (*left*). Arrange the stuffed tomatoes on a platter (*above*).□

3
Pastry and Dough
Versatile Vehicles

Crisp and golden after their brief baking, folded phyllo triangles (*page 60*) are arranged on a serving platter. Inside the buttery phyllo coils and triangles shown here is a rich and highly seasoned mixture of spinach and *feta* cheese.

Bread and pastry doughs provide great scope for improvisation in the making of snacks, varying from doughs strong enough to support substantial stuffings of meat or vegetables to the puffiest of pastries that need only be flavoured or filled with a light sauce or spread.

Bread dough (*page 42*) must be thoroughly kneaded to distribute yeast and to develop gluten—the substance in flour that gives the dough its strength and elasticity. As well as using the dough to bake bread, you can shape it into discs and bake them with toppings to make pizzas (*page 62*).

The pastry doughs in this chapter can be divided into two types: strong doughs that are kneaded to develop gluten, and tender doughs that are handled very lightly. The strong, flaky crusts of *samosas* (*page 55*)—stuffed deep-fried pastries—are formed by combining flour with liquid fat and kneading the mixture (*page 42*). Kneaded flour and water dough (*page 46*) can simply be flavoured and fried in a coil. This dough—containing no fat—is also elastic enough to be stretched into paper-thin sheets known as phyllo. Once formed, phyllo sheets are very fragile. To keep the layers separate, each sheet is brushed with melted butter before being folded round a filling, and the dough cooks to form buttery, flaky pastry of great delicacy (*opposite and page 60*).

Shortcrust and rough-puff doughs (*page 44*) contain high proportions of fat and must be handled very lightly: too much handling would develop the gluten and make the pastry tough. Tender yet sturdy, these are the most versatile doughs: they can be wrapped round solid ingredients, such as small sausages (*page 50*), and shaped into cases that can be covered with pastry lids or left open to display their fillings (*pages 52-59*).

Rich, sticky choux paste contains eggs and a large amount of water, beaten into the flour and fat over heat (*page 44*). During cooking, the water becomes steam, causing the dough to expand into an airy, hollow crust—a perfect vehicle for flavouring or stuffing (*page 48*).

Fillings for any of these doughs include meat, fish, vegetables, sauces and savoury custards (*recipes, page 121-136*). All you need to remember is to match the consistency of the filling to the container: fragile sheets of phyllo, for example, are best wrapped round solid ingredients that will hold their shape, while pre-baked shortcrust cases are crisp enough to contain even a liquid sauce without becoming soft.

A Pair of Kneaded Doughs

Sandwiches, canapés, pizza and countless other snacks begin with some form of dough, such as those shown here and on the following pages. All doughs contain flour and liquid; they have strikingly different characteristics, however, according to whether the mixture is leavened, what amount of fat is added—if any—and how the dough is handled.

Leavening flour and liquid with yeast creates a bread dough (*right; recipe, page 164*); adding fat to flour and binding with water produces a basic pastry dough. Unlike bread, pastry doughs are usually handled very lightly and kept cold, so that they will bake to a tender crust. But the pastry dough shown on this page (*right, below; recipe, page 128*) is deliberately strengthened so it can be stuffed and deep fried in hot oil without crumbling.

To make bread dough, yeast—dried or fresh—must first be activated by being dissolved in tepid water. It is then combined with flour, more water and salt. The next step is kneading, which disperses water through the flour, activating flour proteins called gluten. Gluten forms a microscopic three-dimensional mesh that holds the dough together. Kneading also distributes the yeast, a necessity if the bread is to have an even texture.

After it is kneaded, the dough must be left to rest so that the yeast can grow. Feeding on the starch in the flour, the organisms give off the carbon dioxide gas that expands the dough. To break the gas bubbles down and to spread them more evenly, thus producing a finer texture, the risen dough is kneaded and left to rise again. Then the dough is shaped and baked—as a crisp-crusted loaf, as small rolls or, with the addition of a little oil, as a base for a pizza topping.

The crisp, strong pastry dough is made by rubbing liquid fat—melted clarified butter or oil—into the flour. The liquid fat is evenly and rapidly distributed, giving each particle of flour a thorough coating. After binding with water, the dough is kneaded, like bread, for at least 10 minutes, which develops and strengthens the gluten. When it has rested, the dough is strong enough to be rolled out very thinly to enclose a filling.

Producing a Basic Bread Dough

1 **Mixing yeast and flour.** In a large bowl, combine the yeast with tepid water. Stir the mixture briefly, then allow it to rest in a warm place—25°C (77°F) is ideal—for 10 to 15 minutes, until it is frothy. Stir in the flour and salt (*above*).

2 **Blending the ingredients.** Stir in more tepid water until the mixture becomes a stiff, shaggy dough. Squeeze the dough with your hands (*above*) to blend the ingredients thoroughly, then gather the sticky mass into a ball.

Crisp Pastry Dough for Deep Frying

1 **Adding butter to flour.** Melt clarified butter (*page 20*). Measure water into a jug. Mix flour and salt together in a large bowl. Spoon the melted clarified butter into the bowl (*above*).

2 **Rubbing in the fat.** Pick up a handful of flour and rub the butter into it with your fingertips (*above*). Continue until all of the butter is evenly distributed and the mixture looks like coarse oatmeal.

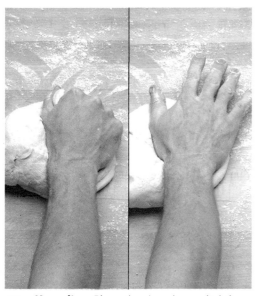  

3 **Kneading.** Place the dough on a lightly floured work surface. Flatten it with the heel of your hand; then fold the dough towards yourself, turn it so that the fold is at one side, and push it down and away (*above, left*). Continue to fold, turn and push the dough until It is smooth and elastic (*above, right*)—10 to 15 minutes.

4 **Punching down.** Gather the dough into a ball and place it in a clean, oiled bowl. Cover the bowl and put it in a warm, draught-free place. Leave the dough for about 1½ hours, until it has doubled in volume. Plunge your fist into the risen dough to deflate it (*above*).

5 **Kneading again.** Place the dough on a lightly floured surface and knead as before, working for 3 to 4 minutes, until the dough is satiny If you are making a basic bread, flatten the dough with the heel of your hand, then roll it into a ball or cylinder and let it rise for about 1 hour before baking it in the oven.□

 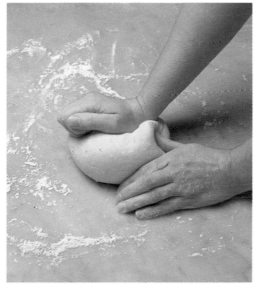 

3 **Binding with water.** A little at a time, pour in water and, with your hands, mix it into the flour and butter (*above*). Continue to add water until the ingredients cohere, forming a smooth, fairly stiff dough.

4 **Kneading the dough.** Gather the dough up into a ball and turn it out on to a lightly floured work surface. Knead it vigorously until it becomes smooth, elastic and glossy—10 to 15 minutes.

5 **Resting the dough.** Shape the dough into a ball and put it in a bowl. Brush a little clarified butter over the surface of the dough. Cover the bowl with a damp cloth and let the dough rest for 30 minutes.□

A Pair of Useful Pastries

Two forms of pastry dough, choux and shortcrust, provide the starting point for a wide range of snacks. Both doughs contain flour, water and butter, but choux also includes a high proportion of eggs. Moreover, the ingredients of the doughs are handled very differently.

Choux dough (*right; recipe, page 165*) is made by beating together over heat butter, flour and large amounts of water, then enriching the mixture with eggs. The dough is too soft and sticky to be rolled out: it has to be spooned or piped on to a tray. During baking, the water becomes steam which—together with the air beaten in during mixing—expands and puffs the choux into hollow mounds.

The first step in making shortcrust dough is to combine flour and butter. The quantity of butter can be varied from half the flour's weight to an equal weight—the more butter, the richer and crisper the pastry. The butter may be either rubbed or cut into the flour. In a rubbed short-

crust the butter and flour are closely intermingled and the result is a crumbly pastry; if the butter is cut in, it remains in distinct pieces and the pastry is flakier. A cut shortcrust such as the one below (*recipe, page 164*), containing equal quantities of butter and flour, can, if you wish, be transformed by repeated folding and rolling into the many-layered dough known as rough-puff (*Steps 5 and 6*).

After the butter and flour have been combined for shortcrust or rough-puff, a minimum of water is added, just enough to make the dough cohere. Too much water will make the dough sticky and difficult to roll out, and the resulting pastry will be tough; too little water will give a dry dough and mealy pastry.

When making a cut pastry dough, always start with chilled butter and cold water, and chill the dough thoroughly before rolling it out: if the butter softens, it will spread and coat the flour instead of remaining in separate particles.

Choux: an Egg-Rich Paste

1 **Adding flour.** Sift flour and salt together. Put water and diced butter into a heavy saucepan and set the pan over a high heat. Bring the water to a rolling boil. When the butter has completely melted, reduce the heat to medium and pour in the flour mixture all at once, stirring rapidly with a wooden spoon.

Shortcrust: a Butter-Flecked Sheet

1 **Cutting in butter.** Sift flour and salt into a mixing bowl. Cut chilled butter into small pieces and drop them into the bowl. Rapidly cut the butter into smaller bits in the flour, using two knives in a crossed slicing motion (*above*).

2 **Binding with water.** When the butter pieces are well coated with flour, use a fork to stir in cold water—a little at a time. Add just sufficient water to make the dough cling together in a mass.

3 **Chilling the dough.** Working quickly and avoiding handling the dough too much, gather up the dough with both hands and firmly press it into a ball. Flatten the ball into a thick cake, wrap it in plastic film and chill it in the refrigerator for at least 1 hour, or in the freezer for about 20 minutes.

2 **Combining the ingredients.** Cook the mixture over a medium heat, stirring constantly with the spoon to blend the flour and liquid together. The mixture will be lumpy at first (*above*), but it will become smooth within a minute or so.

3 **Stirring the mixture.** Continue to beat until the mixture pulls away from the sides of the pan in a smooth mass (*above*). Remove the pan from the heat. Let the mixture cool for about 2 minutes.

4 **Enriching with eggs.** Beat whole eggs, one at a time, into the cooled mixture, making sure each is incorporated before adding the next. As each egg is added the mixture will separate; it will smooth out again when the egg is thoroughly blended in. When all of the eggs are incorporated, the choux paste will be smooth and shiny and ready for use.□

4 **Rolling out the dough.** Place the chilled dough on a lightly floured work surface. Working from the centre in short, light strokes, roll out the dough. If you intend to use it as shortcrust, simply roll it to whatever shape and thickness you need, and it will be ready for use. For rough-puff pastry, roll the dough into a long, narrow rectangle 1 to 1.5 cm (½ to ⅔ inch) thick.

5 **Folding for rough-puff pastry.** On a lightly floured surface, fold one end of the rectangle at a time towards the centre of the dough (*above*). The two ends should meet each other in the centre.

6 **Finishing rough-puff.** Brush off excess flour (*above*). Fold the dough in half to make a package four layers thick. Turn it so that one of the open ends is facing you and roll it out again. Fold, roll and fold again. Wrap the dough in plastic film and chill it. Roll and fold two or three times more; chill thoroughly after every second turn. Roll the dough out for use.□

A Fried Spiral of Pastry

The simplest form of pastry dough—a mixture of flour and water, without added fat—yields a variety of sturdy snacks. Because of its lack of fat, this dough is unsuitable for baking: it would become hard and unpalatable in the dry oven heat. But, shaped and flavoured as shown here, the dough can be fried to make crunchy pancakes (*recipe, page 140*); or it can be filled with a savoury mixture, shaped and deep fried in the same way as the *samosa* pastry shown on page 55.

This basic dough is very easy to make. However, it is important to knead the flour and water mixture thoroughly to activate the gluten in the flour, and then to let it rest before shaping. These steps will ensure that the dough is cohesive and pliable enough to be formed into a thin pancake that will cook through quickly.

An assertive filling will lend flavour to the bland pastry. Here, the dough is brushed with sesame-seed oil and then sprinkled with chopped spring onions. Ham, sausage or shrimps could be used instead of the onions, and olive oil or melted lard could replace the sesame-seed oil.

1 Mixing the dough. Place the flour in a bowl, make a well in the centre and with your fingers gradually stir in sufficient water to form a soft dough. On a lightly floured surface, knead the dough (*page 43*) until it is smooth and elastic—about 3 minutes. Place the dough in an oiled bowl and cover it with a damp cloth.

2 Final kneading. When the dough has rested for about 15 minutes, transfer it to a floured work surface. Knead the dough for 2 minutes, sprinkling it with flour as necessary to keep it from sticking. When the dough feels soft and smooth, gather it together into a ball.

6 Forming a cylinder. With your fingers, roll up the rectangle of coated pastry dough across its width to form a long cylinder (*above*). Pinch both the ends and the long open edge closed.

7 Forming a coil of dough. Starting at one end of the sealed cylinder of pastry dough, wind it with your fingers into a coil (*above*). Tuck the loose end of the dough cylinder underneath the finished coil.

8 Rolling out the coil. Flatten the coil of dough slightly with the palm of your hand. Roll it out with a rolling pin to make a pancake about 5 mm ($\frac{1}{4}$ inch) thick. Cover the pancake with a cloth to keep it moist and then repeat the procedure with the remaining dough rectangles.

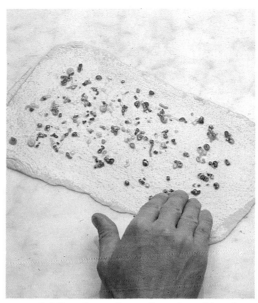

3 **Rolling out the dough.** Cut the ball of dough into four quarters. On a floured surface, roll each quarter into a rectangle about 3 mm (⅛ inch) thick. Sprinkle each rectangle with salt and roll it once more to press the salt into the dough.

4 **Coating the dough.** Clean spring onions and trim them, then slice them across into fine pieces. Set them aside. Brush each of the dough rectangles with a thin coat of sesame-seed oil (*above*).

5 **Adding the spring onions.** Sprinkle a few of the spring onion pieces evenly over the entire surface of one of the rectangles of dough. Pat the onions and press them into place on the dough (*above*).

9 **Frying the pancakes.** In a heavy frying pan, heat a thin layer of oil. Add a pancake and fry it over medium heat for about 5 minutes, turning it once, to brown both sides. Transfer the fried pancake to paper towels to drain (*left*) and then fry the remaining pancakes. Cut them into quarters (*above*) and serve them hot.□

Ethereal Confections from Choux

Choux paste (*page 44*) expands dramatically during baking to make a rich, light vehicle for flavourings and fillings.

The cook may, for instance, incorporate cubes of cheese into the choux paste and shape it into a ring to produce *gougère* (*right; recipes, page 138*), a savoury Burgundian dish. The traditional *gougère* is made with cubed Gruyère cheese, but other firm cheeses may be used instead; for a richer *gougère*, milk can be used instead of water in the dough. An alternative way to treat choux paste is to form it into small spheres. As they swell in the oven's heat, the spheres become hollow balls—useful containers for many different fillings (*box, below*).

To form either balls or rings, you can spoon mounds of the paste on to a prepared baking sheet. For particularly neat balls, or miniature rings, pipe the paste through a piping bag.

Both rings and balls must be baked at a steady high temperature to ensure that they rise properly. Do not open the oven door until the end of the cooking time: even a slight drop in temperature could cause the choux to collapse. When the pastries are done, they should be dried to keep them light and crisp. Pierce them to provide vents for steam, and leave them in the turned-off oven for a few minutes to dry out. A *gougère* should remain slightly moist, but choux balls must be quite dry inside to be successful containers.

If you intend to serve choux balls with a cold filling, leave them to cool completely before filling them. Fairly solid fillings such as the chicken in mayonnaise shown below should be spooned into the balls after their tops have been sliced off. More liquid fillings, such as a cheese mixture (*upper demonstration, page 18*) or a shellfish purée (*page 39*) can either be spooned in, as below, or piped from a piping bag through the hole in each ball.

1 **Adding cheese.** Cut cheese—Gruyère is used here—into small cubes; add about two-thirds of the cubes to prepared choux paste. Season the mixture with salt and pepper and, if you like, a little dry mustard (*above*). Stir the mixture to blend all the ingredients thoroughly.

Piping Tiny Puffs

1 **Piping choux balls.** Fit a piping bag with a round-tipped nozzle. Fill the bag with choux paste, twist the bag closed and pipe balls 1 cm (½ inch) in diameter about 8 cm (3 inches) apart on a prepared baking sheet. Brush the tops of the balls with egg glaze (*Step 2, opposite page*).

2 **Filling the balls.** Bake the balls in a preheated 190°C (375°F or Mark 5) oven for 15 to 20 minutes or until golden. Prick the balls with a knife and let them dry out in the turned-off oven for 20 minutes. Take them out and leave them to cool. Slice off the tops of the balls and spoon in a filling—here, chicken in mayonnaise. Replace the tops and serve.

4 **Smoothing the ring.** Either leave the ring of paste in mounds, or, as here, smooth the surface of the circle with a spatula or the flat of a knife. Brush the top of the *gougère* with the egg glaze, taking care that none drips on to the baking sheet.

2 Making a pattern and an egg glaze. Coat a baking sheet with butter and flour, or line it with buttered greaseproof paper. Use a saucepan lid as a guide to draw a circle on the paper or to stamp a circle into the flour. Beat an egg with milk, cream or water to make a glaze for brushing over the top of the *gougère*.

3 Forming a ring. Scoop up large spoonfuls of paste and arrange them in mounds in a ring on the baking sheet, using the circle as a guide for the ring's outer edge. Place a second ring of smaller spoonfuls on top of the first, centring them between its mounds.

5 Baking the gougère. Sprinkle the rest of the cubed cheese over the *gougère* (*above*). Bake it in a preheated 190°C (375°F or Mark 5) oven for 35 to 40 minutes—it should be firm to the touch when pressed lightly with a finger. Using a knife, pierce the top of the ring in several places. Leave it in the turned-off oven for 5 to 10 minutes. Serve in wedges.□

Mass-Producing Pastry Wrappers

Shortcrust and rough-puff pastry doughs can easily be wrapped round any of a variety of fillings to produce small, savoury packages. But if the pastry parcels are to be properly crisp yet tender, care must be taken in choosing the filling, assembling the packages and baking the assemblies. Here, shortcrust wrappers are shaped into crescents and baked.

The crescents begin from a sheet of chilled pastry dough, rolled out as described on page 45. To divide the sheet into portions, cut it into strips, then stack the strips and cut through the stack, forming triangles. Use a pastry wheel or a very sharp knife for cutting: a dull blade will pull and wrinkle the dough.

In addition to pork sausages shown here, the choice of fillings for the pastry

parcels can also include mixtures based on minced or chopped seasoned meats, chopped vegetables such as mushrooms or spinach—first parboiled and squeezed—leftover meats and vegetables, and even chopped nuts. Breadcrumbs soaked in cream, or *ricotta*, curd or grated Parmesan cheese are often added, both for flavour and to stiffen mixtures, and egg yolk is useful for binding.

Use only fillings that are fairly firm and dry—a very liquid filling might seep through the dough wrapper. And remember that oven heat takes time to penetrate an enclosed stuffing: any filling which would not cook through in the brief period needed to bake the pastry crescents must be cooked in advance. In this demonstration, the small pork sausages are poached in water and white wine. Always allow a cooked filling to cool before wrapping

pastry dough round it, or the heat from the filling may melt the butter in the dough, causing it to run out.

As a further precaution against leaks the cut edges of the crescents should be sealed. To encourage the edges to stick together, moisten them with water, raw egg white, or egg yolk mixed with milk or water. Next, brush the egg mixture over the pastry parcels. It will harden to a crisp, shiny glaze during baking.

Baking sheets to be used for pastries should be made of heavy metal—such as the carbon steel used in this demonstration—that will not buckle in the oven's heat. To prevent the pastry crescents from sticking while they are baking, grease and flour the sheet, or cover it with greaseproof paper or aluminium foil.

1 Preparing small sausages. Fill sausage casings with a pork mixture (*page 16*). To separate long pork sausages into small links, twist them at intervals of 2.5 cm (1 inch) (*above*). In a partly covered pan, simmer the sausages in a mixture of equal parts of water and white wine for 12 to 15 minutes. Drain the sausages; cut through the twists to separate the links.

2 Cutting strips of dough. To make about 20 sausage crescents, roll 500 g (1 lb) of shortcrust pastry dough into a rectangle 50 cm (20 inches) long, 30 cm (12 inches) wide and no more than 5 mm (¼ inch) thick. Square off the edges with a pastry wheel or a sharp knife. Cut the dough into strips 10 cm (4 inches) wide.

3 Cutting triangles. Dust the strips with flour and stack them. Press the pastry wheel diagonally across the stack of strips to cut the dough into triangles 10 cm (4 inches) wide at their bases, then separate the triangles and lay them out in rows on a lightly floured surface.

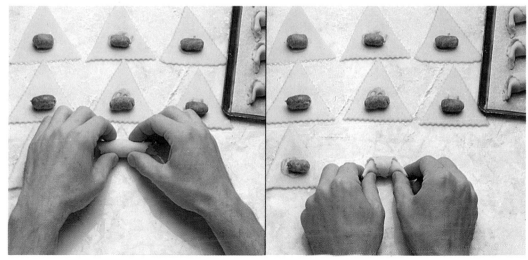

4 **Filling the triangles.** Put a small dab of mustard near the base of each triangle and lay a sausage on it. Using a pastry brush or your finger, damp the triangle's edges with water, egg white or a mixture of egg yolk and water (*above*).

5 **Forming crescents.** Working from the base (*above, left*) roll each triangle up round its sausage. Pinch the ends of the roll firmly together and bend them down to form a crescent (*above, right*). Place the filled crescents on a prepared baking sheet.

6 **Baking the parcels.** Brush each crescent with a mixture of egg yolk and water (*below*). Chill them for about 20 minutes. Place the baking sheet in a preheated 220°C (425°F or Mark 7) oven. After 3 to 4 minutes, lower the heat to 190°C (375°F or Mark 5) and bake the crescents for a further 25 minutes, until golden. Transfer them to a tray and serve at once.□

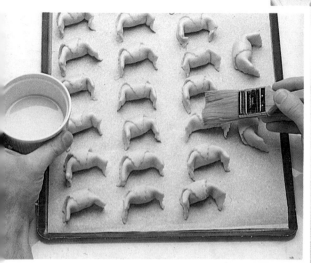

A Catalogue of Parcels

A variety of pastry parcels may be formed from circles, squares and rectangles of shortcrust or rough-puff pastry dough. You can either fold a single dough shape to make a turnover or roll that encloses a stuffing, or seal together two shapes with stuffing between them.

No matter how the parcel is formed, direct handling of the dough should be kept to a minimum, to prevent the butter from softening and the pastry from becoming tough. Various types of equipment may be employed to help keep warm hands away from the dough itself. Greaseproof or wax paper, for example, can be used to lift and move large pieces of dough without damaging them (*page 54, Step 1, above*). (A paper wrapping also prevents dough made in advance from drying out.)

Metal tools can be used to shape and decorate dough: edges can be sealed with pincer-like pastry crimpers (*Step 4, right, below*), turnovers such as Cornish pasties (*right; recipe, page 122*) can be crimped with a fork, and layered packages can be stamped and sealed with metal cutters (*page 54, Step 2, below*).

The sealed edges of the packages demonstrated here and on pages 54-55 allow greater leeway in the choice of fillings than is possible with rolled pastry wrappers (*page 50*). Liquid, if it is properly handled, can be used to enrich fillings without damaging the packages. The liquid can be funnelled in after the pastry has set (*Step 4, right, above*) or, as in the pies in the lower demonstration—which can be covered, as here, or left without lids (*recipe, page 133*)—the liquid may be combined with such thick, starchy ingredients as parboiled potatoes, which will absorb any excess.

Once filled and sealed, most of these pastries are, like the wrappers, brushed with an egg glaze (*page 49, Step 2*) and then baked. Notable exceptions are the *samosa* pastry parcels demonstrated on page 55 (*recipe, page 128*), which are deep fried in hot oil. For these, the egg glaze is omitted, since the oil might burn it.

Filling and Folding Circles

1 **Cutting circles.** Roll out dough—in this case, rough-puff—into a rectangle 3 mm (⅛ inch) thick. Use the rim of a bowl or tin to stamp out circles about 12 cm (5 inches) in diameter, or use a plate as a pattern and cut round it with a pastry wheel or a knife. If you wish to cut smaller circles, use a biscuit cutter or the rim of a glass.

2 **Filling the pastries.** Prepare a filling; the one used here includes finely chopped beef, potatoes and onions. Place 2 to 3 spoonfuls of filling slightly off-centre on each circle of dough, and top the filling with butter. Paint the rim of the dough with egg glaze. Fold the uncovered half of the dough over the filling; crimp the edges with the prongs of a fork.

Making Miniature Pies

1 **Filling the pies.** From rolled-out dough— here, rough-puff—stamp circles to fit the cups of a tartlet mould and an equal number of slightly smaller circles. Press the larger circles into the cups. In each, place grated, parboiled potatoes and chopped truffles or mushrooms.

2 **Enriching the pies.** Spoon more grated potatoes into the pies. Then spoon or pour in some double cream seasoned with salt and pepper. Fill the pies to within 5 mm (¼ inch) of the top.

3 **Baking the turnovers.** Paint the pastries with egg glaze. With a fork, prick the top of each turnover, so that steam can escape. Bake them for 45 minutes in a preheated 170°C (325°F or Mark 3) oven.

4 **Enriching the filling.** Take the turnovers out of the oven. Pierce a small hole in the top of each turnover with the neck of a funnel, and pour in about 2 tablespoons of double cream. Do not allow the cream to drip on to the pastry.

5 **Completing the baking.** Replace the turnovers in the oven and bake for 15 minutes more, until the pastry is crisp and golden-brown. If you like, place sprigs of fresh rosemary or thyme in the holes made by the funnel.□

3 **Covering the pies.** Place a smaller circle of dough on top of each of the filled pies. But do not press the smaller dough circles down, in case you make the filling leak from the edges of the pies.

4 **Crimping the edges.** Use pastry crimpers to seal the lid and base of each pie. Paint the pies with egg glaze. Bake at 200°C (400°F or Mark 6) for 5 minutes, then at 170°C (325°F or Mark 3) for about 30 minutes, until the pies are golden-brown and shrink from the sides of the cups.

5 **Removing the pies.** Lift each pie carefully from its cup and transfer it to a wire rack. When the pies have cooled slightly, put them on a serving plate (*above*) and serve them immediately.□

Forming Triangular Turnovers

1 Preparing the triangles. Cut rolled-out dough—in this case, rough-puff—into 12 cm (5 inch) squares. Spoon filling—here, drained marinated oysters (*recipe, page 125*) and lemon rind slivers—diagonally along one half of each square. Paint the square's edges with egg glaze; using wax paper, fold over the uncovered half.

2 Decorating. Press the edges closed, then slash them with a knife to form a decorative border. Make a slit in each triangle to allow steam to escape. Cut leaf shapes out of dough scraps. Brush the turnovers with egg glaze; place the leaves on them and glaze them again.

3 Baking the triangles. Put the turnovers on a prepared baking sheet (*page 50*). Chill them for about 20 minutes. Bake them in a preheated 230°C (450°F or Mark 8) oven until golden—about 15 to 20 minutes. Use a broad spatula or a fish slice to transfer the turnovers to a serving platter. Serve them immediately.□

Bonding Twin Squares

1 Filling the squares. Cut rolled-out pastry dough—in this case, rough-puff—into 12 cm (5 inch) squares. Place a spoonful of filling—here, chopped leeks stewed in butter and thickened with cream—in the centre of one of the dough squares. Brush a wide egg glaze border round the filling. Cover with another square.

2 Sealing the squares. Press the borders of the pair of squares together. With a pastry wheel or a biscuit cutter, trim off the edges, cutting through the egg glaze border (*above*). Repeat this procedure with the rest of the squares. Paint the filled squares with more egg glaze.

3 Baking the squares. Cut a small cross in the top of each square so that steam can escape. Place the squares on a prepared baking sheet. Chill the pastries for about 20 minutes. Bake them in a preheated 230°C (450°F or Mark 8) oven for 15 to 2 minutes, until they are golden. Transfer the squares to a platter and serve.□

Rolling Up a Filling

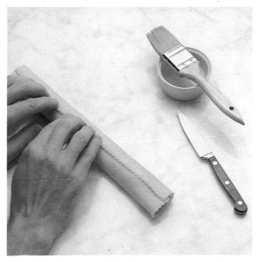

1 Filling a pastry rectangle. Cut rolled-out pastry dough—here, rough-puff—into rectangles 30 cm (12 inches) long and 10 cm (4 inches) wide. Spoon filling—in this instance, minced liver, egg and onion (*recipe, page 130*)—along the centre of each rectangle. Smooth the filling into a cylindrical shape with a spatula.

2 Sealing a roll. Fold one long side of the dough up over the filling. Brush the second side with egg glaze and fold it up to overlap the first; press it lightly to seal the roll. Brush egg glaze inside the open ends of the roll and pinch them together. Place the roll, seam side down, on a prepared baking sheet.

3 Baking. Make deep diagonal slashes in the roll at 2.5 cm (1 inch) intervals. Fill, fold up, seal and slash the other rectangles. Paint the rolls with egg glaze. Chill them, then place them in a preheated 220°C (425°F or Mark 7) oven. After 5 minutes, reduce the heat to 190°C (375°F or Mark 5); bake for 40 minutes. Cut through the slashes to give diagonal slices.□

Deep Frying Stuffed Cones

1 Cutting the dough. Roll out *samosa* pastry dough (*page 42*) to a thickness of 3 mm (⅛ inch). With the rim of a tin or a bowl, cut out circles about 12 cm (5 inches) in diameter. Divide each circle in half with a sharp knife or a pastry wheel. Paint the edges of each half with water.

2 Filling the samosas. Fold each semicircle in half and press the straight edges together to form a cone. Spoon filling into the cone; a mixture of peas and potatoes (*recipe, page 128*) is used here. Press the top edges of the cone together to seal it.

3 Deep frying. In a deep pan, heat 7.5 cm (3 inches) of oil to 180°C (350°F) or until a bread cube browns in the oil within 35 seconds. Put in a few *samosas*. The oil temperature will drop to about 150°C (300°F); maintain this temperature by adjusting the heat. A few at a time, deep fry *samosas* for 12 minutes, turning once. Remove them with a skimmer and drain.

Savoury Custards for Pastry Cases

Open pastry cases filled with a smooth egg custard mixture offer rich opportunities to combine flavours, colours and garnishes in a broad assortment of small baked pastries.

The choice of possible additions to an egg custard is wide. While some of the custard here is left plain, some is coloured with a sweet red pepper purée to make a pink mixture, and the rest is speckled green with courgette shreds and threads of parsley. You could also add tomato sauce, sorrel stewed in butter, spinach purée, a purée of broccoli or peas—even puréed crayfish carcasses (*page 22*).

Choose garnishes whose colours and flavours blend or contrast attractively with that of the custard. Some of the pink custards here, for example, are garnished with shrimp tails, others with sweet red pepper strips and olive halves. Diced bacon, asparagus tips, squares of Gruyère cheese, slices of tomato or courgette appear on the other quiches. Alternative possibilities for garnishes include sliced sautéed mushrooms, chopped truffles and parboiled and sautéed cauliflower florets.

1 Preparing an egg custard. Break eggs into a large bowl. Season them with salt and pepper and a little nutmeg and cayenne. Pour in double cream—about 12.5 cl (4 fl oz) of cream for each egg—and whisk the mixture thoroughly.

2 Preparing courgettes. Wash, top and tail courgettes. Cut them into chunks and shred them, using a hand grater, a rotary shredder or a food processor. Put the shreds in a bowl, sprinkle them with salt and leave them for about 30 minutes; the salt will draw out their liquid. Squeeze the shreds (*above*) and put them in a clean bowl. Discard the liquid.

5 Preparing garnishes. Remove the rind of a slab of bacon; dice the bacon finely. Parboil, refresh, drain and dry the diced bacon, then sauté it. Cut the tips from asparagus; peel and slice the stems. Parboil, refresh, drain, dry and sauté asparagus tips and slices. Remove the heads from cooked shrimps and shell the tails. Roast, peel and seed sweet red peppers; cut them into strips. Reserve the asparagus tips, half the shrimp tails and half the pepper strips. Place diced bacon, asparagus slices, shrimp tails or pepper strips in two-thirds of the cases; leave the remaining cases empty.

6 Adding the custard. Fill the pastry cases containing the diced bacon and those containing the asparagus with the plain custard. Spoon the pink mixture into the pastry cases containing shrimp tails or pepper strips. Fill the empty pastry cases with the green-speckled mixture.

3 **Colouring the custard.** Chop parsley finely and add it to the courgettes. Roast, peel and seed sweet red peppers (*page 7*). Cut them into small pieces and, using a pestle, purée them through a sieve. Ladle a third of the egg custard into the bowl containing the courgettes and parsley (*above*) and stir them together so that the custard is speckled with green. Mix half of the remaining custard into the red pepper purée to make the pink mixture.

4 **Moulding pastry cases.** Cut rolled-out shortcrust dough (*page 44*) into rounds slightly larger than your tins; here, rounds 9 cm (3½ inches) in diameter are cut to fit tins 7 cm (2¾ inches) across and 1 cm (½ inch) deep. Press a round into each tin.

7 **Applying top garnishes.** Top the plain custard quiches with diced bacon or asparagus tips and the pink ones with shrimp tails or olive halves and pepper strips. Peel, seed and slice tomatoes; salt the slices to draw out excess liquid; pat them dry. Top the speckled quiches with the tomato slices and thin squares of Gruyère cheese (*above*) or with courgette slices and olive halves. Sprinkle the olive-garnished pastries with grated Parmesan cheese. Bake all the filled pastries at 220°C (425°F or Mark 7) for 15 minutes, until the custard is set and the tops are brown (*right*). □

Filling Pre-Baked Cases

Shortcrust pastry cases that are baked empty make suitable containers for fillings that do not need to be cooked, or that have cooking requirements different to those of the pastry. The pastry cases can be wholly baked or partially cooked and then later returned to the oven with a filling added to them.

Pastry cases are usually shaped individually, as demonstrated on page 57, but you can shape and cut a number of cases at once by the method shown here. The dough is rolled out thinly, loosely draped over the tins and pressed down with a rolling pin so that the edges of the tins cut their own shape out of the dough. The excess dough will drop off the sides.

If pastry dough is not weighed down, it tends to blister during baking: to prevent this, pastry cases that are to be baked without filling can be lined with grease-proof paper and filled with dried beans or peas. A simpler way of achieving the same result is to stack the dough-lined tins on top of one another so that each weighs down the dough in the tin beneath. In this demonstration, the pastries are baked in a stack for 15 minutes, then unstacked and returned briefly to the oven to brown.

Because fillings for pre-baked cases are prepared separately from their pastry containers, there need be no restriction on what type of filling you choose. Any of the fillings for toast or bread cases (*recipes, pages 156-157*) would be suitable. For garnishes, you might like to try sautéed mushroom slices or any of the garnishes used for open tarts (*page 56*).

In the demonstration here, caviare and salmon roe are the fillings chosen. Fine caviare is enhanced by mild-flavoured garnishes such as the butter and hard-boiled eggs used here, while the rougher taste of salmon roe can support stronger flavours. Here, diced onions, lemon slices, parsley and chervil are used to garnish the barquettes filled with salmon roe.

1 Laying dough over tins. Make shortcrust pastry dough (*page 44*) and roll it out thinly. Arrange small tins in rows. Wrap the dough loosely round a rolling pin and unroll it over the tins (*above*). With your fingers, press the dough into each tin.

2 Cutting pastry shapes. Roll the pin back and forth over the dough until the sharp edges of the tins cut through the dough (*above*). Pick up the lined tins one by one and press the dough against the walls and bottom of each tin to ensure that the dough is firmly in place.

6 Preparing garnishes. Cut hard-boiled eggs in half; remove the yolks and press them through a sieve with a wooden spoon. Slice the egg whites paper-thin and cut the slices into tiny sticks. Dice onions very finely. Wash parsley, dry it with a towel and chop the leaves finely. Slice a small lemon thinly and halve the slices. Pull off the leaves from chervil sprigs. Mix softened butter with spinach juice to colour it green (*pages 9 and 6*). Place lines of diced onion down the centre of some of the barquettes with salmon roe filling and sprinkle the finely chopped parsley on top.

3 **Stacking the tins for baking.** To prevent the pastry dough from rising as it bakes, stack the dough-lined tins on top of each other. Place an empty tin on each stack to weigh down the dough in the top tin.

4 **Baking the empty cases.** Place the lined tins on a baking sheet and bake the stacked pastry cases for 15 minutes in an oven preheated to 220°C (425°F or Mark 7). Remove and unstack the tins and return them to the hot oven for about 5 minutes, until the pastry is crisp and golden. Slide the cases out of the tins on to a wire rack and allow them to cool.

5 **Filling the cases.** Tumble caviare and salmon roe from their containers into small bowls. If you try to spoon them straight from tightly packed containers you may break the grains. Fill half of the cases with caviare, carefully spooning it out of the bowl and letting it tumble loosely into the cases. Fill the remaining cases with salmon roe.

7 **Garnishing.** Cut the halved lemon slices in the middle from the straight edge almost to the rind; twist them into curls. Place the curls on the rest of the cases with salmon roe filling and add chervil leaves. Lay the strips of egg white on some of the caviare-filled cases. Using two small knives, guide the sieved yolk into lines down the middle of the other cases. Fill a piping bag fitted with a nozzle with the green butter and pipe it thinly round the edges of the cases filled with caviare (*above*). Arrange the garnished barquettes on a serving plate (*right*).□

The Special Demands of Phyllo

Light and very crisp pastry packages are produced from sheets of phyllo, a paper-thin flour and water pastry that is popular in Greece and the Middle East. Phyllo is difficult to make at home, but ready-made phyllo dough is available, either fresh or frozen, at delicatessens and shops specializing in Middle Eastern foods.

The dough is sold in stacks of rectangular sheets sealed in plastic to keep them moist. Because the dough contains no fat, the sheets quickly become dry and unmanageably brittle when exposed to the air. Fresh phyllo can be kept for as long as five days in the refrigerator. Frozen phyllo keeps four to five months; it should be defrosted in the refrigerator for 24 hours before being unwrapped.

Once phyllo dough is taken out of its wrapping it should be used immediately. Remove the number of sheets required, keeping them in a stack, and return the rest in their wrapping to the refrigerator. Use scissors or a very sharp knife to cut the sheets into the strips from which the packages will be fashioned. Then peel off phyllo strips one by one. If you work slowly, cover the stack of dough with a damp towel to keep the sheets flexible.

Before filling the sheets of phyllo, brush each one generously with melted butter. The butter will crisp the pastry during cooking, and ensure that each delicate layer remains separate.

The filling can consist of almost any well-seasoned mixture. For the two demonstrations on the right, chopped spinach is combined with cheeses and beaten eggs (*recipe, page 126*). For the third demonstration (*box, opposite page*), equal parts of grated cheese and sautéed, chopped mushrooms are topped with an egg.

To make the packages, the filling is placed near one end of a strip of dough. The dough is then rolled or repeatedly folded to form a many-layered envelope that can be cylindrical, triangular or square in shape. The sealed packages may be either baked or deep fried.

Repeated Folds That Yield a Triangle

1 **Filling a piece of phyllo.** Cut phyllo into strips about 15 cm (6 inches) across and at least 40 cm (16 inches) long. For each triangle, brush a phyllo strip with melted butter and put filling—here, spinach and cheese—near the bottom end, slightly left of centre. Hold the left corner and fold the right corner over towards the left edge of the strip, forming a triangle.

2 **Folding a phyllo strip.** Hold the edges of the triangle to keep the filling in place. For the second fold, fold the triangle along its top edge straight up over the phyllo strip, aligning the triangle's left edge with the left edge of the phyllo strip. For the third, fold the triangle towards the right edge of the phyllo strip (*above*); for the fourth, fold the package straight up again.

A Cylinder Curled Back on Itself

1 **Adding filling.** Cut phyllo into rectangles about 25 cm (10 inches) wide and at least 40 cm (16 inches) long. For each coil, brush one rectangle with melted butter (*above*). Spoon a line of filling—here, a spinach-based filling—across the lower end, leaving margins of dough 2.5 cm (1 inch) wide on the sides and bottom.

2 **Rolling a tube.** Fold the long sides of the dough towards the centre to cover both ends of the line of filling; the folds should extend the length of the phyllo. Brush the edges with melted butter. Roll the dough up from the bottom to enclose the filling in a tube (*above*). Press the end flap on to the filled tube to seal it.

3 **Finishing the package.** Repeat the four steps, folding the triangle over until you reach the top of the strip. Press the loose end of dough at the top gently on to the triangular package to seal it (*above*).

4 **Baking the triangles.** Brush the triangles with melted butter on all sides and put them on a baking sheet. Bake them in a preheated 220°C (425°F or Mark 7) oven for 5 minutes; reduce the heat to 190°C (375°F or Mark 5) and cook them for 7 to 10 minutes more. Using tongs to avoid piercing the delicate pastry, transfer the triangles to a serving platter.☐

A Square with Egg Inside

1 **Filling.** Cut a double thickness of phyllo and butter the top. Spread mushroom and cheese filling 10 cm (4 inches) from one end. Fold in the long sides. Break an egg on the filling; fold over the short end.

2 **Folding.** Working gently to avoid breaking the egg, fold the filled square of phyllo over and over until you reach the end of the strip. In a deep pan, heat oil to 190°C (375°F).

3 **Forming coils.** Bring the ends of the tube together to form a circle. Tuck one end under the other; press the top end down over it to keep it in place. Brush the coils all over with melted butter and place them on a baking sheet.

4 **Baking the coils.** Bake the coils in a preheated 220°C (425°F or Mark 7) oven as for the triangles (*Step 4, above*). Transfer the coils carefully to a platter and serve them immediately.☐

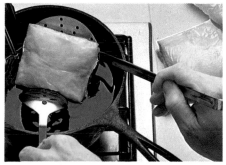

3 **Deep frying.** Using a spatula, slide each phyllo square into the hot oil. Deep fry the pastry for 4 to 6 minutes or until it is golden, turning it once with two slotted spatulas or spoons. Drain on paper towels.

Pizza: a Bread Platform for Hearty Sauces

A thin round of yeast-leavened dough topped with a savoury mixture bakes to create the hearty Neapolitan snack that is known throughout the world as pizza (*recipes, pages 136-137*). The dough is essentially bread dough (*page 42*), but it calls for some minor modifications in both ingredients and handling.

First, pizza dough may be enriched by adding a couple of tablespoons of olive oil when you combine the flour and salt with the yeast mixture. Then, to produce the coarse texture characteristic of pizza, let the kneaded dough rise only once before flattening it into a disc. The disc should not be shaped until you are ready to place the pizza in the oven; if it were left for any length of time, the yeast would cause the disc to rise and become distorted.

Traditionally, pizza is baked on hot bricks or tiles, causing a crisp crust to form. To simulate a brick oven, line the middle shelf of the oven with unglazed quarry tiles. Heat them in the oven for at least 30 minutes before you place the pizza on them. You will need some means of sliding the unwieldly disc in and out of the oven. A bread board will suffice, or you can use the wooden paddle—known as a peel—shown in this demonstration.

Many of the toppings used for pizza dough have a foundation of tomatoes—either fresh, ripe tomatoes, skinned, sliced and strewn over the dough, or a sauce made from fresh, canned or bottled tomatoes (*recipe, page 166*). Most pizza toppings also include cheese—*mozzarella* or Parmesan, for example—and herbs such as oregano or basil. More elaborate pizzas may have added layers of mushrooms, sweet green or red peppers, dried sausage, or even cooked seafood.

1 Kneading the dough. Mix bread dough, adding a little olive oil to the flour (*page 42, Steps 1 to 2, above*). With the heel of your hand, knead the dough on a lightly floured work surface for 15 minutes, or until the dough feels silky, elastic and not sticky. Gather the dough into a ball.

2 Leaving the dough to rise. Coat the inside of a bowl with olive oil. Place the ball of dough in the bowl and roll it round to coat it with the oil. Cover the bowl with a damp towel and put it in a warm, draught-free place for 2 hours, or until the dough doubles in volume. Punch the dough down (*page 43, Step 4, above*).

5 Assembling the pizza. Spread tomatoes—a thick tomato sauce is shown here—over the dough without dampening the rim. Sprinkle any other toppings—here, shredded *mozzarella* and grated Parmesan cheese, chopped basil, whole basil leaves, salt and pepper—on to the tomatoes. Dribble olive oil on top.

3 **Rolling and shaping the dough.** Divide the dough into fist-sized balls and let them rest for a few minutes. On a lightly floured surface, roll or press each ball of dough into a disc 3 mm ($\frac{1}{8}$ inch) thick (*above, left*). Then, with your fingertips, gently push some dough outwards from the centre of the disc (*above, right*) to build up a rim round the outside edge that will retain the topping.

4 **Transferring the dough to a peel.** Dust a wooden peel or bread board lightly with cornmeal, as here, or coarse semolina. Grasp the dough with your fingertips and—using the motion you would use to shake out a wet cloth—fling the disc on to the peel. Carefully smooth out any wrinkles in the disc with your fingers.

6 **Baking the pizza.** Set the edge of the peel on the tile-lined shelf of a preheated 230°C (450°F or Mark 8) oven. Jerk the peel or use a wooden spatula to push the pizza on to the tiles (*above*). Bake for 15 to 20 minutes. Lift the pizza with the spatula to check the bottom (*right*); when it looks crisp and browned, the pizza is done. Serve immediately.□

4
Bread Bases and Cases
The Simple Sandwich: Theme and Variation

Many people think of a sandwich as just two slices of bread with a filling between them. In fact, the term encompasses dozens of culinary creations, from open sandwiches that display a plenitude of ingredients on thin slices of bread, to substantial, multi-layered constructions such as the double-decker American "club"; it even includes entire loaves, stuffed and served in slices. The smallest, most elegant open sandwiches are bite-sized canapés—shaped bread or toast bases with delicate toppings.

The character of sandwiches depends as much on the bread chosen as on the way it is sliced, shaped, topped, filled or garnished. The most versatile bread is a firm, close-grained, rectangular sandwich loaf that can be sliced thinly and that also toasts well (*page 66*). It can often be replaced, however, by loaves made from whole wheat or rye flour. Breads of contrasting colour can be arranged in combination to yield sandwiches with attractive patterns (*page 70*). French or Italian long loaves are especially well suited to being stuffed whole: their strong crusts provide sturdy shells to hold the fillings (*page 68*).

Bread-based snacks are served both hot and cold. Small rolls, cut in half and hollowed out, can be packed with a sauced filling, baked and served straight from the oven (*page 72*), while a simple topping of grated cheese can be sprinkled on a slice of bread and heated beneath a grill until it bubbles (*page 73*). Sandwiches in which the filling is securely enclosed can be deep fried or sautéed: cheese fillings melt smoothly while the outer surface of the bread becomes crisp (*page 74*).

Most open sandwiches are served cold, and their exposed toppings and garnishes give them instant appeal. The collages of meats, seafood, vegetables and eggs that characterize the Danish sandwiches known as *smørrebrød* (*pages 76-79*) are arranged to be visually attractive as well as to combine complementary flavours and textures. Canapés may be as simple as small rounds of toast topped with a flavoured butter or spread and garnished with finely chopped herbs or vegetables (*pages 80-83*). For a more elaborate effect, tiny morsels, such as quail's eggs (*opposite*) and crayfish tails, are set off by delicate pipings of flavoured, coloured butter; while thin slices of cooked meat, first dipped in a thick, creamy sauce known as *chaud-froid*, then garnished and glazed, create a colourful assortment of the tastiest party food (*pages 84-86*).

A quail's egg, poached and trimmed, then strewn with finely chopped parsley, is placed on a canapé. Thin white bread and Parma ham have been shaped with a cutter; the bread, lightly toasted, is then spread thinly with butter and the ham pressed on top. The canapé could be enhanced with pipings of flavoured butter.

The Simple Sandwich: Theme and Variation

A Light Filling of Cucumber Slices

At its simplest, a sandwich need consist only of a single ingredient between two slices of buttered bread. Light, delicate cucumber sandwiches, for example, are ideal as a tea-time snack (*right*). But this simple structure is also the basis for more elaborate presentations.

By combining two or more different fillings, using breads of different flavour or texture—such as rye or wholemeal—or increasing the number of bread layers, you can build a wide variety of colourful and substantial sandwiches. The "double-decker" (*opposite page, below*), containing fillings of bacon, lettuce, tomato and chicken between layers of toast, is hearty enough to form a light meal in itself.

Your choice of bread will depend on the filling you are using, and how substantial you want the sandwich to be. For very thin, light sandwiches, a close-grained white bread is a good choice. The bread should be slightly stale, about a day old. The crumb will then be firm enough for you to cut very thin slices; fresher bread would tear beneath the knife.

Butter, spread on the bread, serves several purposes. It prevents the bread from absorbing moisture from the filling, and also ensures that filling and bread will stick firmly together. And, of course, it contributes its own flavour. Here, parsley butter adds piquancy to the mild taste of cucumber. To complement different fillings, you can use mayonnaise instead of butter. However, it is best to use mayonnaise with toast, since it would seep into bread and make the sandwich soft.

The list of ingredients that can serve as sandwich fillings is virtually endless; it includes thick purées made from meat or fish (*pages 20 and 22*), crisp salad vegetables, slices of cooked meat or poultry, or any combination of these. Ingredients containing a lot of moisture, such as slices of cucumber, can, if you wish, be drained and dried beforehand.

To hold the finished sandwiches firmly together, you can chill them briefly in the refrigerator so that the butter hardens slightly. If you are making very thin sandwiches, weight them before serving to give them an even shape.

1 Slicing the cucumber. Peel a cucumber and halve it lengthwise. Run a finger down the centre of each half, scooping out all the seeds and the water that comes with them. Slice the cucumber halves thinly (*above*).

2 Draining the cucumber. Layer the slices of cucumber in a bowl, sprinkling each layer with a little fine salt. Leave them to stand until their liquid is drawn out— about half an hour. Then squeeze the slices over the bowl, a handful at a time (*above*), and spread them on a towel. Roll up the towel tightly to dry them.

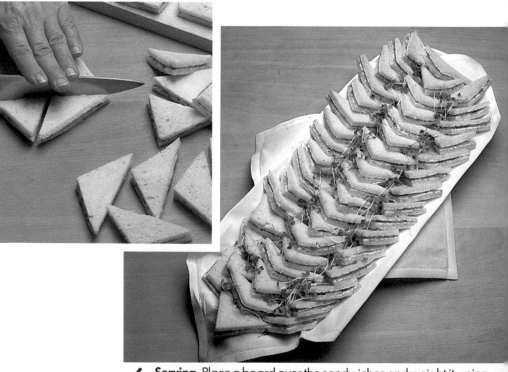

6 Serving. Place a board over the sandwiches and weight it, using scale weights or unopened cans; leave them under weights for at least an hour. Cut the sandwiches into quarters (*inset*); cover with a damp cloth until it is time to serve them. Arrange the sandwiches on a napkin-lined platter and decorate with mustard and cress.□

3 **Slicing the bread.** Using a sharp knife, remove the crusts from a loaf of bread and cut it into 8 mm (⅓ inch) slices. If the bread is too fresh or too crumbly to be sliced so thinly, put the loaf into the freezer for up to an hour to firm it.

4 **Buttering the slices.** Chop fresh herbs—here, parsley—into fine threads. Soften butter (*page 6*); mix it with the chopped herbs. Spread the herb butter evenly over one side of each slice of bread.

5 **Assembling the sandwiches.** Unroll the towel that contains the cucumber. Cover half the buttered slices of bread evenly and thinly with the cucumber slices. Lay the remaining slices of bread, buttered side down, on top of the cucumber.

A Hearty Double-Decker

Assembling the layers. Wash and dry lettuce leaves; fry bacon rashers; cut tomatoes and cooked chicken breasts into thin slices. Spread mayonnaise on one side of three slices of toast; place a layer of each filling on the mayonnaise on one slice. Cover with the second slice of toast, mayonnaise-side down. Spread more mayonnaise on the top; add more filling (*left*). Top each sandwich with the third slice of toast, mayonnaise-side down; cut into quarters. □

Constructing the Super-Sandwich

One way to produce large quantities of sandwiches quickly and easily is to put the filling inside a whole loaf and then cut the loaf into slices for serving. You can hollow out the crumb of a crusty loaf and pack a stuffing into the shell (*right*), or halve a long, thin loaf lengthwise and enclose a filling between the halves (*below*).

The hollowed loaf should be spread with butter on the inside to seal it. Choose a soft, homogeneous stuffing that can be piped into the crust and that will become firm when chilled. A spread containing butter or cheese is the best choice—here, raw minced steak is mixed with butter. Chilling hardens the stuffing so that it will not crumble and will stay bonded to the bread when the loaf is sliced.

Virtually any ingredient can be used in a halved loaf sandwich; no special method of introducing the filling is required. Here, olive oil complements the flavours of onions, sweet red peppers, anchovies and black olives. To mingle the flavours and hold the assemblage together, weight the filled loaf before slicing.

Hollowing a Crusty Cylinder

1 **Hollowing the loaf.** Cut off the tapered ends of a long loaf; if the remainder of the loaf is more than 30 cm (12 inches) long, cut it in half. Using a long, flexible knife and working from each end, hollow out the crumb (*above*), leaving just the crusty shell. With the same knife, spread the inside of the cavity with softened butter.

2 **Stuffing the loaf.** Prepare a spread of raw minced steak, replacing the olive oil with softened butter (*page 17*). Using a piping bag with a wide nozzle, pipe the stuffing into each end of the hollowed loaf; round off the exposed filling. Wrap the loaf in plastic film. Leave in the freezer for about 1 hour, until partially frozen, or in the refrigerator for about 3 hours.

Layering a Long Loaf

1 **Oiling bread.** Slice a long, crusty loaf lengthwise into halves. If the bread is very fresh, place the halves in an oven set at 170°C (325°F or Mark 3) for about 5 minutes to dry the cut surfaces. Rub the surface of each half with a cut garlic clove, then dribble over some olive oil. Sprinkle salt over each of the halves.

2 **Preparing fillings.** Peel an onion and cut it into thin slices. Roast, seed and peel sweet red peppers (*page 7*), then cut the peeled peppers into strips about 2.5 cm (1 inch) wide. Lay the onion slices on one half of the bread and place the pepper strips on top of them.

3 **Adding layers.** Soak and fillet anchovies (*page 6*). Place the anchovy fillets in a criss-cross pattern on top of the pepper strips (*above*). Remove the stones from black olives; cut each olive in half.

3 **Slicing rounds.** When the stuffing has become very firm, slice the loaf into rounds about 1 cm (½ inch) thick (*above*). Place the slices on a tray lined with a napkin. If the loaf has been partially frozen, leave the sliced rounds at room temperature for 15 to 20 minutes before serving them (*right*).□

4 **Completing the sandwich.** Arrange the olive halves in the spaces between the anchovies on top of the pepper strips. Cover the filling with the other half of the loaf (*above*), pressing it down lightly.

5 **Weighting the sandwich.** Place a wooden board on the sandwich (*above*) and put two or three weights on top. Leave the sandwich under the weighted board for at least 2 hours, until the assemblage holds firmly together. Then cut the compressed sandwich into portions; if you like, serve them garnished with watercress (*inset*).□

A Play of Geometry

For colourful, patterned sandwiches, you can put together layers of bread and filling in such a way that, when sliced, they reveal geometric designs.

Any two breads of similar texture but contrasting colour may be used to produce chequered sandwiches (*right*). Stacked slices of alternating colour, joined with butter, can be cut into striped slices and these, in turn, can be stacked and cut again, forming chequerboards.

To make spiral-patterned sandwiches, a thin slice of close-textured bread—cut lengthwise from the loaf—is covered with a spread containing a high proportion of butter (*page 20*) or with butter and a thin, pliable topping, such as prosciutto or smoked salmon (*below*). The open sandwich is rolled into a cylinder that yields coils when diagonally sliced.

The construction of both chequerboards and spirals relies on the adhesive effect of butter, which hardens when chilled. Coloured butters—such as those mixed with spinach juice or sweet red pepper (*page 7*) are especially attractive.

Two-Bread Chequerboards

1 Assembling layers. Trim the crusts from two rectangular loaves—here, dark rye and white bread. Cut the loaves into slices about 1 cm (½ inch) thick. Starting with white bread, butter and stack the slices—in this case, herb butter is used (*page 7*)—alternating the colours and ending with an unbuttered slice of rye.

2 Slicing the loaf. Wrap the stacked loaf in plastic film and chill it for at least an hour to firm the butter. Then, using a sharp bread knife, cut through the loaf at 1 cm (½ inch) intervals to form ribboned slices.

Spiralling Slices

1 Flattening bread slices. Cut a light rye loaf lengthwise into slices 8 mm (⅓ inch) thick. Trim the slices into rectangles; press them very hard with a rolling pin to make them thin and supple (*above*). Cover the bread with a dampened towel to prevent it from becoming dry.

2 Adding filling. Spread softened butter—in this case, butter tinted green with spinach juice (*page 9*)—on each bread slice. Place smoked salmon on top, using as many slices as necessary to cover the bread in one even layer. Trim the edges and use the salmon trimmings to fill any uncovered areas of bread.

3 Spreading butter. Spread more butter over the surface of the salmon. To help you roll up the sandwich tightly, make a dent across the width of each bread slice close to one end, using the blunt edge of a knife blade. Lift up the end to form the beginning of a roll (*above*).

3 **Creating chequered slices.** Spread a layer of butter on one ribboned slice. Place a second slice on top of the first, turned so that the rye strips rest on top of the white strips. Continue to butter and layer the remaining slices in the same way (*above*). Wrap the assembled loaf in plastic film and chill until firm. Unwrap the loaf and slice it (*right*); halve each slice diagonally to make triangles.□

 4 **Rolling the sandwiches.** Fold the end of each sandwich tightly over the dent. Roll up the sandwiches (*above*); wrap them securely in plastic film. Freeze the rolls for at least an hour, until they are partially frozen and very firm to the touch.

5 **Cutting rounds.** Remove the rolled sandwiches from the freezer when you are ready to cut them. Unwrap each roll and, with a sharp knife, cut it diagonally into slices about 5 mm (¼ inch) thick. Arrange the slices on a napkin-lined platter for serving.□

Toasted Shells for Creamy Sauces

Warm sandwich fillings and toppings call for equally warm bread that has been toasted to crispness so that the filling does not make it soggy. One such combination is demonstrated here: hollowed, buttered and oven-crisp halved rolls are packed with a mixture of shallots, garlic, mushrooms, tongue, cream and egg yolks (*recipe, page 156*), then they are baked in the oven until piping hot.

Halved baps or simple bread slices could also be used as bases. The possibilities for fillings are extensive: as well as the mixture shown here, you could try diced cooked game or fish in velouté sauce (*recipe, page 166*), or chicken in a béchamel sauce (*recipe, page 166*).

Toast the rolls in the oven, where the even heat will crisp the bread on every side. They may be baked in any rack position, or on two racks if the number of pieces warrants it. For extra crispness and flavour, brush the bread with oil or melted butter before toasting it.

1 Preparing the filling. In a wide pan, sauté chopped shallots in butter for 5 minutes. Stir in finely chopped garlic and sliced mushrooms, cover the pan and cook over a low heat for 3 to 4 minutes to soften the mushrooms. Season, then stir in double cream and diced, cooked, smoked tongue. Simmer the mixture for a few minutes to blend the flavours.

2 Thickening the filling. Stir a little of the simmering sauce into lightly beaten egg yolks to raise their temperature so that they will not curdle when added to the pan. Blend the mixture gradually into the filling. Stir over a low heat until the sauce thickens—do not let it return to the boil. Adjust the seasoning.

3 Toasting roll shells. Slice the tops off crusty rolls. Pull out the crumb, leaving shells about 1 cm (½ inch) thick. Brush them all over with melted butter; place them on a baking sheet and bake in a preheated 230°C (450°F or Mark 8) oven for 5 to 10 minutes, until brown and crisp.

4 Filling the shells. Spoon the mushroom filling into the baked roll shells, dividing the mixture equally among them and mounding the filling slightly. Return the filled shells to the baking sheet.

5 Heating the shells. Heat the filled shells in the oven for 5 minutes, or until the tops are bubbly and lightly browned. Arrange the hot shells on a warmed serving plate and serve them at once.□

A Golden Blanket of Cheese

One of the most delicious cooked sandwiches is produced by sprinkling grated cheese over crisp bread and grilling the assembly so that the cheese melts into a golden mass. Nothing could be simpler. Nonetheless, close attention to the cooking is essential, since the heat of a grill is so intense that the cheese can quickly overcook and become leathery.

Most types of bread are suitable—French, sandwich, light or dark rye, or the potato bread shown here. But whatever bread you use, it should be sliced no more than 1 cm (½ inch) thick, so that it heats through in the time that the cheese takes to melt. And, to make sure it stays crisp, it should be toasted before the cheese topping is added. To add extra flavour, the toast may be brushed with melted butter or with olive oil, or it can be spread with a soft topping such as anchovy paste.

Cheshire, Edam, Gouda, Parmesan, Gruyère or the Cheddar cheese used here, are all good choices. Or you could use a mixture of leftover cheeses.

1 Preparing the bread. Cut bread into slices about 1 cm (½ inch) thick. Toast the slices. While the toast is still warm and absorbent, brush the tops of the slices with olive oil. The oil used here has been flavoured with garlic cloves which were steeped in it for several days.

2 Grating the cheese. Using a box grater or, as above, a rotary grater, grate the cheese into fine shreds. Alternatively, cut the cheese into small chunks and then grate them in a food processor.

3 Making the sandwiches. Using a fork or your fingers, sprinkle a thick layer of cheese over the toast (*left*). Cover each slice to the edges so that the crusts will not burn under the grill. Place the cheese sandwiches on a baking sheet and set them 10 cm (4 inches) below the grill. Grill for about 1 minute, until the cheese melts and begins to bubble (*above*).□

Fried Sandwiches: Hot, Crisp and Tasty

A wide array of fried sandwiches feature cheese as their main ingredient. For the lightest versions of these sandwiches, the cheese is placed between two slices of bread and the sandwich is then sautéed in a little butter; or the bread can be buttered on the outside and the sandwich cooked on an ungreased griddle. For a more robust sandwich, demonstrated here, the assemblage is dipped into beaten egg and then deep fried (*recipe, page 150*).

Sandwiches that are dipped in egg before frying should be made with a bread that is firm enough in texture to soak up the egg without disintegrating. To ensure even absorption of the egg, the crusts of the bread should be removed when you shape the slices. Here, both bread and cheese are cut into circles, but triangles or rectangles would do just as well.

Any firm cheese that slices easily and melts readily is suitable for filling the sandwich. *Mozzarella*, Gruyère, Cheddar, Cantal, Gouda, Edam or Taleggio are the commonest choices. To make a more substantial sandwich with extra flavour, sliced tomato or ham can be layered together with the cheese filling (*recipe, page 152*) before the sandwich is fried.

Moistening the sandwich with beaten egg ensures that a seal is formed round the sandwich as it fries, preventing the oil from permeating the bread. The egg also helps hold an edging of breadcrumbs that adds crunchiness and prevents the cheese from oozing out as it melts.

The egg-coated sandwiches need only a very brief period of frying—just enough to brown the surface and melt the cheese. Drain the sandwiches and serve them at once, while they are still hot. Deep-fried cheese sandwiches may be accompanied by a sauce: a piquant tomato sauce (*recipe page 166*) combines well with a mild cheese, as does the anchovy sauce shown here (*recipe, page 102*).

1 Shaping bread and cheese. Cut cheese—here, *mozzarella*—into 5 mm (¼ inch) thick slices. Cut twice as many slices of the same thickness from a loaf of bread. Using biscuit cutters, shape both the bread and cheese into circles, making the cheese rounds about 1 cm (½ inch) smaller in diameter than the bread rounds. Place a round of cheese between each pair of bread rounds.

2 Soaking the sandwiches. Prepare fine crumbs from day-old bread. In a shallow dish, beat together a couple of eggs, a teaspoon of water and a pinch of salt. Dip each sandwich into the egg mixture and turn it to moisten the edges. Leave the sandwich to soak in the egg mixture for a few seconds until the bread is well moistened.

3 **Sealing the sandwiches.** As soon as each sandwich is coated with the egg mixture, lift it out of the dish and roll it in the breadcrumbs until the edges are thoroughly coated with crumbs. As you work, set the coated sandwiches aside on a platter.

4 **Frying the sandwiches.** In a frying pan, heat 2.5 cm (1 inch) of olive oil until it is hot but not smoking. Lower the sandwiches into the oil with a spatula and fry them for about 1 minute on each side, or until they are golden. Lift the fried sandwiches out of the oil between tongs or spatulas. Drain the sandwiches on paper towels and transfer them to a warmed serving dish.

5 **Making anchovy sauce.** Soak and fillet anchovies (*page 6*); pound them in a mortar with some olive oil until they form a coarse purée. Transfer the purée to a saucepan; pour in vinegar or, as here, lemon juice (*left*). Over a medium heat, let the sauce warm through gently; do not let it boil. Remove the sauce from the heat and spoon or pour a little of it over each fried sandwich (*below*).□

The Sandwich as a Still Life

In an open sandwich, a single slice of bread makes a showcase for an elaborate topping. Ingredients for the topping—chosen for their visual characteristics as well as for their flavours—are arranged with meticulous care to produce a harmonious and colourful pattern. The nine sandwiches displayed below, and prepared opposite and overleaf, are typical of the Danish sandwiches known as *smørrebrød*. But they are a few among many possibilities; you can vary the ingredients and arrangements at will to produce innumerable sandwiches.

An open sandwich must be put together at the last possible moment so that it does not dry out. To taste their best, all the ingredients must be served at room temperature; if any have been refrigerated, remove them from the refrigerator in plenty of time.

The first step in assembling the sandwich is usually to spread softened butter over a slice of bread. The bread can be sour rye, pumpernickel, trimmed white bread, toast or crispbread. Whatever sort you choose, it should be sliced about 8 mm (⅓ inch) thick. Butter brings a rich taste while sealing the bread's surface. Mayonnaise may be substituted in cases where its sharper taste would better comple-

ment a topping; however, mayonnaise will seep into the bread, softening it.

Almost anything may be included in the topping for an open sandwich. Most toppings combine meat, fish, cheese or eggs with raw or cooked vegetables. Fresh herbs, pickles or twists of lemon provide decorative garnishes.

Open sandwiches are usually eaten with a knife and fork. One notable exception is the combination of caviare or lumpfish roe and a shell-cupped raw egg yolk presented on crispbread (*below, bottom left*). The diner pours the yolk into the hollow made in the roe by the egg shell, then picks up the sandwich in his hand to eat it.

A selection of open sandwiches. The common denominator of these open sandwiches—prepared on the following pages—is the careful arrangement of the toppings. Clockwise from top left are prune-stuffed pork with red cabbage; prawn salad with salmon roe, garnished with lemon and dill; liver loaf with diced aspic and pickles; herring with beetroot and egg slices; prawns with dill; roast beef with fried onions; hard-boiled egg with sprats; dill-marinated salmon, and lumpfish roe with raw onion rings and an egg yolk.

Stuffed Pork with Red Cabbage

1 Stuffing pork. Pierce a boned pork loin with a sharpening steel. Stuff it with stoned prunes; roast at 170°C (325°F or Mark 3) for 25 minutes per 500 g (1 lb).

2 Buttering bread. Cool, then slice the pork. Butter trimmed white bread. At one end, mound red cabbage cooked with apples (*recipe, page 163*).

3 Completing the sandwich. Prop slices of pork, overlapping each other, against the mound of cabbage. Garnish the open sandwich with a sprig of parsley.☐

Prawn Salad with Salmon Roe

1 Spooning on salmon roe. On buttered toast, spread a layer of diced, cooked prawns mixed with mayonnaise (*page 8*). Place salmon roe on the centre.

2 Making a lemon twist. Cut a lemon slice half way through and twist the halves in opposite directions. Place the twist of lemon at one edge of the sandwich.

3 Garnishing the sandwich. Lay a sprig of fresh dill opposite the twist of lemon. Serve the garnished prawn and salmon roe sandwich immediately.☐

Liver Loaf with Aspic

1 Slicing loaf. Cut uniform slices from a liver loaf (*recipe, page 97*). As you work, dip the knife blade into hot water to keep it from sticking to the loaf.

2 Dicing aspic. Set lettuce and tomato on one side of a slice of buttered bread and place a slice of liver loaf on top of the bread. Garnish with sliced pickles and parsley. Dice aspic (*recipe, page 165*).

3 Finishing the sandwich. With a spatula, transfer diced aspic to the sandwich. Position it round the liver loaf, opposite the lettuce and tomato.☐

Beetroot, Herring and Hard-Boiled Egg

1 **Spreading the salad.** Prepare a salad of diced herring and beetroot (*recipe, page 163*); slice a herring fillet. Set a lettuce leaf on buttered dark rye bread and spoon the salad on top of it.

2 **Piping soured cream.** Place the herring slices across the salad. Then pipe a swirl of soured cream on to the lettuce leaf. For extra colour, the soured cream may be tinted with beetroot juice.

3 **Adding garnishes.** Prop two slices of hard-boiled egg alongside the sliced herring (*above*). Tuck a sprig of fresh dill in the lettuce under the soured cream. □

A Pinwheel of Prawns with Dill

1 **Preparing prawns.** Poach fresh prawns in a court-bouillon (*recipe, page 166*) until pink; drain, shell and de-vein them. Spread mayonnaise (*page 8*) on toast. Arrange the prawns in a ring.

2 **Adding the garnish.** Fill the centre of the ring with more prawns. For the garnish, tuck some sprigs of fresh dill into the crevices between the prawns.

3 **Seasoning the prawn sandwich.** Grind a generous amount of black pepper over the prawns. Squeeze fresh lemon juice over the completed sandwich. □

Roast Beef with Herb Mayonnaise

1 **Making mayonaise.** Prepare a basic mayonnaise (*page 8*), flavouring the egg yolks with a pinch of mustard and a little sugar before whisking in the oil. Add some finely chopped dill.

2 **Preparing the topping.** Fry thinly sliced onion rings in butter or oil; drain them. Slice rare roast beef and cut a tomato in wedges. Butter a slice of dark rye bread.

3 **Arranging the sandwich.** Place a lettuce leaf, a tomato wedge and parsley on a corner of the bread. Fold roast beef slices to fit on the bread, add the mayonnaise and garnish with the onion rings. □

An Assembly of Egg and Fish

1 **Shaping bread.** Assemble the toppings: drained sprats, sliced hard-boiled egg, tomato wedges, lettuce and dill. Cut a circle of bread with a biscuit cutter or a glass—as here—and butter it.

2 **Arranging the egg slices.** Put a lettuce leaf on the circle of buttered bread and place the hard-boiled egg slices over it, overlapping the slices.

3 **Adding the sprats.** Cross a pair of sprats over the row of egg slices. Tuck a tomato wedge behind the eggs and garnish the assembly with fresh dill.□

Salmon Marinated in Dill

1 **Slicing the salmon.** Coat filleted fresh salmon with seasonings and sugar, layer with dill, place under weights and chill for one to two days (*recipe, page 163*). Drain and wipe it; cut it in thin slices.

2 **Arranging the salmon.** Place lettuce at one end of a slice of buttered crispbread. Lay salmon slices on the crispbread, covering some of the lettuce to anchor it.

3 **Adding sauce.** Garnish the sandwich with a lemon twist and chopped dill. Spoon dill-flavoured mayonnaise (*page 8*) on to the fish; grind pepper over it.□

A Bed of Roe for a Cupped Egg Yolk

1 **Buttering crispbread.** Assemble all the toppings: lumpfish roe, lettuce, onion rings and a small egg. Butter a piece of crispbread; put a lettuce leaf on one end.

2 **Spreading the roe.** Smooth a generous portion of the lumpfish roe over the crispbread, covering part of the lettuce to anchor it. Spread the roe lightly, to avoid damaging the eggs as far as possible.

3 **Separating the yolk.** Place fresh onion rings on top of the roe. Break an egg and separate the yolk from the white. Stand the half-shell containing the yolk beside the lettuce leaf, settling it in the roe.□

A Practical Approach to Canapés

The small open sandwiches known as canapés provide the imaginative cook with unlimited opportunities to experiment with toppings, decorations and garnishes. As the examples here and overleaf show, canapés can be made with almost any food: meat, poultry, fish, eggs, vegetables, fresh herbs and flavoured butters.

The bread that provides the bases for canapés should be cut very thinly. To get the maximum number of bases with the least waste, cut a whole loaf lengthwise. For perfect slices, have the loaf cut on a machine by your baker. Toast the slices lightly for crispness and extra flavour.

Any of the ingredients used for the open sandwiches shown on pages 76-79 are suitable toppings for canapé bases; the only requirement is that they be as delicate as possible. Butters and spreads must be smooth and soft, so they can be applied evenly. Meat, fish and poultry must be sliced finely; prosciutto—used here (*right*)—is ideal. Raw or cooked vegetables should be cut into tiny pieces; small ingredients, such as shrimps and quail's eggs, can be left whole.

There are two methods of assembling canapés. To create rounds, ovals and crescents, stamp out bases from the toast with a biscuit cutter, and butter and decorate each one individually. For straight-sided shapes, apply the topping to whole slices of toast and then cut them into sections.

If you are making individual canapés, solid toppings, such as slices of meat or fish, must be cut out separately to fit the toast bases exactly. For straight-sided canapés made by the second method, you can apply butter and other spreads to the unsectioned slices—a mixture of finely chopped olives, gherkins and salami is shown here (*right*). If you wish to add slices of meat or fish to the toast at this stage, be sure that they are supple enough to be easily and cleanly sliced. If in doubt, leave the topping to be applied after the canapés are cut.

To decorate the assembled canapés, use fresh herbs—either whole leaves or finely chopped. Flavoured butter—piped to emphasize the shape of the base or to highlight the contour of the topping— provides a final flourish of colour.

Stamping Out Uniform Shapes

1 Cutting out ovals. Using a sharp knife, cut a loaf of bread lengthwise into 8 mm (⅓ inch) slices. Toast the slices lightly under the grill or in an oven preheated to 230°C (450°F or Mark 8). While they are still warm, stamp out ovals with a biscuit cutter (*above*). With the same cutter, stamp out ovals from the topping—here, thin slices of prosciutto are used.

2 Preparing a garnish. Squeeze lemon juice into a bowl. Wash small button mushrooms and wipe them dry. Cut the mushrooms into thin slices (*above*); put the slices in the lemon juice to keep them white. Holding chives in a bunch, cut across their stems with scissors or a sharp knife to make very fine pieces; mix them with the mushroom slices.

An Efficient Scheme for Cutting

1 Fashioning a base of toast. Cut a loaf of sandwich bread lengthwise into slices about 8 mm (⅓ inch) thick, or ask the baker to do it for you. Toast the slices lightly. Using a sharp knife, trim off the crusts (*above*); cut each slice in half lengthwise.

2 Applying the topping. Spread flavoured butter—in this case, sweet red pepper butter (*page 7*)—on the toast. Prepare a mixture of finely chopped ingredients— here, equal amounts of salami, olives and gherkins. Using a knife with a long blade, apply the mixture from the blade down the centre of the toast. Use a second knife to guide the first (*above*).

3 **Assembling the canapés.** Spread the toast ovals thinly with softened butter (*page 6*). Carefully aligning the edges, lay a prosciutto oval on top of each piece of buttered toast (*above*). Gently press the prosciutto into place.

4 **Piping decorations.** Place mushroom slices in the centre of each canapé, overlapping them slightly. Fit a piping bag with a 5 mm ($\frac{1}{4}$ inch) nozzle and fill it with softened butter—here, butter tinted with spinach juice (*page 9*). Pipe the butter round the edge of each canapé (*above*). Arrange the canapés on a plate lined with a napkin (*inset*).☐

3 **Finishing the edges.** Prepare another flavoured butter—saffron butter is used here. Fit a piping bag with a broad nozzle with three parallel holes and fill it with the butter. Pipe the butter in bands down each side of the topping (*above*).

4 **Dividing into sections.** Using a sharp knife, cut across the strips to divide them into bite-sized pieces (*above*). Present the finished canapés on a plate lined with a folded napkin (*inset*).☐

A Sumptuous Topping of Crayfish

Garnishing with sprigs of dill. Cook and shell crayfish (*page 22*); split and reserve the tails. Purée the rest of the flesh; combine it with softened butter. Using a biscuit cutter, stamp out circles of toast; move the cutter's rim to the centre of each circle and stamp again to form crescents. Spread the crayfish butter on the crescents. Pipe red pepper butter (*page 7*) round each canapé; lay a crayfish tail, cut side down, in the centre; garnish with dill.□

Almond-Stuffed Olives as Centrepieces

Decorating edges with parsley. Soak and fillet anchovies (*page 6*); halve them lengthwise. Stone black olives; stuff each with a blanched almond; halve them crosswise. Cut trimmed slices of toast into squares. Spread the tops and side edges with red pepper butter (*page 7*). Press the edges into finely chopped parsley; pat the parsley into place with a knife blade. Wrap each olive half with an anchovy strip; place one, cut surface up, in the centre of each square.□

Asparagus Tips on a Tapenade Base

Piping thin lines of saffron butter. Parboil asparagus tips for 2 minutes; refresh them in cold water; drain and dry them. Halve trimmed slices of toast lengthwise. Spread the toast with *tapenade* butter (*page 6*). Fit a piping bag with a fine nozzle; pipe lines of saffron butter across each buttered toast strip, piping beyond the edges. To make diamond-shaped canapés, cut diagonally across each strip at 4 cm (1½ inch) intervals. Garnish with the asparagus tips.☐

A Smoked Salmon Setting for Quail's Eggs

Circling eggs with butter. Poach quail's eggs; dip them in cold water to arrest their cooking. Lay the eggs on a damp towel; trim the edges of the whites. With a biscuit cutter, stamp out circles of toast and thinly sliced smoked salmon. Spread the toast with softened plain butter. Lay a salmon circle on each piece of toast; centre a quail's egg on top. Fit a piping bag with a star nozzle; pipe saffron butter round each egg and then round the canapés.☐

A Silken Coat of Jellied Cream

A gelatinous stock is the basis for the deliciously creamy sauce known as *chaud-froid* (*right; recipe, page 166*). The sauce takes its name—meaning "hot-cold"—from the fact that it is first heated to thicken it and then cooled to set it. The result is a firm, rich jelly—an ideal coating for canapé toppings of meat, fish or poultry, such as the turkey breast used here.

To ensure that *chaud-froid* contains enough gelatine to set properly, it is cooked in two stages. First, a reduced veal stock is simmered with a flour and butter roux to make a velouté. Jellied stock is then added, a spoonful at a time, so that the sauce can be rapidly reduced after each addition, thus reinforcing the gelatine content without diluting the sauce. Blended with cream to add flavour, the finished sauce can be used as it is or coloured with herbs, saffron, tomato purée (*page 8*) or—as in this demonstration—with a purée of sweet red peppers.

Gelatine dissolves completely at high temperatures, but quickly starts to set again as the finished sauce cools. To control this gelling process, transfer the hot sauce to a metal bowl and stir it continuously over ice (*Step 5*). Metal is a rapid conductor of temperatures, so the sauce will cool quickly; the stirring will ensure that the sauce cools evenly, and also that no skin forms on its surface.

To coat the meat, the sauce should be just thick enough for you to feel the spoon pulling slightly as you stir it: it will then adhere closely to the surface of the topping and form an even coating. If, while you are working, the sauce continues to cool and becomes too thick, thin it by stirring it briefly over hot water. You may then need to stir it over ice again until it has reached just the right consistency.

Once the toppings are coated, you can refrigerate them to allow the sauce to finish setting quickly. Simple garnishes—such as herbs or thin slices of hard-boiled egg white—will stay firmly in place on top of the *chaud-froid* if they are first dipped in a little melted jelly (*Step 8*). A final coating of jelly spooned over the toppings will give them a gleaming, jewel-like finish. Just before serving, transfer the toppings to buttered toast bases and decorate them (*Step 11, overleaf*).

1 **Preparing toppings.** Cook buttered and boned turkey breasts in a tightly covered casserole in an oven set at 180°C (350°F or Mark 4), allowing 20 minutes per 500 g (1 lb). Refrigerate the breasts; cut them into 5 mm (¼ inch) slices. Cut ovals from each slice with a biscuit cutter (*above*); wrap the ovals in plastic film until needed.

2 **Making a velouté.** Boil a veal stock (*page 25*) until reduced by about a third; reserve it. In a heavy pan, melt butter over a low heat. Stir in flour; cook, stirring continuously, for 3 to 4 minutes to make a roux. Whisk in stock (*above*). Continuing to whisk, increase the heat until the sauce comes to the boil, then reduce the heat so that the sauce simmers.

5 **Cooling the sauce.** Pour the sauce into a metal bowl set in a larger bowl filled with ice. If—as here—you intend to colour half the sauce, cool only half; leave the rest in the pan set over a low heat and stir it occasionally. With a wooden spoon, stir the sauce in the metal bowl (*above*) until it has completely cooled, then remove the bowl from the ice and set it aside.

6 **Colouring the sauce.** Pour the remaining sauce into another metal bowl. Add a colouring—here, a purée of sweet red peppers (*page 7*)—stirring it in with a spoon (*above*). To cool the coloured sauce for immediate use, set the metal bowl in a bowl of ice and stir the sauce as in Step 5 until it is just thick enough to coat the spoon. Remove the bowl from the ice.

3 **Cleansing the velouté.** Set the pan half off the heat. Skim off the skin of fat and impurities that forms on the cooler side of the liquid (*above*). Simmer, skimming regularly, until no more fat rises and the liquid has reduced by about a third—approximately 40 minutes.

4 **Finishing the sauce.** To give additional body to the sauce, add jellied stock, a chunk at a time (*above, left*), reducing the sauce after each addition. Gradually add cream (*above, right*) along with the final addition of jelly. Continue to cook the sauce gently, repeating the skimming (*Step 3*) to remove any fat that rises to the surface, until the sauce's consistency resembles that of a thick cream.

7 **Dipping the ovals.** Unwrap half of the turkey ovals. Using a fork, dip each oval in the sauce (*above*). Place the ovals on a rack set over a tray; refrigerate each rack as you fill it. Unwrap the remaining ovals to dip them in the reserved, uncoloured sauce. Set the bowl of sauce in a larger bowl of hot water; stir the sauce to melt it.

8 **Decorating the ovals.** Dip tarragon sprigs in boiling water; refresh them in cold water; pinch off the leaves and lay them on a towel to dry. Cut truffles and hard-boiled egg whites into thin matchsticks. Melt jelly in a pan; flavour it with sherry; stir a small quantity in a metal bowl over ice to cool and thicken it. Dip the decorations in the jelly and lay them on the ovals—here, truffle strips and egg white on the coloured canapés, and truffle strips and tarragon leaves on the plain ones. Refrigerate each rack of ovals as you finish them. ▶

9 **Glazing the ovals.** Transfer more melted jelly to a metal bowl; stir it over ice until it cools and begins to thicken. To seal in the garnish and give the toppings a glossy finish, pour a little of the cooled jelly over the ovals from a spoon (*above*). Refrigerate the ovals for 10 minutes to set the coating; coat and refrigerate again. To prepare the bases, slice a sandwich loaf lengthwise; toast the slices.

10 **Assembling the canapés.** With a biscuit cutter—here, a fluted oval—1 cm (½ inch) larger all round than the jellied toppings, cut out bases from the toast; let them cool and butter them lightly. Using a small knife, remove the jellied ovals from the racks, gently prising them loose; place one on each of the buttered toast bases (*above*). Reserve the jelly that has collected in the trays beneath the racks to use in another preparation.

11 **Piping decorations.** Prepare flavoured butter—here, pale green butter made with spinach juice (*page 9*). Fit a piping bag with a fluted nozzle; spoon in the butter. Holding each canapé by the edges, pipe butter round the topping (*left*). If possible, serve the canapés immediately; otherwise, keep them in a cool place for up to half an hour.□

Anthology
of Recipes

The snack and canapé recipes in the Anthology that follows have been selected by the Editors and consultants from among the best published during the past two centuries. In all, the work of 170 authors is represented; the choices range from the elegant canapés of the 1920s cocktail era to the rustic pizzas and hero sandwiches that Italian cooks have popularized around the world. A number of the recipes have been chosen from rare and out-of-print books in private collections, and some of them have never before been published in English.

Throughout the Anthology of recipes, as in the demonstrations in the first half of the book, the emphasis is on how to ring the changes upon such fundamentally simple ideas as the sandwich, the dip and the filled pastry; on vivid contrasts in flavour, texture and colour; and on the selection of fresh ingredients of high quality. Since many early cookery writers did not specify amounts of ingredients for their recipes, the missing information has been judiciously included and, where appropriate, introductory notes printed in italics have been added by the Editors.

Modern terms have been substituted for archaic language, but to preserve the character of the original recipes and to create a true anthology, the authors' texts have been changed as little as possible. Some instructions have necessarily been expanded, but in cases where the cooking directions seem somewhat abrupt, the reader need only refer to the appropriate demonstration in the front of the book to find the technique in question explained in words and pictures. Cooking terms and ingredients that may be unfamiliar are explained in the combined General Index and Glossary that appears at the end of the book.

The Anthology is organized into separate categories according to ingredients (Eggs and Omelettes; Stuffed Vegetables), cooking methods (Fried Foods) or the end results of the recipes (Spreads, Dips and Sauces). Bread-based recipes form the largest group (Sandwiches and Canapés). Recipes for standard preparations—basic doughs, flavoured butters, sauces—appear at the end of the Anthology. The serving suggestions included in some recipes are, of course, optional.

All recipe ingredients are listed in order of use, except for the main or title ingredient, which appears at the head of the list. Metric and imperial weights and measures for each ingredient are given in separate columns. The two sets of figures are not exact equivalents, but are consistent for each recipe. Working from either metric or imperial weights and measures will produce equally good results, but the two systems should not be mixed for the same recipe. All spoon measures are level.

Spreads, Dips and Sauces

Avocado Dip

Guacamole

The word *guacamole* comes from the Nahuatl words for "avocado" (*ahuacatl*) and "mixture" or "concoction" (*molli*)—and what a beautiful "concoction" *guacamole* is, pale green sparked with the coriander's darker green and the red of the tomato. *Guacamole* is usually eaten in Mexico at the beginning of a meal with a pile of hot, freshly made tortillas and other *botanas* (snacks) like crisp pork skins (*chicharrónes*) or little pieces of crispy pork (*carnitas*). It will also often accompany a plate of *tacos*. It is so delicate that it is best eaten the moment it is prepared. There are many suggestions for keeping it—covering it airtight, leaving the stone in, and so forth—but they will help only for a brief time; almost immediately the delicate green will darken and the fresh, wonderful flavour will be lost.

To make 500 g (1 lb) dip

2	avocados	2
1/4	small onion, finely chopped	1/4
2	serrano chili peppers or any other fresh hot green chili peppers, finely chopped	2
4	large sprigs fresh coriander, leaves only	4
1/4 tsp	salt	1/4 tsp
1	large tomato, skinned, seeded and chopped	1
	Garnish	
1/4	small onion, finely chopped	1/4
6	sprigs coriander, leaves only, roughly chopped	6

In a mortar, grind the onion, chili peppers, coriander and salt together until they are almost smooth.

Cut the avocados in half. Remove the stones, scoop out the flesh with a wooden spoon and mash it roughly into the ingredients in the mortar. Mix well together to make sure that the ingredients are thoroughly incorporated, then stir in the chopped tomato. Adjust the salt, if necessary. Sprinkle with the garnish of onion and coriander, and serve at once.

DIANA KENNEDY
RECIPES FROM THE REGIONAL COOKS OF MEXICO

Egg and Avocado Appetizer

Picante de Huevos

To make about 1 kg (2 to 2½ lb) spread

6	eggs, hard boiled and chopped	6
2	avocados, halved, stones removed, peeled and finely chopped	2
1	chili pepper, finely chopped, or ¼ tsp cayenne pepper	1
1	onion, finely chopped	1
3 tbsp	chopped parsley	3 tbsp
2 tbsp	vinegar	2 tbsp
1½ tsp	salt	1½ tsp

Combine the eggs, avocados, chili or cayenne pepper, onion, parsley, vinegar and salt. Mix well and chop until smooth and well blended. Chill. Serve on toast or lettuce leaves.

MYRA WALDO
THE COMPLETE ROUND-THE-WORLD COOKBOOK

Fresh Herb Dip

To make about 250 g (8 oz) dip

1 tbsp	finely chopped chives	1 tbsp
1 tbsp	finely chopped parsley	1 tbsp
1 tbsp	finely chopped dill	1 tbsp
1	garlic clove, crushed or finely chopped	1
175 g	soured cream	6 oz
60 g	yogurt	2 oz
	lemon juice	
	salt and pepper	

Thoroughly mix all of the ingredients. Taste and adjust the seasonings. Refrigerate. Serve as a dip with raw vegetables.

WOLF TRAP ASSOCIATES
WOLF TRAP PICNIC COOKBOOK

Cucumber Yogurt Dip

Tzatzíki Soúpa

To make about ½ litre (16 fl oz) dip

1	large cucumber, peeled and finely grated	1
½ litre	yogurt	16 fl oz
1 tbsp	olive oil	1 tbsp
¾ tbsp	wine vinegar	¾ tbsp
	salt	
½ tsp	finely chopped mint	½ tsp
1	small garlic clove, crushed	1
	chopped parsley	

Blend together the yogurt, olive oil, vinegar, salt to taste, mint and garlic. Add the grated cucumber, stir well and chill the dip for at least 1 hour. Before serving, sprinkle chopped parsley over the top.

ANNE THEOHAROUS
COOKING THE GREEK WAY

Garlic Sauce

Skorthalia

This sauce may also be made by omitting the soaked bread and increasing the quantity of potatoes to 350 g (12 oz). The soaked bread may also be replaced by 90 g (3 oz) of ground walnuts, almonds or pine-nuts.

To make ½ litre (16 fl oz) sauce

6	garlic cloves	6
	salt and pepper	
250 g	mashed potatoes	8 oz
2	slices stale white bread, crusts removed, soaked in cold water and squeezed dry	2
5 tbsp	olive oil	5 tbsp
1 tbsp	lemon juice	1 tbsp
1 tbsp	vinegar	1 tbsp

Pound the garlic with ½ teaspoon of salt in a mortar until smooth. Add the mashed potatoes and continue to pound and stir with the pestle. Add the soaked bread, pounding and stirring until smooth. Gradually add the olive oil, lemon juice and vinegar, stirring vigorously. When smooth and light, add salt and pepper to taste. Chill in a covered bowl before using. Serve with hot or cold seafoods and fried or boiled vegetables.

TESS MALLOS
GREEK COOKBOOK

Garlic Sauce with Pine-Nuts

Skordalia

Pine-nuts, often marketed under their Italian name pignolia, are the small, cream-coloured, slightly oil-flavoured kernels from the cones of the stone pine. They are available where Mediterranean foods are sold.

To make about 1 litre (1¾ pints) sauce

6	garlic cloves	6
60 g	pine-nuts	2 oz
1 tsp	salt	1 tsp
3	medium-sized potatoes, boiled, peeled, mashed and cooled	3
12.5 cl	vinegar or lemon juice	4 fl oz
60 cl	olive oil	1 pint
1	egg	1
12.5 cl	warm water (optional)	4 fl oz

In a mortar mash the garlic with the salt. Add the pine-nuts and pound until they are well blended. Add the mashed potatoes. Transfer the mixture to a bowl. Clean the mortar with the vinegar or lemon juice and add this liquid to the mixture. Gradually add the olive oil, beating with an electric beater. When all of the oil is absorbed, add the egg and continue beating until the sauce is smooth. For a thinner sauce, beat in the warm water.

THE WOMEN OF ST. PAUL'S GREEK ORTHODOX CHURCH
THE ART OF GREEK COOKERY

Courgette and Sesame Dip

M'tabbal Koussa

Cauliflower, cooked in lightly salted boiling water, can be prepared in the same way.

To make about ¾ litre (1¼ pints) dip

1 kg	small courgettes, scraped and cubed	2 to 2½ lb
4 tbsp	sesame-seed oil	4 tbsp
8 cl	lemon juice	3 fl oz
4	garlic cloves, crushed (optional)	4
½ tsp	salt	½ tsp
1 tbsp	chopped parsley	1 tbsp

Cook the courgettes in a very little water, in a tightly covered pan, for 10 to 15 minutes or until tender. Remove from the pan with a skimmer, in case any liquid remains. Mash with a fork. Combine the oil, lemon juice, garlic (if used) and salt, and beat into the courgettes. Sprinkle with parsley and serve.

FAYEZ AOUN
280 RECETTES DE CUISINE FAMILIALE LIBANAISE

Sunflower Seed Dressing

Created as a dressing for coleslaws and green salads, this mixture of sunflower seeds and yogurt also makes a tangy dip for raw vegetables.

To make about 35 cl (12 fl oz) dip

60 g	shelled sunflower seeds	2 oz
1	garlic clove	1
	salt, preferably sea salt	
	freshly ground pepper	
1 tbsp	chopped herbs (parsley, tarragon, thyme, dill)	1 tbsp
2 tbsp	lemon juice	2 tbsp
¼ litre	yogurt	8 fl oz

In a blender or food processor, grind the sunflower seeds finely, almost to a butter. Add the garlic, salt and pepper and herbs, then blend in the lemon juice and the yogurt, and mix until you have a smooth sauce. Adjust the seasoning.

MARTHA ROSE SHULMAN
THE VEGETARIAN FEAST

Aubergine Filling

Berinjela

This mixture may be used as a sandwich filling or canapé topping, or even as a dip.

To make about 250 g (8 oz) filling

250 g	cooked aubergine, chopped	8 oz
3	green olives, stoned	3
¼	garlic clove	¼
½ tsp	vinegar	½ tsp
	salt and pepper	
2 to 3 tbsp	mayonnaise (*page 167*)	2 to 3 tbsp

Blend the aubergine with the olives and garlic in a blender or chop the mixture very fine. Add vinegar and season to taste. Mix well with enough mayonnaise to bind the mixture.

MARGARETTE DE ANDRADE
BRAZILIAN COOKERY

Chick Peas with Tahini

Hummus bi Tahina

Tahini is a paste made from ground sesame seeds. It is obtainable in Middle Eastern food shops.

This *tahini* salad makes an excellent appetizer served as a dip with Arab bread or pitta, fish, aubergines—practically anything—and can also be used as a salad with a main dish.

An alternative, rather stronger cream is made by using a generous pinch of cayenne pepper instead of paprika. Some of it is mixed into the cream, the rest is sprinkled over the top together with a little ground cumin, in a star design or alternating red and brown.

To make 500 g (1 lb) dip

125 to 175 g	chick peas, soaked overnight	4 to 6 oz
2 or 3	lemons, juice strained	2 or 3
2 or 3	garlic cloves	2 or 3
	salt	
15 cl	*tahini*	¼ pint
	Garnish	
1 tsp	paprika	1 tsp
1 tbsp	olive oil	1 tbsp
1 tbsp	finely chopped parsley	1 tbsp

Boil the chick peas in fresh water for about 1 hour, or until they are soft. The cooking time will depend on their age and quality. Drain the chick peas and put aside a few whole ones to garnish the dish. Press the rest through a sieve or pound them in a mortar; or, better still, use an electric processor or blender to reduce them to a purée. In this case, you will have to pour the lemon juice and a little water into the mixing bowl or blender container first to provide enough liquid for the puréeing to be successful. If you are using a processor or blender, add the remaining ingredients (excluding the garnish) and blend to a creamy paste, adding more water if necessary.

If you are blending by hand, crush the garlic cloves with salt, add them to the crushed chick peas and pound them together until well mixed. Add the *tahini* gradually, followed by the lemon juice, and mix vigorously. If the paste seems too thick, beat in a little water to thin to the consistency of a creamy mayonnaise. Keep tasting and adjusting the seasoning, adding more lemon juice, garlic or salt if necessary.

This is one of the dishes which, for centuries, have been traditionally decorated in the same manner. Pour the cream into a serving dish and dribble a little red paprika mixed with olive oil over the surface. Sprinkle with the parsley and arrange a decorative pattern of whole chick peas on top.

CLAUDIA RODEN
A BOOK OF MIDDLE EASTERN FOOD

Burghul and Chick Pea Savoury

Safsouf

Traditionally, *safsouf* is spooned up with small vine leaves or cos lettuce leaves rolled into separate cones.

To make 250 g (8 oz) savoury

60 g	fine *burghul* soaked in cold water for 30 minutes and squeezed	2 oz
60 g	dried chick peas, soaked overnight in cold water	2 oz
1 tbsp	dried crumbled mint	1 tbsp
4 tbsp	olive or soy-bean oil	4 tbsp
4 tbsp	lemon juice	4 tbsp
½ tsp	salt	½ tsp
¼ tsp	pepper (optional)	¼ tsp

Simmer the chick peas in water for 2 to 3 hours or until soft. Drain, cool, and remove the skins. Mix all the ingredients together, adjusting the seasoning according to taste.

FAYEZ AOUN
280 RECETTES DE CUISINE FAMILIALE LIBANAISE

Bread and Vegetable Dip

Panzanella

The authentic flavour of *panzanella* was given by the rough grey bread of olden times, but bread made with stone-ground flour will give very good results. The proportions of the vegetables may be varied according to taste.

To make 750 g (1½ lb) dip

4	slices country bread, toasted and soaked in water until soft	4
2 tbsp	vinegar	2 tbsp
500 g	tomatoes, finely chopped	1 lb
4	sticks celery, finely chopped	4
1 tbsp	chopped fresh basil	1 tbsp
1	small onion, finely chopped	1
4 tbsp	olive oil	4 tbsp
	salt and pepper	

Drain and squeeze the slices of toast. Sprinkle them with the vinegar and cut them into cubes. Mix the tomatoes, celery, basil and onion. Add the toast cubes, olive oil, salt and pepper, and mix together. Chill before serving.

GIOVANNI RIGHI PARENTI
LA CUCINA DEGLI ETRUSCHI

Mushroom Paste

To make 500 g (1 lb) paste

500 g	mushrooms, sliced	1 lb
1	small onion, chopped	1
60 g	butter	2 oz
2	rashers bacon, chopped	2
250 g	tomatoes, skinned, seeded and chopped	8 oz
2	eggs, beaten	2
1 tsp	salt	1 tsp
	cayenne pepper	

Brown the onion lightly in a little of the butter. Add the rest of the butter and immediately stir in the bacon, tomatoes and mushrooms. Cook for about 15 minutes. When everything is well cooked, put it through a food mill, or liquidize in a blender. Mix with the eggs and stir over a low heat until the mixture thickens (do not let it boil).

Season with salt and a dash of cayenne pepper. Store in jars, refrigerated, and serve with toast.

JANE GRIGSON
THE MUSHROOM FEAST

Celery, Apple and Watercress Sandwich Spread

To make about 350 g (12 oz) spread

100 g	celery, chopped	3½ oz
100 g	unpeeled apple, diced	3½ oz
½ bunch	watercress	½ bunch
5 tbsp	mayonnaise (*page 167*)	5 tbsp
¼ tsp	salt	¼ tsp

Wash the cress and look it over for any bad or yellowed leaves. Drain it and chop finely. Mix with the other ingredients.

FLORENCE BROBECK
THE LUNCH BOX AND EVERY KIND OF SANDWICH

Dill Butter

Dillsmör

To make about 250 g (8 oz) butter

2 tsp	finely chopped dill	2 tsp
100 g	butter	3½ oz
2	eggs, hard boiled and coarsely chopped	2
	thin slices white bread, or rye crackers	
	cooked crab claws	

Whip the butter until creamy, then mix it with the eggs and dill. Spread the dill butter on white bread or rye crackers and decorate with crab claws.

GRETE WILLINSKY
KULINARISCHE WELTREISE

Peanut Butter

You can substitute almonds, cashew nuts or hazelnuts for the peanuts; a combination of almonds and hazelnuts is especially good. Don't overbrown any of the nuts; hazelnuts should be roasted just until their skins crack. After roasting hazelnuts, rub off as much of the skins as possible.

To make about 500 g (1 lb) butter

500 g	shelled peanuts	1 lb
½ to 1 tsp	salt	½ to 1 tsp
½ to 1 tsp	sugar	½ to 1 tsp
2 tbsp	peanut oil	2 tbsp

Preheat the oven to 150°C (300°F or Mark 2). Spread the nuts in a Swiss roll or roasting pan and roast them for 20 minutes, shaking the pan now and then; they should be light gold. Remove the nuts from the oven and cool them.

For creamy peanut butter, first put half of the cooled nuts in the container of a food processor (or the jar of a blender) with half of the salt, sugar and oil. Process the mixture to a creamy consistency (stopping the action and scraping down the sides of the container often with a spatula), then empty the peanut butter into a bowl and process the remaining nuts, salt, sugar and oil.

For chunky peanut butter, use the processor to chop about one-third of the nuts coarsely; set them aside, then process the remaining nuts to a creamy consistency with the salt, sugar and oil. Stir the mixture together with the chopped nuts. Or use a blender by processing half of the nuts at a time and scraping down the sides of the container and under the blades several times. Process the mixture into as crunchy a texture

as you wish. It is not necessary to chop part of the nuts first for blender-made chunky peanut butter.

Store the peanut butter in a covered jar in the refrigerator; it will keep for about two weeks.

HELEN WITTY AND ELIZABETH SCHNEIDER COLCHIE
BETTER THAN STORE-BOUGHT

Farmer's Wife Butter

Beurre Fermière

To make 350 g (12 oz) butter

5	hard-boiled egg yolks	5
250 g	unsalted butter, softened	8 oz
	salt and freshly ground black pepper	
	cayenne pepper	
3 tbsp	dry white wine	3 tbsp
	lemon juice	
1 tsp	mustard (optional)	1 tsp

Put the egg yolks through a sieve into a bowl and blend in the butter. Add salt and pepper to taste, a dash of cayenne, the wine, lemon juice to taste, and mustard if desired. Mix well.

HENRI PAUL PELLAPRAT
THE GREAT BOOK OF FRENCH CUISINE

Hop Butter

Hops contain a yellow powder called lupuline, which is deposited in minute yellow adhesive globules underneath the bracts of the flower tops. This powder has a powerful aromatic smell. It contains hop resin, tannic acid and hop oil, giving a bitter flavour familiar to all beer drinkers and which acts not only as a stimulant, but as a restorative.

Dandelions, endive and other bitter herbs lend themselves to the same treatment.

To make 300 g (10 oz) butter

30 g	young hop leaves, finely chopped	1 oz
250 g	salted butter	8 oz
30 g	lettuce leaves, finely chopped	1 oz

Cream the butter and work in the hop leaves and lettuce.

ARNOLD SHIRCLIFFE
THE EDGEWATER SANDWICH AND HORS D'OEUVRES BOOK

Green Butter

The butter you use must be the best possible, firm and cold. Novelty rests with yourself: you can ring the changes upon pounded anchovies, sardines, soft herring roe, lobster, crab, prawns and shrimps; you can use capers, parsley, chervil, watercress, cress, gherkins and olives. By the judicious selection of your ingredients, all of which are agreeable in fancy butter, you will avoid sameness and secure success.

To make about 125 g (4 oz) butter

About 250 g	spinach	About 8 oz
125 g	unsalted butter	4 oz
4	salt anchovies, soaked, filleted, rinsed and drained	4
About 30 g	parsley sprigs	About 1 oz
1 tsp	finely chopped capers	1 tsp

Boil the spinach, drain it thoroughly, squeeze the leaves through a piece of muslin and save all the green colouring so obtained in a bowl or saucer. Pass the anchovies through a fine-meshed sieve and save the pulp. Blanch the parsley, drain, and mince as finely as possible enough parsley to fill a tablespoon. Pound the capers to a paste.

Having these ingredients ready, first colour the butter by working into it, as lightly as you can, enough of the spinach colouring to secure the tint you require. Always order a little more spinach than you think you may want, to be on the safe side. Let the colour be pale green rather than dark green.

Lastly, add the other things by degrees and, when they are thoroughly incorporated, trim the butter into a neat shape or sundry pretty patlets, and set it in the icebox or over a dish containing crumbled ice.

A. KENNEY-HERBERT (WYVERN)
COMMON-SENSE COOKERY FOR ENGLISH HOUSEHOLDS

Soused Camembert

To make one 12.5 cm (5 inch) cheese

2	ripe Camembert cheeses	2
15 cl	dry white wine	¼ pint
125 g	butter, softened	4 oz
	salt	
	cayenne pepper (optional)	
	brandy	
350 g	fresh white breadcrumbs, toasted	12 oz
6 tbsp	finely chopped parsley	6 tbsp

Scrape the crusts from the cheeses; cut the cheeses into quarters and soak them overnight in the white wine.

Remove the cheeses from the wine; dry them gently and cream them thoroughly with the softened butter and, if desired, a little of the marinating liquid. Add a little salt and cayenne, if necessary, and flavour with a little brandy. Press the cheese mixture into a plain round 12.5 cm (5 inch) flan ring set on a foil-lined baking sheet. Chill until the cheese is firm, about 4 hours.

Turn the cheese upside down on to the toasted breadcrumbs and remove the flan ring and foil. Coat the bottom of the cheese with the toasted breadcrumbs and the sides with the parsley. Serve with bread or crackers.

ROBERT CARRIER
ROBERT CARRIER'S ENTERTAINING

Liptauer Cheese

The classic accompaniment is long white radishes, but red radishes, cucumber sticks, celery and fennel can all be used. The best bread to serve with this dish is thin caraway rye.

To make 1 kg (2 to 2½ lb) spread

500 g	cream cheese	1 lb
125 g	unsalted butter	4 oz
125 g	cottage cheese	4 oz
2 tbsp	double cream	2 tbsp
1 tbsp	anisette	1 tbsp
2 tsp	caraway seeds	2 tsp
1 tbsp	medium-sweet Hungarian or other paprika	1 tbsp
175 g	onions, finely chopped	6 oz
10	anchovy fillets, chopped	10
125 g	capers, rinsed and drained	4 oz
2	bunches white radishes	2

With an electric mixer, beat the cream cheese and butter until very light and creamy. Add the cottage cheese and whip until fluffy. Thin with the cream and flavour with the anisette. Add the caraway seeds and mix well.

Mound the cheese decoratively on a serving plate. Use a spatula to smooth the surface and to make decorative indentations around the sides. Dust the top with paprika.

This recipe may be made up early in the morning and refrigerated until evening; just be sure to cover it. Take it out of the refrigerator about 30 minutes before serving.

When serving, set out small dishes containing chopped onion, chopped anchovies and drained capers as condiments for the Liptauer cheese. Also set out ice-cold white radishes.

JULIE DANNENBAUM
JULIE DANNENBAUM'S CREATIVE COOKING SCHOOL

Cheese Brick

Mimolette cheese is a deep orange, Cheddar-like French cheese. The author suggests that the cheese brick might alternatively be coated with chopped or ground walnuts, cashew nuts or pistachio nuts, paprika, or very finely chopped fresh herbs such as fennel, dill, basil or chervil.

American chili powder, as called for in this recipe, is a blend of hot and sweet peppers and is much milder than the chili powder available here. If American chili powder is not available, use a mixture of half cayenne pepper and half paprika.

To make one 25 cm (10 inch) cheese brick

250 g	Mimolette or Cheddar cheese, grated	8 oz
90 g	cream cheese, softened	3 oz
$\frac{1}{4}$ tsp	crushed garlic	$\frac{1}{4}$ tsp
30 g	pecan nuts, chopped	1 oz
$1\frac{1}{2}$ tbsp	chili powder	$1\frac{1}{2}$ tbsp
$\frac{1}{2}$ tbsp	ground cumin	$\frac{1}{2}$ tbsp

Blend the cheeses well and add the garlic and pecan nuts. Form this mixture into a brick about 25 cm (10 inches) long, and chill long enough for it to hold its shape. Mix the chili powder and cumin, and spread it on wax or greaseproof paper. Press the cheese brick in the mixture and coat it evenly. Chill, and cut into slices when ready to serve.

ANITA MAY PEARL
COMPLETELY CHEESE: THE CHEESELOVER'S COMPANION

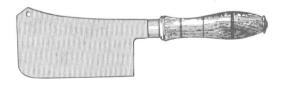

Cheese of the Seven Herbs

To make about 250 g (8 oz) cheese

125 g	Cheddar cheese, grated	4 oz
2 tbsp	double cream	2 tbsp
3 tbsp	sherry or cider	3 tbsp
2 tbsp	finely chopped mixed herbs (parsley sage, thyme, tarragon, chives, chervil and winter savory)	2 tbsp
	salt and pepper	

Put the cheese, cream, sherry or cider, and herbs into the top part of a double boiler set over simmering water. Season, and stir over very gentle heat until the mixture is creamy and pale green in colour. While the mixture is still warm, pour it into small pots. Cool before serving.

BEE NILSON (EDITOR)
THE WI DIAMOND JUBILEE COOKBOOK

Liptó Cheese Spread

Körözött Júhtúró

The cheese that is the base of the spread originally came from the northern Hungarian area called Liptó. The Austrians, who made a similar mixture, called the spread itself Liptauer, or, more correctly, Liptauer *garniert*. Since in Hungary Liptó is the name only of the cheese itself, this causes undue mix-ups in non-Hungarian recipes. If you are unable to buy the real sheep's milk cheese, a very similar product called *brinza*, which comes from Romania, can generally be purchased in the better cheese stores.

The same cheese spread was made in Trieste with Gorgonzola cheese substituting for the sheep's milk cheese and *mascarpone*, a fresh cream cheese, replacing the butter.

To make 500 g (1 lb) spread

250 g	Liptó or *brinza* cheese	8 oz
125 g	butter, softened	4 oz
1 tsp	paprika	1 tsp
$\frac{1}{2}$ tsp	mustard	$\frac{1}{2}$ tsp
$\frac{1}{2}$ tsp	crushed caraway seeds	$\frac{1}{2}$ tsp
1	small onion, grated	1
$\frac{1}{2}$ tsp	anchovy paste	$\frac{1}{2}$ tsp

Sieve the cheese and mix it with the softened butter and all of the other ingredients until the spread is light red in colour and evenly mixed. Refrigerate. Serve with wedges of good crusty bread or toast, accompanied by young radishes, sweet green peppers or spring onions.

GEORGE LANG
THE CUISINE OF HUNGARY

Roquefort with Pine-Nuts

Roquefort aux Pignons

To make 400 g (14 oz) spread

250 g	Roquefort cheese	8 oz
60 g	pine-nuts	2 oz
100 g	butter	$3\frac{1}{2}$ oz
2 tbsp	brandy	2 tbsp

Mash the cheese with a fork and mix it with the butter. Add the brandy and mix again. Place the mixture on a plate and shape it into a small mound. Stick the pine-nuts all over the surface to give a hedgehog effect.

FLORENCE DE ANDREIS
LA CUISINE PROVENÇALE D'AUJOURD'HUI

Herbed Cream Cheese

I like to mould this in a ring, then shortly before serving unmould it on to a platter and garnish it with herbs and fresh vegetables. To unmould, dip the mould in warm water for 10 seconds and invert it on to your platter. Refrigerate immediately to stop the surface from melting.

To make 350 g (12 oz)

250 g	cream cheese, softened	8 oz
3 or 4	spring onions, including the green tops, chopped	3 or 4
2	small garlic cloves, finely chopped or crushed	2
½ tsp	dry mustard	½ tsp
½ tsp	Worcestershire sauce	½ tsp
30 g	parsley, chopped	1 oz
30 g	dill, chopped (optional)	1 oz
2 to 4 tbsp	basil, chopped (optional)	2 to 4 tbsp
30 g	olives, chopped	1 oz
1 to 2 tbsp	lemon juice	1 to 2 tbsp
	salt, preferably sea salt	
	freshly ground pepper	

In a large mixing bowl, whip the softened cheese and add the other ingredients. Mix well, then add salt and pepper to taste. Mould in a bowl or ring, or in a mound on a platter. Cover and refrigerate, or serve immediately. (If the cream cheese is runny or soft, 15 minutes in the refrigerator will stiffen it up.)

MARTHA ROSE SHULMAN
THE VEGETARIAN FEAST

Good Health Cheese

Le Fromage de Santé

This cheese should be eaten from the pot in which it matures. It once had the reputation of combating all ills.

To make about 500 g (1 lb)

250 g	dry goat cheese, grated	8 oz
About 15 cl	goat's milk, or milk mixed with double cream	About ¼ pint
1 tbsp	Roquefort cheese, scraped from the slice with a knife	1 tbsp
About 5 tbsp	marc or brandy	About 5 tbsp

Soak the goat cheese in the goat's milk or in the milk and cream mixture for 30 minutes. Knead the cheese mixture to a smooth paste. It should be soft, but not runny. When well mixed, add the Roquefort, which should be creamy and very blue; knead again and place the mixture in a bowl in a cool place, covered with a cloth, for 24 to 48 hours.

After this, take a tall glazed earthenware pot and moisten the inside well with marc or brandy. Stir 4 tablespoons of marc or brandy into the cheese and pack it into the pot, pressing well down to avoid air bubbles. If the paste has become too thick, which is unusual, thin it with a little more of the milk. Cover the top with greaseproof paper soaked in marc or brandy, then put on the lid.

Store the cheese in a cool place for 15 days before using. It is ideal spread on country bread or rye bread for picnics, on its own or with freshly ground pepper added.

ALBIN MARTY
FOURMIGUETTO: SOUVENIRS, CONTES ET RECETTES DU LANGUEDOC

Persian Yogurt Cheese with Cucumbers

To make about 500 g (1 lb) cheese

1 litre	yogurt	1¾ pints
2	medium-sized cucumbers, peeled, seeded (if seeds are large) and finely chopped	2
60 g	red onion, very finely chopped	2 oz
4	radishes, grated	4
60 g	walnuts, finely chopped	2 oz
30 g	currants	1 oz
1 tbsp	finely chopped dill	1 tbsp
1 tbsp	finely chopped mint	1 tbsp
	salt	
	lettuce leaves	

Line a strainer or colander with a clean muslin cloth wrung out in cold water or with a few layers of dampened cheese-cloth. Stir the yogurt and pour it into the cloth. Tie the opposite corners of the cloth together securely to form a bag. Suspend the bag from a hook for 8 hours or overnight, placing a bowl underneath to catch the drippings. The whey will drain away, leaving a soft, creamy white cheese. When the yogurt has become firm enough to spread, remove it from the muslin bag and place it in a dish.

To flavour the yogurt cheese, combine all the ingredients except the lettuce and mix thoroughly. With an ice-cream scoop, shape the mixture into balls and arrange them on a serving platter lined with the lettuce leaves. Serve chilled.

SONIA UVEZIAN
THE BOOK OF YOGURT

Yogurt Cheese Cubes

The first time you try the recipe, do it a couple of days ahead of time so you can see how it works for you. The cheese will keep that long in cold water in the refrigerator if you change the water once a day. If the cheese does not become firm enough to cube, pack it into a small dish and serve it with a spreader.

To make about 750 g (1½ lb) cubes

1 litre	yogurt	1¾ pints
3 tbsp	ground aniseeds	3 tbsp
	salt	
350 g	walnuts, chopped	12 oz

Line a colander or sieve with three thicknesses of clean cheesecloth or muslin. Blend the yogurt with the ground aniseeds and salt to taste, and pour the mixture into the cheesecloth. Pull the ends of the cheesecloth together and tie them. Do this around noon and allow the cheese to drain at room temperature overnight. In the morning, the cheese should be firm enough to cut into cubes. Heap the cubes on a serving plate and sprinkle generously with the walnuts.

GERI HARRINGTON
THE SALAD BOOK

Chopped Chicken Livers

To make about 600 g (1¼ lb) spread

250 g	chicken livers, cleaned and quartered	8 oz
4 tbsp	rendered chicken fat or butter	4 tbsp
1	medium-sized onion, diced	1
2	eggs, hard boiled and chopped	2
½ tsp	salt	½ tsp
¼ tsp	pepper	¼ tsp
	thyme	

Melt the fat or butter in a frying pan; sauté the livers and onion for about 8 minutes, or until the livers are cooked and the onion is golden. Drain the livers and onion, reserving the fat. Cool. Chop the livers and mix them with the onion and the fat. Combine the liver mixture with the eggs; stir in the salt, pepper and a pinch of thyme. Chill. Serve the mixture in lettuce-lined cups or as a spread for bread or crackers.

IDA BAILEY ALLEN
BEST LOVED RECIPES OF THE AMERICAN PEOPLE

Chicken Liver Mousse

La Mousse de Foie

In case the association of *foie gras* producers is thinking of suing me, I never actually said that this preparation can replace *foie gras*. . . .

To make 400 g (14 oz) spread

100 g	pale chicken livers, trimmed and soaked in milk overnight	3½ oz
2 tsp	oil	2 tsp
	salt and pepper	
15 cl	port	¼ pint
About 300 g	butter, softened	About 10 oz

Rinse the livers in cold water until the water runs clear, and drain them. Heat the oil in a pan, add the livers and sauté until they are hazelnut brown. Drain the livers, put them in a bowl, season with salt and pepper, and cover with port. Leave to marinate overnight.

Drain the livers and discard the marinade. Purée the livers in a blender or food processor; then, without stopping the blender, add the butter and process until it has been completely absorbed. Correct the seasoning, transfer the mixture to a terrine and refrigerate until serving time. Serve with toast.

DANIEL BOUCHÉ
INVITATION À LA CUISINE BUISSONNIÈRE

Unrefined Pâté

Pâté Pas Raffiné

To make 600 g (1¼ lb) pâté

500 g	very pale poultry livers, half chicken, half duck, goose or turkey, membranes removed	1 lb
125 g	unsalted butter	4 oz
1	apple, peeled and diced	1
3 tbsp	calvados	3 tbsp
1 tbsp	very finely mashed onion	1 tbsp
2 tbsp	very finely mashed shallots	2 tbsp
	salt and pepper	
	ground allspice	
12.5 cl	double cream	4 fl oz
1 tbsp	soured cream	1 tbsp
50 g	clarified butter or lard, melted	2 oz

Heat 30 g (1 oz) of the butter in a frying pan and sauté the diced apple over a high heat so that it colours very fast. Add 1 tablespoon of the calvados to the hot frying pan, stir fast and remove all the contents of the pan to a small bowl.

Heat another 30 g (1 oz) of butter in the same pan until it turns nut-brown. Add the onion; sauté 2 minutes. Add the shallots and immediately add the livers and sauté over a high heat until they turn uniformly grey outside but remain rare at the centres. Add salt, pepper and allspice. Add the remaining calvados and set alight. Mash all the ingredients together with a fork while still hot to obtain a semi-liquid, quite rough purée. Strain through a conical wire strainer, pushing hard with a wooden spatula.

Cool the liver purée thoroughly. Cream the remaining butter. Gradually add the liver purée, using an electric mixer if you wish, or beating with a wooden spatula. Add the diced apple with its calvados. Mix well. Mix together the double and soured cream. Beat until the mixture mounds slightly. Fold into the liver pâté.

Pack the pâté into a ½ litre (16 fl oz) soufflé dish or earthenware terrine. Cool and pour the clarified butter or lard over the surface of the pâté to seal it.

MADELEINE M. KAMMAN
WHEN FRENCH WOMEN COOK

Liver Spread

Kenömájas

To make about 750 g (1½ lb) spread

400 g	pig's liver, cut into thin strips	14 oz
50 g	onion, chopped	2 oz
3 tbsp	oil, or 50 g (2 oz) lard	3 tbsp
15 cl	water	¼ pint
100 g	smoked streaky bacon or pork fat, diced	3½ oz
2	potatoes, boiled and mashed (optional)	2
100 g	butter, softened	3½ oz
2 tsp	soured cream	2 tsp
	salt and pepper	
1	lemon, rind grated	1

Cook the onion gently in the oil or lard for about 10 minutes or until soft. Add the liver, water and bacon or pork fat. Cook gently for 10 to 15 minutes or until the liver is cooked through. Allow to cool, then put the whole mixture twice through the

fine disc of a meat grinder. Add the potatoes to thicken the mixture if desired. Mix the butter and soured cream and stir these into the meat mixture. Add salt, pepper and lemon rind to taste. Press into a dish and chill. Serve very cold.

ILONA HORVÁTH
SZAKÁCSKÖNYV

Liver Loaf

Maksapasteija

This is almost a "must" item for the *voileipäpöytä* (bread-and-butter table). It makes an excellent appetizer when served on a platter surrounded with salty crisp crackers; and it is excellent as a sandwich filler.

To make 1 kg (2 to 2½ lb) spread

500 g	calf's liver, sliced	1 lb
30 g	butter	1 oz
1	small onion, grated	1
¼ litre	single cream	8 fl oz
4 tbsp	dry breadcrumbs	4 tbsp
2	eggs, lightly beaten	2
2 tsp	salt	2 tsp
1 tsp	sugar	1 tsp
1 tsp	ground ginger	1 tsp
½ tsp	ground white pepper	½ tsp
3 tbsp	anchovy paste, or 2 tsp minced anchovies (optional)	3 tbsp
350 g	streaky bacon, thinly sliced	12 oz

Put the liver through a meat grinder with a fine blade (this is easier to do if the liver is partially frozen) or remove all the membranes and whirl in a blender until fine but not foamy. Heat the butter in a frying pan, brown the onion and add to the liver with the cream, breadcrumbs, eggs, salt, sugar, ginger, pepper and, if desired, the anchovy paste or minced anchovies. Mix until thoroughly combined.

Line a 12.5 by 22.5 cm (5 by 9 inch) bread tin with the bacon, being sure to cover all surfaces completely. Pour in the liver mixture. Cover the top of the tin securely with greaseproof paper or foil and tie the covering on with string. Set in a pan of water and bake in a preheated 180°C (350°F or Mark 4) oven for 1½ hours or until the loaf is firm. Let cool in the water bath with the cover on, then remove the cover and turn the loaf out on to a serving platter. Chill. Cut into slices to serve.

BEATRICE A. OJAKANGAS
THE FINNISH COOKBOOK

Potted Rabbit

Rillettes de Lapin

This dish is as good made with wild rabbits as with hutch-raised ones. It will keep for six weeks if sealed in fat and stored in a cool, dry place. The quantity given below may be doubled.

To make 1 kg (2 to 2½ lb) spread

750 g	rabbit, with bones, cut into 3 or 4 pieces	1½ lb
1	onion, quartered	1
¼	bay leaf	¼
1	very small sprig thyme	1
1	clove	1
1	garlic clove	1
5	white peppercorns	5
¼ litre	hot water	8 fl oz
300 g	green streaky bacon with rind, cut into 2 cm (1 inch) pieces	10 oz
500 g	very fatty chine or neck of pork, cut into 5 cm (2 inch) pieces	1 lb
	salt and pepper	
250 g	lard, melted	8 oz

Put the onion, bay leaf, thyme, clove, garlic and white peppercorns into a piece of muslin. Tie the muslin in a knot.

Pour the hot water into a stew-pan. Place the pan over a low heat and add the bacon. When the bacon begins to render its fat, add the rabbit and pork pieces and put the muslin bundle in the centre. Salt and pepper the meat; cover and cook over a very low heat for 5 hours. Stir from time to time, making sure nothing sticks to the bottom. When the meat is completely cooked and has fallen off the bones, remove the muslin bundle and press it with a skimmer to squeeze out the fat. Using the skimmer, remove the meats to a chopping board. Scrupulously remove all bones and chop the meats roughly. Return the meats to the stew-pan, which still contains the fat. Correct the seasoning and, off the heat, crush the meats with a mushroom-shaped pestle as the fat begins to congeal.

Amalgamate well and, before the mixture is completely cool, pack it into little stoneware pots, which must be completely dry. Let the meat cool completely and cover the surface with the lard to a thickness of 5 mm (¼ inch). Cover this with a round of greaseproof paper and put the lids on the pots. Keep in a cool, dry place or in the refrigerator.

RENÉE DE GROSSOUVRE
LES RECETTES D'UNE GRAND'MÈRE ET SES CONSEILS

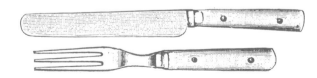

Potted Grouse

If the bird is young, you can roast it or stew it in butter, but if it is old it should be braised, covered, over a low heat until tender, then drained carefully.

To make about 600 g (1¼ lb) spread

1	grouse, cooked, boned and chopped	1
125 g	mild cooked ham, chopped, or 90 g (3 oz) ham and 30 g (1 oz) tongue, chopped	4 oz
250 g	butter, softened	8 oz
	lemon juice	
	salt	
	cayenne pepper	
	Tabasco sauce (optional)	
	clarified butter, melted	

Pound the chopped grouse and ham, or ham and tongue, in a mortar with the softened butter, or put in a processor and blend. Add a few drops of lemon juice, salt if necessary, a few grains of cayenne pepper and a drop of Tabasco sauce if you like. Pour into small pots. Pour on a layer of tepid clarified butter in order to seal the pot.

JULIA DRYSDALE
THE GAME COOKERY BOOK

Potted Tongue

To my mind this is the best and most subtle of all English potted meat inventions. My recipe is adapted from John Farley's *The London Art of Cookery*, published in 1783.

Venison can be potted in the same way as tongue, and makes one of the best of all sandwich fillings. Salt beef makes another excellent potted meat.

To make 500 g (1 lb) spread

250 g	cooked, brined and/or smoked ox tongue, chopped	8 oz
250 g	clarified butter	8 oz
¼ tsp	ground mace	¼ tsp
⅛ tsp	freshly ground pepper	⅛ tsp

In a blender or food processor, reduce the tongue and 150 g (5 oz) of the clarified butter to a paste; season it, pack it tightly down into a pot or pots, smooth over the top, cover and leave in the refrigerator until very firm. Melt the remaining clarified butter, cool it until it is tepid and pour it over the tongue paste, so that it sets in a sealing layer about 3 mm (⅛ inch) thick. When completely cold, cover the pots. For short-term storage it is not necessary to keep potted tongue in the refrigerator, but it is desirable to serve it chilled. If, therefore, the pots are stored in a larder, transfer them, as required, to the refrigerator for at least 1 hour before the meal.

ELIZABETH DAVID
ENGLISH POTTED MEATS AND FISH PASTES

Tongue Spread

To make about 500 g (1 lb) spread

250 g	cooked, smoked tongue	8 oz
1 tbsp	finely chopped gherkin	1 tbsp
1 tbsp	finely chopped chives or shallot	1 tbsp
1	egg, hard boiled and finely chopped	1
1 tsp	Dijon mustard	1 tsp
	mayonnaise (*page 167*)	

Chop the tongue very finely. Add the gherkin, the chives or shallot, the hard-boiled egg and the mustard. Bind this with sufficient mayonnaise to make a stiff paste.

JAMES BEARD
HORS D'OEUVRE AND CANAPÉS

Potted Ham

Any tender and well-roasted meat, taken free of fat, skin and gristle, as well as from the dry outsides, will answer for potting admirably. The quantity of butter required will depend upon the nature of the meat; ham and salted beef will need a larger proportion than roast meat, or than the breasts of poultry and game; white fish, from being less dry, will require comparatively little. Salmon, lobsters, prawns and shrimps are all extremely good, prepared in this way. For these, and for white meats in general, mace, nutmeg and cayenne or white pepper are the appropriate spices. Ground cloves may be added to hare and other brown meat.

To make about 900 g (1 lb 14 oz) spread

500 g	cooked lean ham, all fat and skin removed	1 lb
175 g	roast lean veal, all fat and skin removed	6 oz
250 g	unsalted butter	8 oz
1 to 2 tsp	ground mace	1 to 2 tsp
$\frac{1}{2}$	large nutmeg, grated	$\frac{1}{2}$
$\frac{1}{4}$ to $\frac{1}{2}$ tsp	cayenne pepper	$\frac{1}{4}$ to $\frac{1}{2}$ tsp
125 g	clarified butter, melted	4 oz

Mince the ham and the veal together quite fine with an exceedingly sharp knife, taking care to cut through the meat and not to tear the fibre, as on this much of the excellence of the preparation depends. Next put it into a large stone or marble mortar, and pound to the smoothest paste with the butter, which must be added by degrees. When nearly smooth, mix together the mace, nutmeg and cayenne pepper, and strew over the meat mixture. It is better to limit the spice to this quantity in the first instance, and to increase afterwards either of the three kinds to the taste of the parties to whom the meat is to be served. We do not find $\frac{1}{2}$ teaspoon of cayenne pepper and nearly 2 teaspoons of mace more than is generally approved. After the spice is added, keep the meat often turned from the sides to the middle of the mortar, that the mixture may be seasoned equally in every part. When perfectly pounded, press into small pots and pour the clarified butter over the top. If kept in a cool and dry place, this meat will remain good for a fortnight, or more.

ELIZA ACTON
MODERN COOKERY

Italian Veal Pâté

Pâté di Fesa

To make 1 kg (2 to 2½ lb) pâté

500 g	boned leg of veal, cubed	1 lb
300 g	butter	10 oz
1	stick celery, chopped	1
1	carrot, chopped	1
1	onion, chopped	1
6 tbsp	double cream	6 tbsp
4 tbsp	grated *grana* or Parmesan cheese	4 tbsp
1 tbsp	brandy	1 tbsp
50 g	pistachio nuts, blanched	2 oz
200 g	lean prosciutto, thinly sliced	7 oz

Melt 60 g (2 oz) of the butter in a frying pan. Add the veal, celery, carrot and onion, and cook slowly without browning until the meat is very tender, 20 to 30 minutes. Put the meat and vegetables through a meat grinder three times. Beat the remaining butter and add to the meat with the cream, cheese, brandy and pistachio nuts. Mix thoroughly, then shape into a large sausage. Wrap in the prosciutto slices, then in greaseproof paper. Tie and refrigerate until firm. Remove the greaseproof paper, slice thinly and arrange on a serving dish.

OTTORINA PERNA BOZZI
VECCHIA MILANO IN CUCINA

Mixed Meat Paté

Húspástétom

To make about 750 g (1½ lb) paté

250 g	veal or beef, diced	8 oz
250 g	pork, diced	8 oz
60 g	smoked streaky bacon or pork fat, diced	2 oz
1	carrot, diced	1
1	Hamburg parsley root or small piece young parsnip, diced	1
1	small onion, diced	1
3 tbsp	oil or 50 g (2 oz) lard	3 tbsp
2	eggs, hard boiled	2
60 g	butter, softened	2 oz
1 tsp	soured cream	1 tsp
	salt and pepper	
	Dijon mustard	

Cook the meats and vegetables gently in the oil or lard until the meats are tender, 20 to 30 minutes. Put the mixture through a meat grinder twice, together with the hard-boiled eggs. Beat in the butter and soured cream, add salt, pepper and mustard to taste, and mix well. Press the mixture into a terrine and chill it. Serve in slices, as part of a cold buffet, or as a spread on open sandwiches.

ILONA HORVÁTH
SZAKÁCSKÖNYV

Beef and Cress Spread

To make about 100 g (3½ oz) spread

60 g	lean beef round	2 oz
15 g	mustard and cress, or watercress	½ oz
30 g	butter	1 oz
	salt and pepper	

Shred the beef by scraping it with the back of a knife. In a mortar, pound the beef to a paste with the butter and a seasoning of salt and pepper. Finally, pound in the watercress or mix in the mustard and cress.

MOIRA MEIGHN
SIMPLIFIED COOKING AND INVALID DIET

Chicken Chestnut Spread

To make 250 g (8 oz) spread

250 g	cooked chicken, chopped	8 oz
4 or 5	peeled, cooked chestnuts	4 or 5
2 tbsp	finely chopped celery	2 tbsp
	salt and pepper	
	mayonnaise (*page 167*)	

Purée the chestnuts. Mix these with the chopped chicken meat, the finely chopped celery, salt and pepper to taste and enough mayonnaise to bind.

JAMES BEARD
HORS D'OEUVRE AND CANAPÉS

Chicken and Almond Sandwich Filling

To make about 500 g (1 lb) filling

175 g	cooked chicken, chopped	6 oz
175 g	almonds, blanched and chopped	6 oz
12.5 cl	double cream	4 fl oz
¾ tsp	salt	¾ tsp
¼ tsp	paprika	¼ tsp
	pepper	

Mix together the chicken and almonds. Blend them with the cream and season with the salt, paprika and a dash of pepper. Use with either white or wholemeal bread.

FLORENCE A. COWLES (EDITOR)
1001 SANDWICHES

Potted Chicken, Partridge or Pheasant

To make about 750 g (1½ lb) spread

500 g	boneless roast chicken, partridge or pheasant breast meat, skin removed, minced	1 lb
About 175 g	butter	About 6 oz
	salt	
About 1 tsp	ground mace	About 1 tsp
About ½ tsp	cayenne pepper	About ½ tsp
90 g	clarified butter, melted	3 oz

Pound the meat very smoothly with the butter, using less butter if the meat should appear of a proper consistence without the full quantity; season it with salt, mace and cayenne pepper, and add these in small portions until the meat is rather highly flavoured with both the last. Press the mixture into small pots, and pour over clarified butter to seal.

ELIZA ACTON
MODERN COOKERY

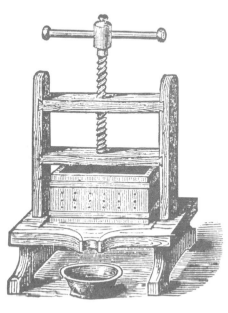

Shrimp or Prawn Pâté

Pâté de Crevettes

A simple standby in which the full flavour of the shrimps or prawns comes through. Try it also with fresh crab meat. Serve the pâté with hot toast.

To make 625 g (1 lb 4 oz) spread

500 g	shelled, cooked shrimps or prawns	1 lb
$\frac{1}{2}$	lemon, juice strained	$\frac{1}{2}$
125 g	butter, softened	4 oz
2 tbsp	sherry or Madeira	2 tbsp
	salt and freshly ground black pepper	
	grated nutmeg	
125 g	clarified butter, melted (optional)	4 oz

Work the shrimps or prawns with the lemon juice, a little at a time, in an electric food processor or blender; they should be coarsely chopped, not puréed. Stir the shrimps or prawns into the butter and season to taste with sherry or Madeira, salt, pepper and a pinch of nutmeg.

Pile the pâté into individual ramekins or a serving crock, cover tightly and chill. If the pâté is to be kept more than 3 to 4 hours, smooth the top and add a thin layer of clarified butter to seal it before covering and chilling.

FAYE LEVY
LA VARENNE TOUR BOOK

Potted Shrimps or Prawns

To make about 500 g (1 lb) spread

1 kg	raw shrimps or prawns, boiled for 5 minutes or until pink, shelled and roughly chopped	2 lb
125 g	unsalted butter	4 oz
$\frac{1}{4}$ tsp	ground mace	$\frac{1}{4}$ tsp
$\frac{1}{8}$ tsp	cayenne pepper	$\frac{1}{8}$ tsp

Put the shrimps or prawns in a mortar and pound them perfectly with the butter, mace and cayenne pepper. When the mixture is thoroughly blended, press it into pots.

ELIZA ACTON
MODERN COOKERY

Prawn Pâté

Cha Tom

If banana leaves are not available, use greaseproof paper. Powdered alum is available from chemists; it is used here to cleanse the prawns but can be omitted.

The balls of pâté may be served hot or cold with a sauce made from lemon or lime juice, garlic and chili pepper.

To make 10 balls

500 g	prawns, shelled, washed in salted water and dried	1 lb
$\frac{1}{2}$ tsp	alum (*phène chua*)	$\frac{1}{2}$ tsp
30 g	pork fat, finely chopped	1 oz
	salt and pepper	
1 tsp	pounded dried onion	1 tsp
10	squares banana leaf	10
4 tbsp	dry white wine	4 tbsp

Add the alum to the prawn washing water and wash the prawns again. Dry them, then pound them to a paste, adding just before this task is finished the pork fat, salt, pepper and dried onion, all of which must be incorporated in the pâté.

Brush fat or oil over the pieces of banana leaf. Place a ball of prawn pâté on each piece of leaf. Beat together the egg yolk and wine. Make a tiny brush of four or five chicken feathers (or use a pastry brush) and use this to coat the balls with the egg yolk mixture, which will give them a golden colour. Then wrap the squares of banana leaf over the balls to make small round packages about 2.5 cm (1 inch) in diameter. Steam the packages for 15 to 20 minutes.

ALAN DAVIDSON
SEAFOOD OF SOUTH-EAST ASIA

Potted Anchovies

To make about 250 g (8 oz) spread

90 g	salt anchovies, soaked, filleted, rinsed, dried, pounded to a paste and sieved	3 oz
About 175 g	unsalted butter	About 6 oz
⅓ tsp	ground mace	⅓ tsp
	cayenne pepper	
	grated nutmeg	
	clarified butter, melted (optional)	

Pound the anchovies with the butter, increasing or diminishing the quantity of butter in proportion as it is wished that the flavour of the anchovies should prevail. Pound in the mace and a pinch each of cayenne pepper and nutmeg; set the mixture by in a cool place for 3 to 4 hours to harden it before it is put into the pots. If clarified butter be poured over to seal, it must be only lukewarm; but the anchovies will keep well in a cool place for two to three weeks without.

ELIZA ACTON
MODERN COOKERY

Celery with Anchovy Dip

Céleri à l'Anchoïade

The anchovy purée can also be made directly over heat, as shown on page 75, where it is used as an accompaniment to fried cheese sandwiches.

To make about ¼ litre (8 fl oz) dip

2	heads celery	2
12	salt anchovies, soaked, filleted, rinsed and dried	12
12.5 cl	olive oil	4 fl oz
2 tbsp	wine vinegar	2 tbsp

Separate the sticks of celery; remove the coarse fibres with a knife and soak the sticks in cold water for 1 hour. Drain and arrange on a serving dish.

In a double boiler, over simmering water, soften the anchovies in the olive oil, crushing them with a fork to obtain a smooth purée. Add the vinegar and keep warm over hot water until ready to serve.

Place the anchovy purée in the centre of the table, so that the sticks of celery may be dipped into it.

FLORENCE DE ANDREIS
LA CUISINE PROVENÇALE D'AUJOURD'HUI

Sardine Rillettes

Rillettes de Sardines Océane

To make about 750 g (1½ lb) rillettes

800 g	fresh sardines, scaled, heads and tails removed	1¾ lb
About 350 g	butter	About 12 oz
	parsley sprigs	

Cook the sardines gently in 60 g (2 oz) of the butter. Let them cool to lukewarm, then skin and fillet them. Weigh the fillets, then mash them with a fork, adding 60 g (2 oz) of softened butter for every 100 g (3½ oz) of fish. Mix well.

Arrange mounds of the rillettes in hors-d'oeuvre dishes, shaping them into ridges. Refrigerate to firm them slightly. Surround with butter curls and parsley sprigs to serve.

ACADÉMIE DES GASTRONOMES, ACADÉMIE CULINAIRE DE FRANCE
LA HAUTE CUISINE FRANÇAISE

Smoked Salmon Butter

Laxsmör

To make 175 g (6 oz) butter

125 g	unsalted butter, softened	4 oz
60 g	smoked salmon, finely chopped	2 oz
	bread, sliced	
	hard-boiled eggs, sliced	

Cream the butter until it is very soft, then stir in the salmon. Spread the mixture on bread and garnish with slices of egg.

GRETE WILLINSKY
KULINARISCHE WELTREISE

Salmon Cream

Laxkräm

To make about 175 g (6 oz) spread

60 g	smoked salmon	2 oz
2	eggs, hard boiled	2
4 tbsp	butter or mayonnaise (*page 167*)	4 tbsp
3 to 4 tbsp	finely chopped dill	3 to 4 tbsp
	salt and pepper (optional)	

Chop the salmon and eggs finely. Mix them with the butter or mayonnaise and the dill. Cream the mixture until it is smooth. Taste for seasoning. Add salt and pepper, if desired.

J. AUDREY ELLISON (TRANSLATOR AND EDITOR)
THE GREAT SCANDINAVIAN COOK BOOK

Salmon Spread

To make about 350 g (12 oz) spread

200 g	cooked salmon, flaked	7 oz
¼ tsp	salt	¼ tsp
¼ tsp	pepper	¼ tsp
75 g	sweet green pepper, finely chopped	2½ oz
60 g	spring onions, finely chopped	2 oz
1 tbsp	lemon juice	1 tbsp
2 to 3 tbsp	mayonnaise (*page 167*)	2 to 3 tbsp
	watercress	
	cucumber slices	

Combine the flaked salmon, salt, pepper, sweet green pepper, spring onions and lemon juice with just enough mayonnaise to bind them. Garnish with watercress and cucumber slices. The spread is delicious on dark or rye bread.

DIANE MACMILLAN
THE PORTABLE FEAST

Conserve of Rascasse

Cassoulet de Rascasse à la Suffren

The rascasse is a bright red-orange fish, native to the Mediterranean. Any other firm-fleshed fish may be substituted.

To make 600 g (1¼ lb) spread

Two 300 to 400 g	rascasses, gutted	Two 10 to 14 oz
2	onions, quartered	2
3	garlic cloves	3
	salt and pepper	
	ground cumin	
3 tbsp	olive oil	3 tbsp
2 tbsp	rum	2 tbsp
	lard, melted	
	parsley	

Fill a fish kettle with cold water and bring it to the boil. Put in the onions and then, 3 minutes later, the fish. Cook for exactly 10 minutes, then drain the fish and remove the skin and bones. Set the fillets aside until they are completely cold.

Pound the garlic in a mortar, then add the fish fillets, crushing them to a moderate extent only and sprinkling on a little salt and some pepper and cumin. When all is well mixed, put the olive oil in a frying pan over a high heat. When the oil "sings" or sizzles, fork the fish mixture into it, and cook, turning as necessary, until it is golden-brown.

Meanwhile, pour the rum into a shallow earthenware terrine and set it alight. When the flames subside, place the fried fish mixture in the terrine and press it down firmly with a fork. Let it cool thoroughly, then cover with 5 mm (¼ inch) of melted lard and decorate with parsley.

70 MÉDECINS DE FRANCE
LE TRÉSOR DE LA CUISINE DU BASSIN MEDITERRANÉEN

Laotian Fish Purée

Ponne Pa

The padek *called for in this recipe is brine-cured fish, with a taste similar to that of salt anchovies, which may be substituted for it.* Mak kheua khao *are round white aubergines; purple-skinned ones may be substituted.* Nam pa *is fish sauce, available bottled in Oriental shops.*

To make about 750 g (1½ lb) purée

500 g	cleaned fish, such as catfish	1 lb
1½ tbsp	*padek*	1½ tbsp
250 g	*mak kheua khao*	8 oz
5	garlic cloves, roasted and roughly chopped	5
2	shallots, roasted and roughly chopped	2
3	dried chili peppers, roasted and pounded to a powder	3
1	spring onion, finely sliced	1
1 tbsp	chopped dill	1 tbsp
	nam pa	

Bring the cleaned fish and *padek* to the boil in 1¼ pints (¾ litre) of water and let it all simmer for 20 minutes. Take out the fish and bone it, leaving the stock to cool.

Meanwhile, boil the *mak kheua khao* in water to cover for about 20 minutes, until they are tender. Then take them out and remove the outer skins.

Now pound the fish, aubergines, garlic and shallots together until they form a smooth paste. Transfer this to a mixing bowl; add some of the fish stock, the pounded chilies, spring onion and dill, and mix it all together. If necessary, to achieve the right consistency (which should be that of thick cream), add more fish stock. Add also a little *nam pa* to taste.

The *ponne pa* is served on a platter, garnished as you please with parsley, coriander, cucumber or dill. Serve it with a good variety of vegetables.

ALAN DAVIDSON
FISH AND FISH DISHES OF LAOS

Estonian Fish Hors-d'Oeuvre

Skoombria

To make about 1 kg (2 to 2½ lb) spread

500 g	cod or other firm white fish, cut into large chunks	1 lb
30 g	flour	1 oz
	salt and pepper	
12.5 cl	vegetable oil	4 fl oz
3	onions, finely chopped	3
4	carrots, grated	4
4	allspice berries	4
1 tsp	paprika	1 tsp
30 cl	tomato sauce (*page 166*)	½ pint
1	bay leaf	1
1 to 2 tbsp	lemon juice	1 to 2 tbsp
	parsley sprigs	
	lemon wedges	

Dredge the cod in the flour that has been seasoned with salt and pepper. Heat half of the oil in a large pot or heavy casserole. Add the cod and cook it over a medium heat for 10 to 12 minutes, until it is barely done. Remove the cod with a slotted spoon and set it aside.

Add to the oil the onions, carrots, allspice berries and paprika. Cook them over a low heat for 5 minutes. Return the cod to the pot. Add the tomato sauce, bay leaf, and salt and pepper to taste. Stir and mash thoroughly. Cover and simmer for 45 minutes, stirring frequently. While the mixture is simmering, add the remaining oil sparingly, as needed, to keep it moist. Remove the bay leaf and allspice berries.

Cover the *skoombria* and refrigerate it for 24 hours. Before serving, add the lemon juice and stir to blend it in thoroughly. Mound the *skoombria* on a serving platter and garnish it with sprigs of parsley and lemon wedges. Serve with thinly sliced black bread and butter.

MELANIE MARCUS
COOKING WITH A HARVARD ACCENT

Lenten Pâté

Pâté di Magro

To make 300 g (10 oz) pâté

100 g	tuna fish in oil	3½ oz
100 g	salt anchovies, soaked, filleted, rinsed and dried	3½ oz
100 g	butter, softened	3½ oz
1	lemon, juice strained	1
	celery sticks	

Sieve the tuna, anchovies and butter together. Add the lemon juice and work the mixture well to form a smooth paste. Rinse out a large cup in cold water, and pack in the paste. Chill for several hours, then turn out on to a dish and surround with celery sticks, the leaves pointing outwards.

OTTORINA PERNA BOZZI
VECCHIA MILANO IN CUCINA

Fish Roe Dip

Taramosaláta

Tarama *is the Greek name for the coral-pink roe of the female grey mullet. It is obtainable, usually salt-preserved in jars, where Greek foods are sold.*

To make 350 to 500 g (12 oz to 1 lb) dip

125 g	*tarama*	4 oz
1	small onion, finely grated	1
¼ to ½ litre	olive oil	8 to 16 fl oz
4	slices white bread, crusts removed	4
2 to 3	lemons, juice strained	2 to 3

Mash the *tarama* and add the grated onion. Add a little of the olive oil and beat the *tarama* mixture to a smooth paste. Moisten the bread by soaking it briefly in water, then squeeze out the excess water. Continue beating the *tarama* mixture, adding small bits of moistened bread alternately with more of the olive oil and lemon juice. When it is ready to serve, *taramosaláta* should be cream-coloured and should have the consistency of a thick mayonnaise.

THE WOMEN OF ST. PAUL'S GREEK ORTHODOX CHURCH
THE ART OF GREEK COOKERY

Fried Foods

Fried Peanuts

Kacang Goreng

This is the simplest possible way of frying peanuts.

To make 500 g (1lb) fried peanuts

500 g	shelled raw peanuts	1 lb
¼ litre	vegetable oil	8 fl oz
	salt	

Heat the oil in a *wok* or deep frying pan. When it is hot, put in half the peanuts and stir-fry continuously for 4 to 5 minutes. Take them out quickly and put them in a colander lined with absorbent kitchen paper. Repeat the process with the remaining peanuts. Dry the excess oil from the peanuts with the kitchen paper, and sprinkle a little salt over them while still hot. Let them cool, then store in airtight containers.

SRI OWEN
INDONESIAN FOOD AND COOKERY

Fried Peanuts, Another Way

Kacang Tujin or Kacang Bawang

To make 500 g (1 lb) fried peanuts

500 g	shelled raw peanuts	1 lb
2	garlic cloves, lightly crushed	2
1 tsp	salt	1 tsp
¼ litre	vegetable oil	8 fl oz

Put the peanuts into a bowl with the garlic and salt. Pour in enough boiling water to cover the nuts. Cover the bowl and let it stand for 30 minutes, then peel off the thin skin from the peanuts—it is usually enough to rub the nut between finger and thumb, the skin will have become very loose. Put the nuts on absorbent paper and, when the peeling is completed, heat the oil in a *wok* or a deep frying pan. Stir-fry the peanuts in this, 250 g (8 oz) at a time, for 5 to 6 minutes. Let the nuts cool before storing them in airtight containers.

SRI OWEN
INDONESIAN FOOD AND COOKERY

Salted Almonds

Salted almonds are not to be bought, but must be prepared at home, and on the day they are to be eaten. Five or 6 hours after the almonds come out of the oven they are at their best. Within 24 hours they have already lost their pristine freshness. The important points about salted almonds are that they squeak as you bite into them; they must be salty in taste but not to the extent that their own flavour is killed.

To make 250 g (8 oz) almonds

250 g	blanched almonds	8 oz
1 tsp	almond oil, olive oil or ground-nut oil, or 5 g (⅛ oz) butter	1 tsp
3 tbsp	kitchen block salt or coarse salt	3 tbsp
	cayenne pepper	

Put the prepared almonds on a baking sheet rubbed with the oil or butter. The sheet then goes into the centre of a very slow oven preheated to about 150°C (300°F or Mark 2). Leave it there for about 45 minutes, until the almonds are a pale toast colour. Have ready on the table a sheet of greaseproof paper sprinkled with the salt. Empty the almonds on to the paper. Swish them round in the salt. Gather up the corners of the paper and twist them so that you have a tightly fastened little parcel. Leave for about 5 hours.

When the moment to set out the almonds arrives, unwrap the parcel, shake the almonds free of excess salt and over them shake an infinitesimal sprinkling of cayenne pepper.

ELIZABETH DAVID
SPICES, SALT AND AROMATICS IN THE ENGLISH KITCHEN

Cheese Balls

Boulettes Jurassiennes

To make 12 cheese balls

125 g	Gruyère cheese, grated	4 oz
2	egg whites, stiffly beaten	2
60 g	dry breadcrumbs	2 oz
	oil for deep frying	
	salt	
	parsley sprigs	

Mix the egg whites with the grated cheese. Form the mixture into 12 small balls; roll them in the breadcrumbs and deep fry in hot oil for 2 minutes or until they are golden-brown. Drain the cheese balls and salt them lightly. Fry the parsley sprigs in the oil until crisp, about 1 minute, and serve the cheese balls accompanied by fried parsley.

LA CUISINE LYONNAISE

Cheese Fritters

Malakoffs

To make 8 fritters

8	slices Emmenthal or Gruyère cheese, 3 mm (⅛ inch) thick	8
125 g	flour	4 oz
¼ tsp	salt	¼ tsp
17.5 cl	warm water	6 fl oz
1 tbsp	olive oil	1 tbsp
3	eggs, well beaten	3
30 g	butter	1 oz
	paprika	

Using a wooden spoon, mix the flour, salt, water and oil to a smooth paste. Fold the beaten eggs into the paste. Melt the butter in a frying pan. Coat the slices of cheese with the batter and fry in the butter on both sides until brown.

Sprinkle with a little paprika and serve immediately.

SIGRID SCHULTZ (EDITOR)
OVERSEAS PRESS CLUB COOKBOOK

Grilled Goat Cheese

Picodons Grillés

Picodon cheeses are small disc-shaped goat cheeses weighing about 100 g (3½ oz) each.

To make 12 cheese slices

6	dry Picodon cheeses	6
1 tbsp	olive oil	1 tbsp
	freshly ground pepper	
	toasted bread	

Cut the cheeses in half crosswise to make thin discs. Place them on a grill rack, brush the cut sides with olive oil and cook over glowing coals or under a grill for 5 minutes. Serve sprinkled with pepper, accompanied by the toasted bread.

FLORENCE DE ANDREIS
LA CUISINE PROVENÇALE D'AUJOURD'HUI

Shrimp Couples

Casadinhos de Camarão

The batter in this recipe may also be used for many kinds of fritters. Add 300 g (10 oz) of highly seasoned, chopped cooked fish, shrimps, ham, chicken, or other meat, and drop by spoonfuls into hot fat or oil.

To make 18 portions

36	shrimps, shelled and marinated in 1 tbsp lemon juice, salt and pepper	36
60 g	rice flour	2 oz
¼ tsp	salt	¼ tsp
1	egg, yolk separated from white, white stiffly beaten	1
12.5 cl	beer	4 fl oz
15 g	butter, melted	½ oz
	oil for deep frying	

Sift the rice flour with the salt. Beat the egg yolk with the beer and add it to the flour. Beat the mixture until smooth, add the butter, and let stand for 1 hour. Fold in the egg white.

Thread two shrimps on to a toothpick, coat with the batter, and deep fry in hot oil. Repeat until all the shrimps are used. Drain on absorbent paper and serve the shrimps with the toothpicks still in them.

MARGARETTE DE ANDRADE
BRAZILIAN COOKERY

Shrimp Appetizers

Bolinhos de Camarão

To make about 20 balls

250 g	shrimps, shelled and de-veined	8 oz
30 g	butter	1 oz
2 tbsp	finely chopped onion	2 tbsp
⅛ tsp	ground coriander	⅛ tsp
	salt and pepper	
250 g	bread, crusts removed, soaked in milk	8 oz
1 tbsp	finely chopped parsley	1 tbsp
3	eggs, lightly beaten	3
60 g	dry breadcrumbs	2 oz
	oil for deep frying	

Sauté the shrimps in the butter with the onion, coriander, salt and pepper. When the shrimps are cooked, after about 2 minutes, cool and mince the mixture in a blender. Mix with the soaked bread, parsley and two of the eggs. Cook over a medium heat until the mixture is thick enough to hold its shape. Adjust the seasoning and allow to cool completely.

Shape the mixture into bite-sized balls, roll in the breadcrumbs, then in the remaining egg and once again in the crumbs. Let stand for 1 hour. Deep fry in hot oil until golden-brown, drain on absorbent paper and serve hot.

MARGARETTE DE ANDRADE
BRAZILIAN COOKERY

Jade Balls

Boulettes de Jade

If you use dried shrimps or prawns for this recipe, use only 100 g (3¼ oz), soak them for 30 minutes in warm water, then drain them carefully before mincing them. If water chestnuts or bamboo shoots are not available, use celery.

To make 20 balls

400 g	shrimps or prawns, shelled, de-veined and minced	14 oz
50 g	pork belly, minced	2 oz
50 g	water chestnuts or bamboo shoots, finely chopped	2 oz
1	egg yolk	1
1 tbsp	flour	1 tbsp
1 tsp	oil	1 tsp
1 tsp	sherry or brandy	1 tsp
¼ tsp	pepper	¼ tsp
1 tbsp	soy sauce	1 tbsp
1 tsp	sesame-seed oil (optional)	1 tsp
¼ tsp	salt	¼ tsp
100 g	almonds, blanched and finely chopped	3½ oz
	oil for deep frying	

Mix the shrimps or prawns, pork, water chestnuts or bamboo shoots, egg yolk, flour, oil, sherry or brandy, and all the seasonings to make a smooth paste.

With oiled fingertips, form the paste into balls the size of strawberries. Roll the balls in the chopped almonds, making sure that the entire surface of each ball is covered and that the almonds adhere firmly.

Deep fry the balls in hot oil for 5 minutes or until they are golden-brown. Remove with a slotted spoon, drain on absorbent paper, and serve hot.

NGUYEN NGOC RAO
LA CUISINE CHINOISE À L'USAGE DES FRANÇAIS

Spiced Prawn Lollipops

Chao Tom

Rose-water may be used instead of the rice spirit in this recipe, and short wooden skewers instead of the sugar cane.

Chao tom are very good eaten just as they are. But they may be wrapped in salad leaves (even wrapped again in rice crêpes) and dipped in fish sauce (*nuoc mam*).

To make about 12 lollipops

750 g	large prawns, shelled, de-veined and pounded	1½ lb
1 tbsp	oil	1 tbsp
1	egg white	1
2	garlic cloves, pounded	2
½ tsp	ground ginger	½ tsp
½ tsp	salt	½ tsp
2 tsp	sugar	2 tsp
1 tbsp	tapioca flour or potato flour	1 tbsp
1 tbsp	rose-perfumed rice spirit (*mai kwai loo*) (optional)	1 tbsp
12	sticks sugar cane, about 15 cm (6 inches) long	12

Mix thoroughly together all of the ingredients except the sugar cane. The mixture must be quite smooth.

Divide the prawn pâté into 12 balls. Encase one end of each sugar cane stick in a ball of pâté. Grill for about 10 minutes or until the pâté is firm and lightly crisp on the outside.

ALAN DAVIDSON
SEAFOOD OF SOUTH-EAST ASIA

Egg Rolls with Pork Stuffing

Egg roll skins may be purchased at Oriental groceries.

To make 20 rolls

20	egg roll skins	20
500 g	minced pork	1 lb
	oil	
500 to 600 g	Chinese cabbage, shredded, mixed well with ⅔ tsp salt, let stand 15 minutes	1 to 1¼ lb
4	spring onions, cut into 5 cm (2 inch) lengths, then into strips	4
1 tsp	minced fresh ginger root, or ½ tsp ground ginger	1 tsp
100 g	bamboo shoots, cut into strips	3½ oz
4 or 5	large dried Chinese mushroom caps, softened in warm water, cut into strips	4 or 5
3 to 4 tsp	salt	3 to 4 tsp
½ tsp	freshly ground black pepper	½ tsp
1½ tbsp	soy sauce	1½ tbsp
½ tsp	sesame-seed oil	½ tsp
4 tbsp	cornflour	4 tbsp

Heat a deep pan to a high temperature. Add 2 tablespoons of oil. Heat for a few seconds. Stir in the pork and cook until the meat changes colour, about 2 minutes. Remove the pan from the heat and cool the pork to room temperature. Squeeze the juice out of the cabbage. Add the cabbage, spring onions, ginger, bamboo shoots, mushrooms, salt, pepper, soy sauce, sesame-seed oil and 2 tablespoons of the cornflour to the pork. Mix the ingredients well.

Divide the stuffing into 20 portions. Place a portion of the stuffing slightly off the centre of each egg roll skin. Roll up the skin to enclose the filling. Tuck in the sides neatly. Combine the remaining cornflour with 12.5 cl (4 fl oz) of water and brush the open edges of the skins with this mixture. Fold and seal. Place each completed egg roll on a platter, sealed edge down. (You may make the rolls ahead and freeze them in a plastic bag, then fry them while still frozen.)

Heat a large pan of oil until a bread cube will brown in it quickly. Deep fry the egg rolls (sealed side down first) for 1½ to 2 minutes on each side, or until they are golden-brown. Drain on paper towels. Serve hot.

EVA LEE JEN
CHINESE COOKING IN THE AMERICAN KITCHEN

Pork Balls

Boulettes Précieuses

To make 20 balls

400 g	boneless pork shoulder, minced	14 oz
50 g	dried shrimps or prawns, soaked in warm water for 30 minutes, drained and minced	2 oz
20 g	dried mushrooms, soaked in warm water for 1 hour, squeezed and roughly chopped	⅔ oz
2	egg yolks, beaten	2
50 g	chives, cut into 1 cm (½ inch) lengths (optional)	2 oz
1 tbsp	oil	1 tbsp
3 tbsp	soy sauce	3 tbsp
¼ tsp	pepper	¼ tsp
1 tbsp	rice wine, dry sherry or brandy	1 tbsp
3 tbsp	flour	3 tbsp
	oil for deep frying	

Mix all the ingredients—except the flour and the frying oil—together to make a smooth, even paste. Form the mixture into small balls the size of strawberries. Roll the balls in the flour.

Deep fry the balls in hot oil for about 5 minutes or until they are golden-brown. Remove them with a slotted spoon and drain on absorbent paper. Serve hot or cold.

NGUYEN NGOC RAO
LA CUISINE CHINOISE À L'USAGE DES FRANÇAIS

Pork and Cheese Strips

Bocaditos de Lomo y Queso

This is one of the few fried *tapas* (snacks) that are just as good cold as hot. Garnish with a little green salad.

To make about 12 strips

500 g	pork fillet, thinly sliced and beaten flat	1 lb
250 g	Gruyère or other mild cheese, sliced to the same size as the pork	8 oz
1	egg, beaten	1
60 g	dry breadcrumbs	2 oz
	oil for deep frying	

Lay half of the pork slices flat and cover them with the slices of cheese. Cover the cheese with the remaining meat and press down lightly. Using a sharp knife, cut these sandwiches in half lengthwise.

Dip each half in the beaten egg, then roll it in the breadcrumbs. Deep fry in oil until golden-brown on both sides, about 2 minutes. Drain on paper towels and serve hot or cold.

GLORIA ROSSI CALLIZO
LAS MEJORES TAPAS, CENAS FRÍAS, Y PLATOS COMBINADOS

Breaded Liver Slices

Higado Empanado

To make about 18 strips

500 g	liver, outer membrane removed, cut into strips 10 cm (4 inches) long	1 lb
1	large onion, thinly sliced	1
30 g	butter	1 oz
1	bay leaf	1
1	egg, beaten	1
60 g	dry breadcrumbs	2 oz
	oil for deep frying	
	salt and pepper	

Fry the onion in the butter for about 15 minutes or until very soft. Add the bay leaf, cover the pan, and keep warm.

Just before serving, dip the liver strips in the egg, then in the breadcrumbs, and deep fry in oil until brown, 2 to 3 minutes. Drain the strips and place on a heated metal serving dish. Cover with the fried onion, season with salt and pepper, place the bay leaf on top, and serve very hot.

GLORIA ROSSI CALLIZO
LAS MEJORES TAPAS, CENAS FRÍAS, Y PLATOS COMBINADOS

Potato Cakes

Pergedel Kentang

To make about 20 cakes

500 g	potatoes, boiled in their skins, peeled and mashed while hot	1 lb
1 tbsp	oil	1 tbsp
6	shallots, finely sliced	6
	salt and pepper	
$\frac{1}{8}$ tsp	grated nutmeg	$\frac{1}{8}$ tsp
4	spring onions, finely chopped	4
2 tbsp	finely chopped flat-leafed parsley	2 tbsp
250 g	minced steak	8 oz
1	egg, beaten	1
1	egg white	1
	vegetable oil for deep frying	

Heat 1 tablespoon of oil in a frying pan and sauté the shallots until soft, about 7 minutes. Drain them and add them to the mashed potatoes. Season with salt, pepper and nutmeg. Mix the spring onions and parsley with the potatoes. Knead the potato mixture and minced meat thoroughly together, then mix in the beaten egg. Pour in the egg white and stir the whole mixture quickly with a fork. Take a dessertspoon of the mixture, roll it into a ball then flatten it slightly with the back of a fork. Continue in this way until all the mixture has been used, then start frying the cakes, a few at a time, in hot oil until golden-brown, about 4 minutes.

They are usually served hot but many people eat them cold.

SRI OWEN
INDONESIAN FOOD AND COOKERY

Ham Curls

Rizos de Jamón

To make 8 to 10 portions

100 g	smoked raw ham or prosciutto, cut into very thin slices 5 cm (2 inches) wide and 10 cm (4 inches) long	3$\frac{1}{2}$ oz
3 tbsp	flour	3 tbsp
2	eggs, beaten	2
60 g	dry breadcrumbs	2 oz
	oil for deep frying	

Flatten the ham slices on the table, then roll them up and skewer them on cocktail sticks. Dip them in the flour, then in the eggs, and roll them in the breadcrumbs. Deep fry them in hot oil for 2 minutes or until golden-brown. Drain them and remove the sticks to serve.

ANA MARIA CALERA
COCINA CASTELLANA

Chick Pea Patties

Panizze

These were sold by street vendors in Corsica. The chick pea flour may be replaced by cornflour.

To make about 12 patties

200 g	chick pea flour	7 oz
1 litre	water	1¾ pints
2 tbsp	olive oil	2 tbsp
¼ tsp	salt	¼ tsp
	oil for deep frying	
	sugar (optional)	

Pour the water into a large saucepan with the olive oil and salt, and bring it to the boil. Pour in the chick pea flour in a steady stream, stirring with a wooden spoon. Let it thicken over a low heat for 6 to 8 minutes, stirring frequently.

Pour the chick pea mixture into shallow oiled moulds about 5 cm (2 inches) in diameter. Allow to cool.

Unmould the patties, detaching them with the point of a knife, and drop them into very hot, deep oil. Cook for about 3 minutes, until golden, then drain and serve hot, plain or sprinkled with sugar.

MARIE CECCALDI
CUISINE DE CORSE

Spinach and Mung Bean Dumplings

Moong Badian

Mung beans are small and green, but are yellow when split. If split mung beans are unavailable, substitute yellow split peas.

To make about 24 dumplings

200 g	split mung beans, soaked for 4 hours	7 oz
125 g	spinach, stemmed and shredded	4 oz
1 tbsp	finely chopped fresh coriander leaves	1 tbsp
1 or 2	green chili peppers, seeded and thinly sliced	1 or 2
⅛ tsp	baking powder	⅛ tsp
¾ tsp	coarse salt	¾ tsp
	oil for deep frying	

Drain and rinse the beans. Purée them to a smooth paste in a blender or food processor for 4 to 5 minutes, adding up to 12.5 cl (4 fl oz) of water to make blending easier. Do not add more liquid than necessary, as the paste should be fairly thick.

Transfer the mixture to a clean bowl and beat it with an electric mixer or a wire whisk for at least 5 minutes, or until very pale, light and fluffy. Cover the paste and let it rest in a warm place (about 26°C or 80°F), such as an unlit oven with the pilot light on, for at least 2 hours.

When you are ready to fry the dumplings, stir the remaining ingredients, except the oil, into the paste. Do not over-blend or the mixture will become dense, which will in turn make the dumplings hard and chewy.

Pour oil to a depth of 5 cm (2 inches) into a frying pan. Heat the oil until hot but not smoking. Drop a heaped teaspoon of the bean mixture into the hot oil. Fry eight to 12 dumplings at a time, making sure not to overcrowd the frying pan. Fry, stirring and turning, until the dumplings are light golden, 4 to 5 minutes. Take them out with a slotted spoon and drain them on paper towels. Continue frying the rest of the bean mixture in the same way. Serve hot.

JULIE SAHNI
CLASSIC INDIAN COOKING

Spiced Bean Rissoles

Ta'amia or Falafel

This is one of Egypt's national dishes. It is also popular in Israel, where it is made with chick peas instead of broad beans. The rissoles may be served with tomato and cucumber salad and tahini, available in jars from Middle Eastern shops. They may also be served in pouches of pitta bread. Dried white broad beans (ful nabed) can be bought in Greek shops and many delicatessens; use the skinless ones if obtainable.

To make about 20 rissoles

500 g	dried white broad beans, soaked for 24 hours	1 lb
2	red or Spanish onions, very finely chopped or grated, or 1 bunch spring onions, finely chopped	2
2	large garlic cloves, crushed	2
1	bunch parsley, finely chopped	1
1 to 2 tsp	ground cumin	1 to 2 tsp
1 to 2 tsp	ground coriander	1 to 2 tsp
½ tsp	baking powder	½ tsp
	salt	
	cayenne pepper	
	oil for deep frying	

Drain the beans and remove the skins if this has not been done. Mince or pound the beans. Mix them with the remaining ingredients, except the oil, and pound to a smooth paste. This will take a long time and much effort, so if a meat grinder is available, put the mixture through twice, using the fine disc, before pounding it. Let the paste rest for at least 30 minutes.

Take walnut-sized lumps of the paste and make flat, round shapes 4 cm (1½ inches) in diameter. Let them rest for 15 minutes longer, then deep fry them in hot oil until they are a dark, rich golden-brown. Serve hot.

CLAUDIA RODEN
A BOOK OF MIDDLE EASTERN FOOD

Sauced and Wrapped Foods

Salami Layers

Neufchâtel is a soft ripened cream cheese made in Normandy.

To make 6 wedges

8	very thin slices salami	8
30 g	Neufchâtel cheese, softened	1 oz
2 tsp	finely chopped chives	2 tsp
2 tsp	finely chopped dill pickle	2 tsp

Spread seven salami slices with the cheese, using about 1 teaspoon for each slice. Sprinkle the cheese with the chives and pickle. Stack the cheese-coated slices one on top of another, and cover the stack with the remaining salami slice. Cut the stack into six equal wedges. Serve on a platter garnished with ripe olives and radishes.

CLARENCE HERISKO
DRINKS AND SNACKS FOR ALL OCCASIONS

Curried Chicken Balls

To make about 60 balls

250 g	cooked chicken, chopped	8 oz
2 tsp	curry powder	2 tsp
250 g	cream cheese, softened	8 oz
175 g	blanched almonds, chopped	6 oz
4 tbsp	mayonnaise (*page 167*)	4 tbsp
3 tbsp	chopped chutney	3 tbsp
1 tsp	salt	1 tsp
125 g	fresh coconut, grated	4 oz

Thoroughly cream the cream cheese, then add the chicken, almonds, mayonnaise, chutney, salt and curry powder. Shape the mixture into walnut-sized balls. Roll each ball in the coconut. Chill the balls until ready to serve.

MARIAN FOX BURROS AND LOIS LEVINE
THE ELEGANT BUT EASY COOKBOOK

Cornets of Smoked Salmon

A cornet, in food terminology, is any food rolled into the shape of a horn. These are most delicious examples.

To make about 40 portions

500 g	smoked salmon, half minced, half thinly sliced	1 lb
	white pepper	
1 tbsp	cognac	1 tbsp
125 g	butter	4 oz
	parsley sprigs or watercress	

Add a dash of pepper and the cognac and butter to the minced salmon and mix well. Cut the sliced salmon into 4 cm (1½ inch) squares. Form the squares into cornets and, with a pastry tube or piping bag, fill each with the minced mixture. Arrange the cornets attractively, spaced well apart, on plates, using a few sprigs of parsley or watercress for garnish.

CHARLOTTE ADAMS
THE FOUR SEASONS COOKBOOK

Paupiettes of Dutch Herrings, Polonaise

Paupiettes de Harengs de Hollande à la Polonaise

To make 16 portions

8	salt herring fillets, soaked in cold water for several hours, drained	8
3	salt anchovies, soaked, filleted, rinsed and dried	3
60 g	butter	2 oz
1 tbsp	lemon juice	1 tbsp
3 tbsp	finely chopped chervil, tarragon and chives	3 tbsp
2	eggs, hard boiled, whites and yolks chopped separately	2
125 g	pickled beetroot, diced or sliced	4 oz
2 tbsp	capers	2 tbsp

Remove the white skin from the herring fillets and halve each fillet lengthwise. Pare the pieces into oblongs. Pound the trimmings in a mortar with the anchovy fillets, butter and lemon juice, then rub the mixture through a sieve. Add 1 tablespoon of the chopped herbs.

Spread a layer of this preparation inside each trimmed herring piece. Roll each piece into a cylindrical shape round its filling and dip the ends in the chopped egg, one end in the white and the other in the yolk. Arrange the paupiettes on a dish, garnishing them with the remaining herbs and surrounding them with the beetroot and capers.

CHARLES RANHOFER
THE EPICUREAN

Devils on Horseback

To make 12 portions

12	large prunes	12
About 30 cl	boiling water or hot red wine	About ½ pint
½	bay leaf	½
12	anchovy fillets, each wrapped round an almond, or 4 tbsp chopped mango chutney, or 12 pimento-stuffed olives	12
6	thin rashers bacon, halved	6
12	slices toast, buttered	12
	watercress	

Pour the water or wine over the prunes; leave for 30 minutes. Simmer the prunes in the same liquid, with the bay leaf, for 20 minutes, or until tender. If wine is used, allow it to be absorbed by the prunes until it has practically disappeared. Drain the prunes, cool and stone them. Fill them with the anchovy-wrapped almonds, the chutney or the olives.

Flatten each half rasher of bacon on a board and wrap it round a prune. Set on a tin and bake in a preheated 220°C (425°F or Mark 7) oven—turning once or twice—for 7 to 10 minutes, or until the bacon is crisp. Set each wrapped prune on a piece of hot buttered toast. Arrange a bunch of watercress in the centre of the dish.

CONSTANCE SPRY AND ROSEMARY HUME
THE CONSTANCE SPRY COOKERY BOOK

Anchovies with Olives

To make 20 portions

10	salt anchovies, soaked, filleted, rinsed and dried	10
20	olives, stoned	20
3	hard-boiled egg yolks, sieved, or 100 g (3½ oz) anchovy butter (*page 167*)	3
4 tbsp	olive oil	4 tbsp

Fill the olives with the egg yolks or anchovy butter. To make a space for the olives, roll each anchovy fillet round a stick of wood 1.5 cm (⅝ inch) in diameter, then remove the stick and place an olive in the centre of the curled anchovy. Range the stuffed anchovy fillets symmetrically on a dish and sprinkle over the olive oil.

CHARLES RANHOFER
THE EPICUREAN

Skewered Dates and Bacon

Pinchos de Datiles y Bacon Fritos

Ham is often substituted for the bacon in this recipe.

To make 12 portions

12	dates, stoned	12
12	thin strips bacon, rind removed	12
	oil for deep frying	

Wrap each date in a strip of bacon and fasten with a toothpick. Fry in hot oil until brown, drain and serve immediately.

SIMONE ORTEGA
MIL OCHENTA RECETAS DE COCINA

Mushrooms with Toast

Crostini con i Funghi

If you are able to obtain fresh ceps, so much the better.

To make 6 to 8 portions

500 g	button mushrooms	1 lb
4 tbsp	oil	4 tbsp
30 g	butter	1 oz
1	garlic clove, finely chopped	1
1	small onion, finely chopped	1
4 tbsp	chopped parsley	4 tbsp
8 cl	meat stock (*page 165*)	3 fl oz
	salt and pepper	
1 tbsp	chopped capers	1 tbsp
6 to 8	slices bread, crusts removed, toasted or fried in butter	6 to 8

Brown the mushrooms in the oil and butter with the garlic, onion and 1 tablespoon of the parsley. After 5 minutes, reduce the heat and add the meat stock, salt and pepper. When the mushrooms are tender, after about 10 minutes, add the capers and the remaining parsley. Stir and leave to cool. Serve surrounded by the toasted or fried bread.

GIOVANNI RIGHI PARENTI
LA CUCINA DEGLI ETRUSCHI

Mushrooms with Garlic

Champiñones al Ajillo

To make 350 g (12 oz) mushrooms

500 g	mushrooms, halved if small, sliced if large	1 lb
2	garlic cloves, finely chopped	2
60 g	butter, or 4 tbsp oil	2 oz
2 tbsp	chopped parsley	2 tbsp
	salt and pepper	
8 cl	dry white wine	3 fl oz

Cook the mushrooms in the butter or oil, over a medium heat, for about 2 minutes or until they have given off their liquid. Add the garlic, parsley, salt and pepper. After about 5 more minutes, when the liquid has evaporated and the mushrooms have begun to brown, pour in the wine. When the excess liquid has evaporated again, after about 5 minutes, the dish is ready to be served. It also reheats well.

GLORIA ROSSI CALLIZO
LAS MEJORES TAPAS, CENAS FRÍAS, Y PLATOS COMBINADOS

———————— ◆ ————————

Sweet-and-Sour Chicken Wings

Ailes de Volaille à l'Aigre-Doux

This dish is eaten with the fingers: one eats the meat and sucks on the bones. Pork spareribs may replace the chicken. Separate the ribs and roll up the meat towards the gristly end.

To make 16 portions

8	chicken wings	8
1½ tbsp	oil	1½ tbsp
1 tsp	flour	1 tsp
½ tsp each	salt and pepper	½ tsp each
1 tbsp	brown sugar, dissolved in 3 tbsp vinegar	1 tbsp

Cut each chicken wing into three portions at the joints, discarding the wing tips. Cut away the meat from the bones of the remaining portions, leaving the meat attached at one end only. Roll up the meat tightly to the end where it is attached, so that it resembles a lollipop.

In a bowl, mix ½ tablespoon of the oil with the flour, salt and pepper. Roll the meaty ends of the wings in this mixture and marinate them for 10 minutes.

Heat the remaining oil in a frying pan over a medium heat. Put in the chicken wings with the marinade that clings to them. Cover and cook for 15 minutes, turning occasionally. Add the sugar and vinegar mixture, and cook for 10 minutes more, basting the wings continually. Serve immediately.

NGUYEN NGOC RAO
LA CUISINE CHINOISE À L'USAGE DES FRANÇAIS

Crab Meat à la Mornay

To make about 1 kg (2 to 2½ lb)

500 g	cooked crab meat, flaked	1 lb
125 g	butter	4 oz
1	small bunch spring onions, finely chopped	1
2 tbsp	flour	2 tbsp
½ litre	cream	16 fl oz
250 g	Gruyère cheese, grated	8 oz
100 g	parsley, finely chopped	3½ oz
1 tbsp	dry sherry	1 tbsp
	cayenne pepper	
	salt	

Melt the butter in a heavy pot and sauté the spring onions until soft but not browned, about 5 minutes. Blend in the flour, cream and cheese, and stir until the cheese is melted. Add the parsley, sherry and the cayenne pepper and salt to taste, and gently fold in the crab meat. Serve in a chafing dish with Melba toast rounds as a dip.

ST. STEPHEN'S EPISCOPAL CHURCH
BAYOU CUISINE

———————— ◆ ————————

Creamed Sweetbreads

To make about 1.5 kg (3 lb) stew

4	pairs calf's sweetbreads	4
45 g	butter	1½ oz
4 tsp	grated onion	4 tsp
1 tbsp	flour	1 tbsp
½ litre	cream	16 fl oz
12	small mushrooms, sliced	12
	salt and pepper	
	paprika	

Soak the sweetbreads in cold water for 1 hour. Parboil them in fresh water for 5 minutes, then drain and let them cool. Remove the membranes and cut the sweetbreads into small pieces. Put the butter in a frying pan and heat it until hot and bubbly. Add the sweetbreads and the grated onion. Fry until the sweetbreads are slightly brown, stirring frequently. Sprinkle the flour over the mixture and stir to blend it in. Then add the cream and mushrooms, mixing thoroughly. Cook over a low heat for about 10 minutes. Season with salt and pepper to taste. Dust with paprika. Serve on hot toast.

NORMA JEAN AND CAROLE DARDEN
SPOONBREAD AND STRAWBERRY WINE

Eggs and Omelettes

Stuffed Eggs with Curry Flavour

The most important thing is to rice the yolks. Two crushed or mashed egg yolks would fill only about 2 tablespoons, whereas two riced yolks fill more than 4 tablespoons. And even after they have been beaten with butter and mayonnaise, riced yolks still retain a much greater volume than if they had been crushed. Do not salt and pepper the basic yolk mixture until after the other ingredients have been added.

To make 16 stuffed egg halves

8	eggs, hard boiled	8
2 tsp	curry powder	2 tsp
15 to 30 g	butter, softened	½ to 1 oz
4 tbsp	mayonnaise (*page 167*)	4 tbsp
1½ tsp	double cream, or 2 tbsp whipped cream (optional)	1½ tsp
	salt and pepper	
1 tsp	finely chopped onion	1 tsp
16	cooked shrimps	16
	dill leaves	

Cut the eggs in half lengthwise, take out the yolks and rice them through a coarse sieve. Stir the curry powder into the soft butter until it is smooth, then whip the butter into the yolks with the mayonnaise, using a fork.

Add the cream, if desired, to make the yolk mixture lighter and smoother. Season the mixture with salt and pepper and add the onion. Pipe the mixture into each egg white through a wide fluted tube, forming a large rosette. Press one shrimp down deep into each rosette and garnish each egg with a little dill pressed down next to one side of the shrimp. Chill the eggs for at least 2 hours before serving.

LILLIAN LANGSETH-CHRISTENSEN
COLD FOODS FOR SUMMER AND WINTER

Tea Eggs

Star anise is a liquorice-flavoured dried spice that looks like an eight-pointed star about 2.5 cm (1 inch) across. Five-spice powder is a combination of five ground spices: anise and fennel seeds, cinnamon, cloves, and the hot but lemony Szechwan pepper. Both star anise and five-spice powder are available at Oriental food stores.

To make 12 tea eggs

12	large eggs, hard boiled	12
2	whole star anise, or 2 tsp five-spice powder	2
2 tbsp	black tea leaves	2 tbsp
1.25 litres	water	2 pints
2 tbsp	salt	2 tbsp

Lightly crack the eggshells with the back of a spoon while the eggs are still warm. (Be sure not to separate the shells from the eggs.) Put the eggs, star anise or five-spice powder, and tea leaves into a 4 litre (7 pint) saucepan. Add the water and salt. Bring the water to the boil, reduce the heat, cover, and simmer for 1½ hours. Remove the eggs from the cooking liquid and refrigerate before serving them.

EVA LEE JEN
CHINESE COOKING IN THE AMERICAN KITCHEN

Pickled Eggs

Oeufs Vieux-Garçons

Pickled in this fashion, the eggs must be refrigerated after the jar in which they are packed is closed. Their flavour will be spicy after five to six days—and will sharpen over the 30-day maximum suggested by the author.

Here is a curious recipe given by E. Richardin in his book, *L'Art du Bien Manger*. The eggs will be best appreciated by lovers of pickles.

To make 12 pickled eggs

12	eggs	12
1 litre	vinegar	1¾ pints
1 tbsp	ground allspice	1 tbsp
1 tbsp	ground ginger	1 tbsp
1 tbsp	freshly ground black pepper	1 tbsp

Boil the eggs for 12 minutes; cool them in cold water and shell them. Bring the vinegar—seasoned with the allspice, ginger and pepper—to the boil, reduce the heat to low and let it cook for 10 minutes. Place the eggs in a jar; pour the boiling vinegar over them. When the vinegar is quite cold, close and seal the jar. These pickled eggs can be kept for a month.

J. BERJANE
FRENCH DISHES FOR ENGLISH TABLES

Stuffed Eggs Delmonico

To make 12 stuffed egg halves

6	eggs, hard boiled	6
60 g	almonds, very finely chopped	2 oz
2 tsp	vinegar	2 tsp
$\frac{1}{8}$ tsp	dry mustard	$\frac{1}{8}$ tsp
$\frac{1}{2}$ tsp	salt	$\frac{1}{2}$ tsp
$\frac{1}{2}$ tsp	Worcestershire sauce	$\frac{1}{2}$ tsp
$\frac{1}{8}$ tsp	Tabasco sauce	$\frac{1}{8}$ tsp
2 tbsp	mayonnaise (*page 167*)	2 tbsp

Cut the eggs in half lengthwise, remove the yolks and put them through a sieve or mash them with a fork. Combine the yolks with the remaining ingredients and blend. Fill the egg-white cavities lightly.

JULIE BENELL
KITCHEN MAGIC

Stuffed Eggs

Telur Isi

Not everyone likes the chewy, flaky consistency of grated coconut. If you want the mixture to be smooth, blend it in a blender before adding the hard-boiled egg yolks; moisten it with a little extra water or, better still, with a little curry sauce or tomato sauce (*page 166*).

To make 24 stuffed egg halves

12	eggs, hard boiled	12
1 tbsp	vegetable oil or 15 g ($\frac{1}{2}$ oz) clarified butter	1 tbsp
3	shallots or 1 onion, finely sliced	3
2	garlic cloves, crushed	2
$\frac{1}{8}$ tsp	ground ginger	$\frac{1}{8}$ tsp
$\frac{1}{8}$ tsp	chili powder or freshly ground black pepper	$\frac{1}{8}$ tsp
3 tbsp	freshly grated or desiccated coconut	3 tbsp
	salt	
3 tbsp	boiled water, still hot	3 tbsp
	parsley sprigs	

Heat the oil or butter in a *wok* or saucepan, fry the shallots or onion until soft, then add the garlic, ginger, chili powder or black pepper and the coconut. Mix well in the pan. Add salt and 2 tablespoons of the hot water. Cook and continue stirring for 4 minutes. The mixture should be moist, so add the remaining hot water. Then put it in a bowl to cool.

Halve the hard-boiled eggs and scoop out the yolks. Mix the yolks with the other prepared ingredients, fill the whites, and garnish with sprigs of parsley.

SRI OWEN
INDONESIAN FOOD AND COOKERY

Totally Stuffed Eggs Indian-Style

To make 6 stuffed eggs

6	large eggs, hard boiled	6
15 g	butter, softened	$\frac{1}{2}$ oz
	salt and pepper	
1 tsp	finely chopped onion	1 tsp
2 tsp	finely chopped capers	2 tsp
1 tbsp	finely chopped sweet pepper	1 tbsp
3	large tomatoes, halved and hollowed out, or 6 lettuce leaves	3
12.5 cl	mayonnaise (*page 167*), flavoured with $\frac{1}{2}$ tsp curry powder	4 fl oz

While they are still hot, cut the eggs in half lengthwise; keep each pair of halves together. Take out the yolks and mash them with the butter, salt and pepper to taste, onion, capers and sweet pepper. Shape the paste into yolk-sized rounds and press them into half of the egg whites. Close each egg white with the second half and wrap each reassembled egg tightly in greaseproof paper. Chill them for at least 1 hour. Remove the greaseproof paper and arrange the eggs on lettuce leaves or in tomato halves and serve them with the mayonnaise.

LILLIAN LANGSETH-CHRISTENSEN
COLD FOODS FOR SUMMER AND WINTER

Red Caviare Roll

To make a roll about 25 cm (10 inches) long

4	eggs, yolks separated from the whites	4
75 g	flour	2½ oz
60 g	butter	2 oz
30 cl	milk, lukewarm	½ pint
	salt	
2 tsp	castor sugar	2 tsp
	grated nutmeg	
4 to 6 tbsp	finely chopped chives	4 to 6 tbsp
	soured cream	
4 tbsp	red caviare (salmon roe)	4 tbsp
	Filling	
3 to 4 tbsp	red caviare (salmon roe)	3 to 4 tbsp
175 g	cream cheese, softened	6 oz
1 to 2 tbsp	lemon juice	1 to 2 tbsp
2 tbsp	soured cream	2 tbsp
	freshly ground black pepper	
17.5 cl	double cream	6 fl oz

Preheat the oven to 200°C (400°F or Mark 6). Line a 26 by 39 cm (10½ by 15½ inch) Swiss roll tin with foil; brush the foil with olive oil and then dust it with 1 tablespoon of the flour, shaking out the excess flour.

To make the roll, first melt the butter in a small saucepan. Add 4 tablespoons of the flour and cook, stirring, over a low heat to blend thoroughly. Gradually stir in the heated milk and cook, stirring constantly, until the sauce thickens—about 2 minutes. Bring to the boil and simmer, stirring, for 3 to 4 minutes. Pour the sauce into a bowl. Beat in a pinch of salt, the sugar and a pinch of nutmeg. Beat the egg yolks lightly. Beating constantly, pour the yolks into the sauce in a thin stream. Cool to lukewarm.

Beat the egg whites with a pinch of salt until stiff but not dry. Fold one quarter of the whites into the lukewarm sauce. Sift in 2 tablespoons of flour, followed by a third of the remaining whites. Repeat with the remaining flour and egg whites. Pour the mixture into the prepared tin; level the top of the mixture with a spatula.

Bake for 5 minutes; reduce the oven temperature to 150°C (300°F or Mark 2) and bake for 50 to 55 minutes, or until the sponge is golden-brown and springy. Turn the sponge out on to a damp cloth lined with greaseproof paper. Remove the foil and trim any crusty edges. Starting at one narrow end, roll the sponge loosely with the cloth and paper. Cool.

To make the filling, first blend the cream cheese, lemon juice and soured cream together. Season to taste with pepper. Whip the double cream until light and fluffy; fold it into the cream cheese mixture, followed by the red caviare. Correct the seasoning and chill the mixture until firm.

Unroll the baked sponge; sprinkle it with the chopped chives; spread with the filling and then roll it up like a Swiss roll. Serve the roll cut into 12 slices, each about 2 cm (¾ inch) thick. Garnish each portion with a little soured cream and 1 teaspoon of red caviare.

ROBERT CARRIER
ROBERT CARRIER'S ENTERTAINING

Chinese Prawn Omelettes

Omelettes Chinoises aux Crevettes

The prawns or shrimps may be replaced by shredded crab meat or chicken breast; the bean sprouts may be replaced by bamboo shoots cut into matchsticks, finely sliced celery, or roughly chopped water chestnuts.

To make 8 omelettes

100 g	prawns or shrimps, shelled, de-veined and roughly chopped	3½ oz
4	eggs	4
4 tbsp	peanut oil	4 tbsp
3	rashers bacon, or 1 slice Bayonne ham, roughly chopped	3
100 g	bean sprouts	3½ oz
2	spring onions, roughly chopped	2
20 g	dried mushrooms, soaked in warm water for 1 hour, dried and roughly chopped, or 50 g (2 oz) button mushrooms, roughly chopped	⅔ oz
¼ tsp each	salt and pepper	¼ tsp each
1 tsp	sesame-seed oil	1 tsp

Heat a frying pan over a high heat for 30 seconds, then pour in 1 tablespoon of peanut oil. Shake the pan until the bottom is covered with the oil, then sauté the prawns or shrimps and bacon for 1 minute, stirring constantly. Add the bean sprouts, spring onions and mushrooms to the pan and cook for 1 minute, stirring constantly. Transfer the mixture to a plate and leave it to cool completely.

Beat the eggs with the salt, pepper and sesame-seed oil. Stir the vegetable mixture into the eggs.

Heat the pan again, adding 1 tablespoon of peanut oil, then reduce the heat to low. Ladle about 4 tablespoons of the egg mixture into the pan and cook for 1 minute or until lightly browned. Turn and cook for 1 minute on the other side. Remove the omelette and keep it hot. Continue making omelettes until all the egg mixture is used, adding 1 teaspoon of peanut oil to the pan before making each omelette.

NGUYEN NGOC RAO
LA CUISINE CHINOISE À L'USAGE DES FRANÇAIS

Stacked Omelettes

Differently coloured and flavoured flat omelettes, cooked on one side only, stacked one on top of the other, given a sprinkling of cheese and baked until set are equally good hot, tepid or cold (room temperature), and provide a perfect luncheon starter if cut into wedges or, when cut into small cubes, a particularly attractive aperitif titbit. Many vegetables form a good omelette base—finely sliced and sautéed artichoke bottoms; peeled asparagus, finely sliced on the bias, parboiled for a minute and rapidly sautéed in butter; parboiled, squeezed and chopped chard leaves; peeled, parboiled and sautéed broad beans heightened with a bit of fresh savory. . . chopped black olives, anchovy, *julienned* or chopped ham, mussels or crustaceans are also good bases.

To make one 20 cm (8 inch) diameter omelette stack

8	eggs, beaten	8
500 g	spinach	1 lb
17.5 cl	olive oil	6 fl oz
1	garlic clove, finely chopped	1
	salt and pepper	
	grated nutmeg	
250 g	mushrooms, finely sliced	8 oz
1	onion, finely chopped	1
2	large ripe tomatoes, skinned, seeded and chopped, or 1 small can Italian plum tomatoes, drained and puréed	2
1	sweet red pepper, roasted, peeled, seeded and cut into fine strips	1
	cayenne pepper	
2 tbsp	chopped basil (optional)	2 tbsp
30 g	Parmesan cheese, grated	1 oz

Parboil the spinach for 1 minute, refresh it in cold water and squeeze it well. Chop the spinach and sauté it in 2 tablespoons of olive oil, with the garlic, for 5 minutes. Season with salt, pepper and nutmeg.

Sauté the mushrooms rapidly in 2 tablespoons of olive oil; season with salt and pepper.

Cook the onion in 2 tablespoons of olive oil for 10 minutes or until it has softened without browning. Add the tomatoes and cook for 5 minutes. Add the sweet red pepper and continue to cook until all excess liquid has evaporated, about 10 minutes. Season the mixture with salt, pepper, a hint of cayenne pepper and, if in season, the chopped basil.

Divide the beaten eggs amongst the three vegetable mixtures. Heat 2 tablespoons of oil in a frying pan, pour in the spinach mixture over a high heat, give it a rapid stir with the back of a fork without scraping it against the bottom of the pan, smooth out the surface of the mixture, cover the pan and cook over a medium-low heat for a couple of minutes or until

the omelette is well set on the bottom and slides easily in the pan but remains moist on the surface. Slide the omelette on to a baking dish, uncooked surface up.

Make the mushroom omelette in the same way and slide it on top of the spinach omelette. Finally, make the more fragile tomato omelette and slide it on top of the mushroom one. Sprinkle the grated Parmesan over the surface of the tomato omelette and bake in a preheated 180°C (350°F or Mark 4) oven for about 20 to 30 minutes or until the omelettes are set and sealed together.

PETITS PROPOS CULINAIRES VIII

Mushroom Roll

For a cool summer lunch, you can spread the surface of the sponge with a mixture of 500 g (1 lb) of flaked, cooked crab meat and ¼ litre (8 fl oz) of soured cream before rolling it up.

To make a roll about 25 cm (10 inches) long

750 g	mushrooms, very finely chopped	1½ lb
6	eggs, yolks separated from whites	6
125 g	butter, melted	4 oz
½ tsp	salt	½ tsp
¼ tsp	freshly ground white pepper	¼ tsp
2 tbsp	lemon juice	2 tbsp
500 g	cooked crab meat, flaked (optional)	1 lb
¼ litre	soured cream (optional)	8 fl oz
4 or 5	sautéed mushroom caps	4 or 5
2 tbsp	chopped parsley	2 tbsp

Brush a Swiss roll tin with vegetable oil, then line it with greaseproof paper, letting the paper extend 10 cm (4 inches) on each end. Brush the paper with vegetable oil and set aside.

Put the chopped mushrooms in the corner of a tea towel a handful at a time, wring them out to remove excess moisture, and put them in a bowl. Beat the egg yolks until fluffy. Add the yolks, melted butter, salt, pepper and lemon juice to the mushrooms. Beat the egg whites until they form soft peaks and fold them into the mushroom mixture.

Pour the mixture into the prepared tin, spread it evenly and bake in a preheated 180°C (350°F or Mark 4) oven for 15 minutes, or until the sponge starts to pull away from the sides of the tin. Turn the sponge out of the tin on to two overlapping sheets of greaseproof paper and, with the paper to help, roll it up like a Swiss roll.

Place the roll on a long narrow platter or board, garnish it with the mushroom caps placed down the centre and sprinkle it with the chopped parsley.

JULIE DANNENBAUM
JULIE DANNENBAUM'S CREATIVE COOKING SCHOOL

Rolled Spinach Omelette

This recipe is by Carol Cutler.

To make a roll about 25 cm (10 inches) long

500 g	spinach, parboiled for 3 minutes, drained, squeezed dry and chopped	1 lb
5	eggs, yolks separated from whites	5
90 g	butter	3 oz
60 g	flour	2 oz
½ litre	milk	16 fl oz
	salt and pepper	
2 tbsp	freshly grated Parmesan cheese	2 tbsp
4	shallots, finely chopped	4
125 g	mushrooms, chopped	4 oz
4	slices ham, finely diced	4
1 tbsp	mustard	1 tbsp
¼ tsp	grated nutmeg	¼ tsp
175 g	cream cheese, softened	6 oz
¼ litre	soured cream	8 fl oz
3 to 4 tbsp	single cream	3 to 4 tbsp

Preheat the oven to 200°C (400°F or Mark 6). Butter a Swiss roll tin. Line the bottom of the pan with greaseproof paper, butter the paper and dust it lightly with flour.

To make the omelette, first melt 60 g (2 oz) of the butter in a saucepan, blend in the flour and cook until foamy. Slowly stir in the milk, then add ½ teaspoon of salt and a large pinch of pepper. Cook for 1 minute. Beat the egg yolks and add a little of the hot sauce. Add the heated yolks to the sauce in the pan and cook the mixture over a medium heat for 1 minute longer, stirring constantly. Do not allow it to boil. Scrape the sauce into a bowl and set it aside to cool, stirring occasionally.

Beat the egg whites until stiff and gently fold them into the sauce. Pour the mixture into the tin and spread it to form an even layer. Sprinkle the omelette with Parmesan cheese. Bake for 20 to 30 minutes, or until puffed and brown.

To prepare the filling, melt the remaining butter, then add the shallots and sauté them for 2 minutes. Next, add the mushrooms to the pan and cook over a medium heat until they give up their moisture, about 4 minutes. Add the spinach, ham, mustard and nutmeg to the pan. Then stir in the cream cheese and season to taste with salt and pepper.

When the omelette is done, turn it immediately on to a clean towel. Spread the top with the spinach filling. Then, with the aid of the towel, roll the omelette into a long cylinder. Slide the omelette on to a serving platter, seam side down. Serve it hot or cold, sliced and accompanied by a sauceboat of soured cream thinned with single cream.

THE GREAT COOKS' GUIDE TO OMELETS FROM AROUND THE WORLD

Stuffed Vegetables

Cheese-Stuffed Mushrooms

This is one of my most successful cocktail goodies. The trick is to use a well-flavoured cream cheese, such as the herb and garlic French Boursin. If necessary, cream cheese can be doctored up with Tabasco sauce, onion juice, a little mashed garlic and whatever herbs one likes. I repeat, the cheese must have plenty of flavour.

To make about 50 stuffed mushrooms

500 g	small mushrooms, all of the same size	1 lb
About 12.5 cl	lemon juice	About 4 fl oz
1	small round Boursin cheese, at room temperature	1

Remove the stems from the mushrooms and dip the mushrooms immediately in the lemon juice on all sides to prevent darkening. Put the prepared mushrooms on kitchen paper to dry. Save the stems for soup. Fill the cavity of each mushroom with a little of the cheese.

Put the mushrooms in a serving dish, cover with plastic film and refrigerate until chilled.

NIKA HAZELTON
THE PICNIC BOOK

Viennese Stuffed Mushrooms

If shallots are unavailable, substitute one small onion.

To make 12 to 16 stuffed mushrooms

12 to 16	large mushrooms, 5 to 7.5 cm (2 to 3 inches) in diameter	12 to 16
250 g	small mushrooms	8 oz
45 g	butter	1½ oz
2	large shallots, finely chopped	2
	salt and freshly ground white pepper	
175 g	cream cheese, softened	6 oz
2 tbsp	finely chopped dill	2 tbsp
2 tbsp	finely grated Parmesan cheese	2 tbsp
	parsley sprigs	

Carefully remove the stems from the large mushrooms, chop the stems finely and set them aside. Wipe the caps of the large mushrooms carefully with damp paper towels. Set the caps aside. Chop the small mushrooms finely.

Heat 30 g (1 oz) of the butter in a small, heavy frying pan. Add the finely chopped mushrooms, the reserved mushroom stems and the shallots, and cook the mixture over a high heat until it is lightly browned and all of the liquid has evaporated. Season with salt and pepper.

In a mixing bowl, combine the cream cheese, dill and the mushroom mixture. Add the Parmesan cheese, then mash the mixture with a fork until it is well blended. Taste and correct the seasoning; chill for 30 minutes.

Preheat the grill. Butter a baking dish with the remaining butter. Fill the reserved mushroom caps with the mushroom and cheese mixture, then place them under the grill and cook for 3 to 5 minutes, or until lightly browned. Do not overcook. Carefully transfer the mushrooms to a serving platter, garnish with sprigs of parsley and serve immediately.

PERLA MEYERS
THE PEASANT KITCHEN

Stuffed Mushrooms

Champignons Farcis

To make 40 to 50 stuffed mushrooms

500 g	very small mushrooms	1 lb
30 g	butter	1 oz
$\frac{1}{2}$	garlic clove, mashed to a paste	$\frac{1}{2}$
	salt and pepper	
1 tsp	finely chopped parsley	1 tsp
About 2 tbsp	dried breadcrumbs, seasoned with oregano and parsley	About 2 tbsp
	oil	

Remove the mushroom stems from the caps, trim off the root ends and chop the stems. Sauté these briefly in the butter. After 2 to 3 minutes, add the garlic, salt and pepper, and the parsley. Cook together for another 2 minutes, remove from the heat, and mix in enough breadcrumbs to make a light stuffing. Fill the caps with this, and put them in a well-oiled shallow baking dish. Pour a few drops of oil over each mushroom and bake them in a preheated 180°C (350°F or Mark 4) oven for 10 to 15 minutes until they are barely soft and the stuffing is lightly browned; they must not be overcooked.

NARCISSA CHAMBERLAIN
FRENCH MENUS FOR PARTIES

Egg and Chicory

To make 12 to 16 stuffed chicory leaves

3	eggs, hard boiled and chopped	3
2 or 3	heads Belgian chicory	2 or 3
2 tbsp	crumbled Roquefort or blue cheese	2 tbsp
About 2 tbsp	mayonnaise (*page 167*)	About 2 tbsp
	salt and black pepper	
$\frac{1}{4}$ tsp	Tabasco sauce	$\frac{1}{4}$ tsp
6 to 8	anchovy fillets, halved lengthwise	6 to 8
	chopped parsley	

Place the eggs in a mixing bowl and add the cheese and mayonnaise. Stir and, if necessary, add more mayonnaise to bind the mixture. Season to taste with salt, pepper and Tabasco sauce. Pull apart the chicory leaves. Spread the egg mixture inside the chicory leaves and lay half an anchovy lengthwise over each filled leaf. Garnish with the chopped parsley. Chill and serve.

JEAN HEWITT
THE NEW YORK TIMES LARGE TYPE COOKBOOK

Courgettes with White Stuffing

Zucchini Ripieni in Bianco

To make 20 portions

10	fairly large courgettes, cooked in boiling salted water for a few minutes	10
300 g	cooked chicken, minced	10 oz
1	egg	1
30 g	Parmesan cheese, grated	1 oz
	salt and pepper	
1 tbsp	chopped parsley	1 tbsp
2 tbsp	oil	2 tbsp
3 tbsp	dry breadcrumbs	3 tbsp

Drain the courgettes carefully, dry them and leave to cool. Cut them in half lengthwise and place them in an ovenproof dish. Using a teaspoon, remove the centre of each half and place the pulp in a bowl. Mix the pulp with the chicken, egg, cheese, salt and pepper to taste, and the parsley. Combine the ingredients thoroughly and use this stuffing to fill the courgette halves. Brush the tops with the oil, sprinkle with the breadcrumbs and bake in a preheated 180°C (350°F or Mark 4) oven for 30 minutes. Serve hot.

MARIA RIVIECCIO ZANIBONI
CUCINA E VINI DI NAPOLI E DELLA CAMPANIA

Filled Cucumber Cups

To make about 16 cups

2	cucumbers, peeled in stripes with a fluted knife	2
¼ litre	vinaigrette (*page 165*)	8 fl oz
2 tbsp	finely chopped parsley	2 tbsp
4	slices smoked salmon, finely chopped	4
About 17.5 cl	tartare sauce (*page 167*)	About 6 fl oz
	grated horseradish	

Cut the fluted cucumbers—the green skin is corrugated with long white lines—across into 2.5 cm (1 inch) slices. Take out the centre of each slice with a large melon scoop, leaving enough cucumber at the sides and bottom to make a thin cup. Marinate the cups in vinaigrette for at least 1 hour, turning them often. Spread the parsley out on greaseproof paper, drain the cucumber cups and dip the top edge of each one into the parsley to make a green border. Bind the chopped salmon with a little tartare sauce and fill the cucumber cups with this mixture. Sprinkle each cup with a few raspings of horse-radish and serve very cold with additional tartare sauce.

LILLIAN LANGSETH-CHRISTENSEN
COLD FOODS FOR SUMMER AND WINTER

Stuffed Celery

To make about 48 pieces

1	celery heart, sticks separated and trimmed	1
175 g	cream cheese	6 oz
1 tsp	white vinegar	1 tsp
1 tbsp	single cream	1 tbsp
1 tsp	curry powder	1 tsp
5 tbsp	finely chopped chutney	5 tbsp

Soften the cream cheese to room temperature. Blend together the vinegar, cream and curry powder. Add the cream cheese and work the mixture into a smooth paste. Stir in the chutney and refrigerate for several hours, overnight if possible. About 1 hour before serving, stuff the mixture into the celery sticks and cut them into 2.5 cm (1 inch) pieces.

ANN ROE ROBBINS
TREADWAY INNS COOK BOOK

Celery Stuffed with Caviare

To make about 48 pieces

2	celery hearts, sticks separated and trimmed	2
75 g	red caviare (salmon roe)	2½ oz
250 g	cream cheese	8 oz
1 tbsp	grated onion	1 tbsp
60 g	parsley, chopped	2 oz
	salt and pepper	

Mix the cream cheese with the onion and parsley until soft, then gently fold in the red caviare. Season with salt and pepper. Stuff the celery sticks with the caviare mixture, cut into 5 cm (2 inch) pieces and refrigerate until serving time.

RENÉ VERDON
THE WHITE HOUSE CHEF COOKBOOK

Celery Stuffed with Roquefort

Céleri au Roquefort

To make about 30 slices

3	heads celery, sticks separated and trimmed	3
250 g	Roquefort cheese, softened	8 oz
250 g	Gruyère cheese, grated	8 oz
150 g	butter, softened	5 oz
	pepper	

Work together the cheeses, butter and pepper. Fill the celery sticks with this mixture. Press together two or three sticks, with the cheese mixture in the middle. Wrap tightly in foil and refrigerate. The next day, cut in crosswise slices about 2.5 cm (1 inch) thick. Keep chilled until serving time.

FLORENCE DE ANDREIS
LA CUISINE PROVENÇALE D'AUJOURD'HUI

Filled Beetroots

To make 24 filled beetroots

24	tiny beetroots, boiled for 30 to 40 minutes, drained, peeled and trimmed	24
¼ litre	vinaigrette (*page 165*)	8 fl oz
90 g	cream cheese, softened	3 oz
4 tbsp	chopped walnuts	4 tbsp

Remove the centres from the beetroots. Toss these beetroot cups with the vinaigrette, cover and marinate for 24 hours. Drain the cups, reserving the marinade, and pat them dry. Mix 2 teaspoons of the vinaigrette with the cream cheese and walnuts. Fill the cups with the cream cheese mixture.

ALICE SCHRYVER AND FRANCILLE WALLACE
THE COMPLETE HORS D'OEUVRES COOKBOOK

Stuffed Aubergine Boats

Milinciani o Tabaccheri Chini

To make about 12 portions

1 kg	small, firm aubergines, stalks removed, halved lengthwise	2 to 2½ lb
1 litre	salted water	1¾ pints
30 g	butter	1 oz
100 g	onion, chopped	3½ oz
30 g	capers	1 oz
50 g	salt anchovies, soaked, filleted, rinsed, dried and chopped	2 oz
50 g	salami, chopped	2 oz
2	garlic cloves, chopped with 1 sprig parsley	2
	salt and pepper	
100 g	breadcrumbs, half toasted	3½ oz
1	egg white, stiffly beaten	1
12.5 cl	olive oil	4 fl oz

Boil the aubergines in the salted water for 10 minutes or until they are tender but still hold their shape. Drain them and scoop out the pulp from the inside.

Heat the butter and cook the onion in it until golden. Add the aubergine pulp, capers, anchovies, salami, garlic and parsley. Season lightly with salt and pepper.

When the ingredients are well mixed and softened, add the toasted breadcrumbs and remove from the heat. Fill the aubergine halves with this mixture. Coat them with the egg white, then with the rest of the breadcrumbs. Heat the oil and fry the aubergine halves in it until golden on both sides.

PINO CORRENTI
IL LIBRO D'ORO DELLA CUCINA E DEI VINI DI SICILIA

Pastries and Breads

Kurland Bacon Cakes

Kurländer Speckkuchen

To make 15 cakes

250 g	smoked streaky bacon, minced or finely diced	8 oz
250 g	onions, finely chopped	8 oz
2 tbsp	chopped parsley	2 tbsp
	pepper	
1	egg, yolk separated from white	1
	Soft yeast dough	
15 g	fresh yeast, or 2 tsp dried yeast	½ oz
¼ litre	milk, lukewarm	8 fl oz
375 g	strong plain flour	13 oz
	salt	
50 g	lard	2 oz

To make the dough, dissolve the yeast in half of the milk. Place the flour in a bowl with the salt and lard. Pour in the yeast mixture and the remaining milk. Knead together to make a soft, smooth dough. Cover the dough and leave it to rise for about 1 hour, until it has doubled in bulk.

Meanwhile, fry the bacon until it begins to render its fat. Add the onions and fry until the onions are soft and transparent but not brown. Season with parsley and pepper.

Roll out the dough into a sheet 5 mm (¼ inch) thick. Cut out 15 rounds 10 cm (4 inches) in diameter. Place a mound of the bacon filling in the centre of each round and brush the edges with the egg white. Fold the rounds into half-moon shapes round the filling and press down the edges carefully. Place the cakes on baking sheets and brush them with the egg yolk. Allow them to rise for 15 minutes, then bake in a preheated 200°C (400°F or Mark 6) oven for 20 minutes or until golden-brown. Serve freshly baked.

HEDWIG MARIA STUBER
ICH HELF DIR KOCHEN

Bacon and Egg Pasty

To make 4 pasties

12	rashers streaky bacon, rind removed, diced	12
4	eggs, hard boiled and chopped	4
2 tbsp	chopped parsley	2 tbsp
	salt and pepper	
500 g	shortcrust dough (*page 164*)	1 lb

Combine the bacon, eggs, parsley, salt and pepper. Roll out the dough and cut it into four circles. Place a quarter of the filling on each circle and fold the dough in half to enclose the filling. Moisten the edges and crimp them to seal. Place the pasties on a baking sheet and bake in a preheated 190°C (375°F or Mark 5) oven for 40 minutes or until golden-brown.

ANN PASCOE
CORNISH RECIPES OLD AND NEW

Cornish Pasties

To make 6 pasties

500 g	beef rump steak, finely diced	1 lb
175 g	potatoes, finely diced	6 oz
175 g	onions, finely chopped	6 oz
½ tsp	thyme	½ tsp
1 tsp	salt	1 tsp
¼ tsp	freshly ground black pepper	¼ tsp
500 g	shortcrust dough (*page 164*)	1 lb
90 g	butter	3 oz
6 tbsp	finely chopped parsley	6 tbsp
1	egg yolk, beaten with 1 tbsp water	1
12.5 cl	double cream	4 fl oz

In a bowl, combine the diced beef and potatoes with the onions. Season with the thyme, salt and pepper.

Roll out the shortcrust dough 3 mm (⅛ inch) thick and cut it into six 12.5 cm (5 inch) rounds.

Spoon 3 tablespoons of the filling on to one side of each round. Dot with 15 g (½ oz) of the butter and sprinkle with 1 tablespoon of the parsley. Moisten the edges of the dough and fold them over into turnovers. Crimp the dough together with a fork. Prick the tops of the turnovers, and brush them with the diluted egg yolk.

Bake in a preheated 170°C (325°F or Mark 3) oven for 1 hour. Fifteen minutes before the pasties are done, make a small hole in the top of the crusts and spoon 2 tablespoons of cream into the holes. (If the crusts brown too quickly during baking, cover the turnovers with foil.)

NANCY FAIR MCINTYRE
COOKING IN CRUST

Herb Pasty

To make 4 pasties

125 g	sprigs parsley	4 oz
125 g	watercress leaves	4 oz
500 g	spinach, stemmed	1 lb
4	shallots or 1 leek, finely chopped	4
1 or 2	thick rashers bacon, finely chopped	1 or 2
500 g	shortcrust dough (*page 164*)	1 lb
1	egg, beaten	1

Chop and scald a quantity of well-washed parsley, watercress and spinach for 1 minute. Drain; press out the excess liquid, and chop the mixture finely. Add the finely chopped shallots or leek and the chopped bacon.

Divide the pastry dough into four pieces. Roll out the pieces and place the vegetable mixture on the rounds of dough, fold the rounds in half, crimp each pasty except at one point and pour into this a small amount of beaten egg. Seal the pasties and bake in a preheated 230°C (450°F or Mark 8) oven until the pastry is pale brown, about 10 minutes. Then reduce the heat to 180°C (350°F or Mark 4) for about 40 minutes.

ANN PASCOE
CORNISH RECIPES OLD AND NEW

Meat Pasty

To make about 6 pasties

350 g	mutton or beefsteak, diced	12 oz
500 g	shortcrust dough (*page 164*)	1 lb
175 g	potatoes, diced	6 oz
1	small onion, finely chopped	1
	salt and pepper	
1	egg, beaten, or 4 tbsp milk (optional)	1

Roll out the dough about 5 mm (¼ inch) thick. Cut it into rounds, using a saucer or a small plate as a guide. Mix the meat, potatoes and onion together very thoroughly. Add salt and pepper and about 3 tablespoons of cold water. Place some of this filling on one half of each circle of dough, damp the edges of the circle with cold water and fold them over to cover the mixture. Press the edges of the dough together and crimp them with your fingers to seal them. Make two or three ventilating slits in the "lid", brush with beaten egg or milk if a glaze is required, and place on a baking sheet. Cook in a preheated 230°C (450°F or Mark 8) oven until the pastry is pale brown—about 10 minutes—then reduce the heat to 180°C (350°F or Mark 4) and cook for about 40 minutes more.

ANN PASCOE
CORNISH RECIPES OLD AND NEW

Priddy Oggies

This pasty was invented by Mr. Paul Leyton for his restaurant at Priddy in Somerset, the Miner's Arms. The shape of it is based on the Cornish oggy or pasty, that convenient arrangement which enabled a miner—or a schoolboy—to take his lunch to work in his pocket.

Before cooking, the pasties can be stored in a refrigerator for three days, or a deep-freeze for three months. In the latter case, give them 15 to 20 minutes in the oven before frying.

To make 8 pasties

One 600 g	pork fillet, halved horizontally and beaten until 5 mm (¼ inch) thick	One 1¼ lb
30 g	very thinly sliced smoked pork, smoked bacon or Bayonne ham, cut into 8 strips	1 oz
1	large egg, beaten	1
90 g	mature Cheddar cheese, grated (or half mild Cheddar, half Parmesan)	3 oz
1	sprig parsley, chopped	1
¼ tsp	salt	¼ tsp
8	drops Tabasco sauce, or ¼ tsp cayenne pepper or freshly ground black pepper	8
	milk	
	fat for deep frying or 90 g (3 oz) lard	

Cheese dough

100 g	mature Cheddar cheese, grated (or half mild Cheddar, half Parmesan)	3½ oz
30 g	butter	1 oz
30 g	lard	1 oz
1	small egg yolk	1
2½ tbsp	water	2½ tbsp
¼ tsp	salt	¼ tsp
250 g	flour	8 oz

Make the pastry dough first. Mix all the dough ingredients, except the flour, in a bowl. It is a good idea to warm the butter and lard slightly. Cool the mixture in the refrigerator until firm. Sieve the flour, and rub the cooled mixture in roughly. Take about 100 g (3½ oz) of this dough and roll it into a 1 cm (½ inch) thick slab, folding and rolling two or three times. Repeat with the remaining dough and stack the slabs, moistening the top of each slab before putting another on it. Press the stack down firmly and cut it into several 100 g (3½ oz) lumps. Repeat the entire rolling process twice more. Leave the dough for 30 minutes in a cold place. Cut into eight pieces. Squeeze each one into a sausage shape, and roll out to measure 10 by 15 cm (4 by 6 inches). Leave to rest for 1 hour.

For the stuffing, set aside half of the beaten egg. Mix the cheese, parsley, salt and Tabasco or pepper into the other half. Spread this mixture evenly over the two cut sides of the pork fillet. Roll each piece up, press down firmly, and leave in the ice compartment of the refrigerator to harden.

To assemble the oggies, cut each roll of fillet into four cross-sections and wrap each piece in a strip of smoked pork, bacon or ham. Lay each little parcel in the middle of a piece of dough and moisten round the edge of the dough with milk. Bring the dough up and over the pork, pressing the two edges together in a scalloped crest, like a Cornish pasty. Press down to flatten the base, and trim where necessary. Brush over with the rest of the beaten egg and bake for 10 minutes in a preheated 180°C (350°F or Mark 4) oven, until the pastry begins to brown. Finish by frying for 5 minutes in deep hot fat; or fry in lard, turning the oggies over until they are golden-brown.

JANE GRIGSON
GOOD THINGS

Lancashire Foot

A Lancashire foot is similar to a very thick pasty, but was elliptical in shape to fit into the oval tins that miners once used to carry their snappin or snap (snack) down the pit. The name foot was given because of the shape and because the miner's wife or mother would usually make a pair. Apparently the plural was not feet, but foots! The dough was rolled into a long oval and cut lengthwise into two, then the rolling pin was placed half way along the length and the dough was just rolled from the centre to the further edge. This gave the foot shape, with the heel nearer to the cook and the sole widening out at the top edge. It was a simple but effective way of keeping the base crust thick, and the upper one thin but also larger to cover the filling.

To make 2 pasties

350 g	lean beef, cut into small pieces	12 oz
2 or 3	medium-sized potatoes, diced	2 or 3
1	large onion, thinly sliced	1
	salt and pepper	
500 g	shortcrust dough (*page 164*)	1 lb

Combine the meat, potatoes and onion, and season to taste. Cook this mixture with a little water in a 180°C (350°F or Mark 4) oven until the meat is tender—about 1 hour. Cool the mixture. When cold, use it to fill the pastry dough, rolled out as above. Bake the foots in a preheated 190°C (375°F or Mark 5) oven until brown, about 40 minutes.

JOAN POULSON
OLD LANCASHIRE RECIPES

Baked Neapolitan Turnovers

Calzoni Imbottiti al Forno

The filling can also be made with leftovers of *provola* or *provolone* cheese, sausage, or mortadella.

To make 6 turnovers

200 g	Neapolitan salami, diced	7 oz
200 g	*mozzarella* cheese, diced	7 oz
300 g	*ricotta* cheese	10 oz
15 g	lard	½ oz
	salt	
2 tbsp	chopped basil	2 tbsp
60 g	Parmesan cheese, grated	2 oz
	pepper	
1 kg	basic bread dough (*page 164*)	2 to 2½ lb

Mix together all the ingredients except the bread dough. When the bread dough has risen once and doubled in bulk, divide it into six equal pieces and roll out each piece into a round about 5 mm (¼ inch) thick. Raise the edges of the dough slightly to hold the filling. Cover half of each round with filling and fold the other half of the round over to make a half-moon shape. Seal the edges of the turnovers carefully, pressing them down with a fork. Place on an oiled baking sheet and bake in a preheated 220°C (425°F or Mark 7) oven for 20 to 30 minutes, or until golden-brown.

MARIA RIVIECCIO ZANIBONI
CUCINA E VINI DI NAPOLI E DELLA CAMPANIA

Spinach Pies

Panadons con Espinacas

To make 12 pies

1 kg	spinach	2 to 2½ lb
	salt	
2	garlic cloves, chopped	2
5 tbsp	olive oil	5 tbsp
100 g	Malaga raisins, halved and seeded	3½ oz
25 g	pine-nuts	1 oz
225 g	flour	7 oz
	oil for deep frying, or 1 egg, beaten, for glazing	

Steam the spinach with salt but without water for 3 minutes. Drain it well and chop roughly.

Fry the garlic in 2 tablespoons of the olive oil until lightly browned. Add the chopped spinach, raisins and pine-nuts.

Cook, seasoning with salt if necessary, for 5 minutes or until all excess liquid is absorbed.

Place the flour in a bowl and pour the remaining olive oil into the centre; add salt and enough water to form a smooth dough. Knead lightly and roll out 3 mm (⅛ inch) thick.

Cut the dough into 12.5 cm (5 inch) rounds. Place a mound of spinach filling on each round, and fold the rounds in half to enclose the spinach, sealing the edges.

Fry the pies in deep hot oil until golden-brown, about 12 minutes. Or brush them with beaten egg and bake them in a preheated 200°C (400°F or Mark 6) oven for 15 minutes.

MARIA PILAR
TU COCINA

Ham Turnovers

Mince the ham and onion through a meat grinder, using the medium disc, or purée them coarsely in a food processor.

To make about 18 turnovers

500 g	cooked ham, minced	1 lb
30 g	butter	1 oz
2 tbsp	flour	2 tbsp
¼ litre	hot milk	8 fl oz
1	small onion, minced	1
	pepper	
	Lard dough	
125 g	lard, softened	4 oz
175 g	flour	6 oz
½ tsp	salt	½ tsp
1 tsp	baking powder	1 tsp
3 to 4 tbsp	cold water	3 to 4 tbsp

Sift the flour, salt and baking powder together. Cut in the lard and add enough cold water to make the dough stick together. Roll out this extra-rich dough on a floured board to a thickness of about 5 mm (¼ inch) and cut it into 8 cm (3 inch) squares.

To make the ham filling, make a white sauce by melting the butter, stirring in the flour until smooth, then adding the milk, stirring constantly as it thickens. Add the ham, onion and a pinch of pepper.

Put a heaped spoonful of filling in the centre of each square, fold it into a triangle and pinch the edges together. Cut a slit in the top of each turnover. Bake on an ungreased baking sheet in a preheated 200°C (400°F or Mark 6) oven for about 15 minutes, or until the turnovers are puffed and golden-brown. Serve hot.

BEATRICE VAUGHAN
YANKEE HILL-COUNTRY COOKING

Cheese Pirozhki

Käsepirogen

To make about 12 pirozhki

100 g	Gruyère or other firm cheese, grated	3½ oz
45 g	butter, softened	1½ oz
3	eggs, 1 lightly beaten, yolks of 2 separated from whites, whites of 2 stiffly beaten	3
	salt and pepper	
	Soured cream dough	
2 tbsp	soured cream	2 tbsp
45 g	butter, softened	1½ oz
150 to 200 g	flour	5 to 7 oz
¼ tsp	salt	¼ tsp

Work all the dough ingredients together, adding enough flour to make a smooth, pliable dough. Leave to rest in a cool place.

For the filling, beat together the butter, two egg yolks and a pinch each of salt and pepper. Add the grated cheese and, finally, fold in the beaten egg whites.

Roll out the dough and cut it into rounds using a large beer glass or biscuit cutter. Place a spoonful of the cheese mixture on each round, fold the *pirozhki* over into a half-moon shape, and press the edges firmly together. Place the *pirozhki* on a greased baking sheet, not too close together, paint with the beaten egg and bake in a preheated 180°C (350°F or Mark 4) oven for 12 to 15 minutes or until brown. Serve immediately.

GRETE WILLINSKY
KOCHBUCH DER BÜCHERGILDE

Oysters Ritz Bar

To make 24 small turnovers

24	small oysters, shelled	24
2 tbsp	wine vinegar	2 tbsp
6 tbsp	olive oil	6 tbsp
¼ tsp	salt	¼ tsp
⅛ tsp	black pepper	⅛ tsp
¼ tsp	dry mustard	¼ tsp
1 tbsp	finely chopped parsley	1 tbsp
250 g	shortcrust dough (*page 164*)	8 oz

Drain the oysters. In a bowl combine the vinegar, oil, salt, pepper, mustard and parsley. Mix well. Marinate the oysters in this dressing for 3 hours in the refrigerator. Drain the oysters and dry them on paper towels.

Roll out the dough on a lightly floured board to a thickness of 3 mm (⅛ inch). Cut the dough into rounds 6 cm (2½ inches) across. Place an oyster on each round. Moisten the edges of each round, fold the dough over the oyster and seal the edges together with a fork. Arrange the turnovers on a baking sheet and cut a small vent in each one.

Bake the turnovers in a preheated 230°C (450°F or Mark 8) oven for 15 minutes, or until the pastry is golden.

NANCY FAIR MCINTYRE
COOKING IN CRUST

Shrimp Curry Puffs

Chia Li Chiao

If you are using cooked shrimps or prawns, it is not necessary to parboil them. Raw shrimps or prawns, if bought in the shell, may be shelled after parboiling.

To make about 60 puffs

500 g	shelled raw shrimps or prawns	1 lb
200 g	onions, finely chopped	7 oz
45 g	lard	1½ oz
2 tsp	Madras curry powder	2 tsp
1 tbsp	salt	1 tbsp
1 tsp	sugar	1 tsp
125 g	mashed potato (about 1 medium-sized potato)	4 oz
500 g	shortcrust dough (*page 164*, but substitute lard for butter)	1 lb
2	eggs, beaten	2

Cover the shrimps or prawns with water and bring them to boiling point. Drain, then mince the shrimps or prawns or chop them finely. Set them in a mixing bowl. Stir-fry the onion with the lard until soft, add the curry powder and stir them together for 1 minute. Pour the onion mixture on to the shrimps or prawns and add salt, sugar and mashed potato. Mix and stir thoroughly. Let the mixture cool, then put it in the refrigerator to chill for 1 hour.

Divide the dough into two balls. Roll out one ball at a time on a lightly floured surface into a sheet about 1.5 mm (1/16 inch) thick. Using a biscuit cutter, cut out circles about 8 cm (3 inches) in diameter. Knead the scraps into the remaining dough to make more circles. Place about one heaped teaspoon of the shrimp or prawn filling in the centre of each round, fold over the dough into a half-moon shape and seal the edges tightly, making a scalloped edge. Place the puffs on ungreased baking sheets and prick each puff with a fork. Brush the tops with the beaten egg. Bake the puffs in a preheated 200°C (400°F or Mark 6) oven for about 20 minutes, or until they turn golden-brown.

FLORENCE LIN
FLORENCE LIN'S CHINESE REGIONAL COOKBOOK

Spinach Cheese Puffs

Spanakópetes

The technique of folding phyllo pastry into triangles is demonstrated on page 60.

To make rolls instead of triangles, cut the sheets of phyllo into quarters crosswise. Brush each quarter sheet as you use it with warm melted butter. Place 1 teaspoon of filling 2.5 cm (1 inch) from the bottom edge of the sheet, fold the bottom up over the filling, then fold the sides in towards the middle. Brush with warm melted butter and roll the sheet loosely. Brush each roll with warm melted butter as you place it, seam side down, on a baking sheet.

To make about 80 triangles

1 kg	spinach	2 lb
500 g	*feta* cheese	1 lb
350 g	*ricotta* or curd cheese	12 oz
6 tbsp	olive oil	6 tbsp
6	spring onions, including the green tops, finely chopped	6
90 g	parsley, finely chopped	3 oz
$\frac{1}{8}$ tsp	white pepper	$\frac{1}{8}$ tsp
1 tsp	dill	1 tsp
6	eggs, beaten	6
250 g	unsalted butter	8 oz
500 g	phyllo pastry sheets, at room temperature	1 lb

Chop the spinach. Heat the oil and sauté the spring onions until soft and wilted. Add the spinach and simmer until all of its moisture evaporates. Rinse the *feta* under cold water, drain, and crumble it into a bowl. Blend in the *ricotta* or curd cheese, parsley, pepper and dill. Add the beaten eggs and mix well. Add the spinach and spring onions and mix well.

Melt the butter in a small saucepan over a very low heat. Do not let it brown. Set it aside. Gently unfold the phyllo sheets and cut them into thirds lengthwise, using scissors and cutting through the entire stack at one time. Wrap two-thirds of the strips in plastic film or greaseproof paper to prevent them from drying out, and refrigerate them until needed. Drape another piece of plastic film over the remaining third. Remove one phyllo strip at a time, lay it on the counter and, with a pastry brush, coat it lightly with melted butter. Fold the two long sides towards the middle, making a strip about 5 cm (2 inches) wide and 28 cm (11 inches) long. Brush the strip with melted butter again. Place a teaspoon of the spinach mixture at the bottom end, slightly left of centre. Pick up the right corner and fold it over so that the bottom edge meets the adjacent side edge and forms a right-angle triangle. Continue folding over from side to side into neat triangles until you reach the end of the strip. Brush the finished triangle with butter and place it on an ungreased baking sheet. Repeat for

each strip of phyllo. Do not let the triangles touch; they will puff up quite a bit during baking.

Bake in a preheated 220°C (425°F or Mark 7) oven for 12 to 14 minutes, or until plump, crisp and golden. Do not turn the triangles over while baking. Arrange the *spanakópetes* on an attractive plate and serve.

ANNE THEOHAROUS
COOKING THE GREEK WAY

Brain and Egg Turnovers

Briks Bil Mohk

The technique of frying these Tunisian turnovers is shown on page 61. The author suggests two other pastry fillings: the first alternative is to fill each turnover with 2 tablespoons of minced beef cooked with a little onion and parsley and seasoned with salt and pepper. Mix in 1 tablespoon of grated Parmesan cheese and a few drops of lemon juice, and use a sliced hard-boiled egg instead of a raw one. The second alternative is to use six anchovy fillets mixed with 1 tablespoon of chopped onion cooked in butter and 1 tablespoon of grated Parmesan cheese for each turnover; season with freshly ground black pepper and top with a raw egg.

To make 4 turnovers

350 g	lamb's, calf's or ox brains	12 oz
4	eggs	4
	salt and freshly ground black pepper	
	vinegar	
30 g	unsalted butter	1 oz
60 g	onion, finely chopped	2 oz
1 tbsp	finely chopped parsley	1 tbsp
1 tbsp	freshly grated Parmesan cheese	1 tbsp
2	phyllo pastry sheets or 4 Chinese spring-roll skins	2
1	egg white, lightly beaten	1
	oil for deep frying	
	lemon quarters	

Soak the brains for 30 minutes in several changes of water. Remove the membranes, then rinse the brains and drain them. In a 2 litre (3½ pint) saucepan bring 1.5 litres (2½ pints) of seasoned and acidulated water to a simmer. Slip in the brains, cover and cook for 20 minutes. Drain, cool and dice the brains.

Melt the butter in the saucepan and cook the onion over a low heat until soft but not browned. Add the brains, parsley, and salt and pepper to taste. Cook gently for 10 minutes, stirring often. Stir in the cheese. Mix and mash, then separate this filling mixture into four equal portions.

Spread out the phyllo sheets and cut them in half crosswise. (Leave spring-roll skins whole.) Fold each of the phyllo strips in half crosswise and place one portion of the filling 5 cm (2 inches) away from one corner. Flatten the centre of the filling slightly to make a hollow. Break an egg into the hollow. Fold over the pastry to cover the egg; dab the edges with the egg white and press the edges so that they adhere. Then fold each rim over 1 cm (½ inch) for a secure closing, being careful not to break the egg inside. Repeat with the three remaining phyllo strips. (If you are using spring-roll skins, fold in the left and right sides of the skins in order to make a square, then proceed as directed above.)

Pour oil to a depth of 2.5 cm (1 inch) into a large deep frying pan. Heat the oil until hot but not smoking, then slide in one *brik*. Lightly push it down into the oil, then press one corner in order to make the *brik* swell. When the *brik* is golden-brown on both sides (after about 2 minutes), transfer it to paper towels to drain. Repeat with the three remaining *briks*. Serve hot with lemon quarters.

PAULA WOLFERT
MEDITERRANEAN COOKING

Meat Squares

Boureka

To make 36 pastries

500 g	lean beef or lamb, minced	1 lb
1	onion, finely chopped	1
2 tbsp	oil	2 tbsp
1 tsp	salt	1 tsp
¼ tsp	pepper	¼ tsp
½ tsp	ground allspice	½ tsp
2 tbsp	chopped parsley	2 tbsp
2	tomatoes, skinned and diced	2
90 g	nuts, finely chopped	3 oz
1	egg, beaten	1
	sesame seeds	
	Dough	
350 g	flour, sifted	12 oz
1 tsp	salt	1 tsp
250 g	butter	8 oz
2 tbsp	oil	2 tbsp
About 15 cl	water	About ¼ pint

To make the dough, blend the flour, salt and butter together until the mixture resembles fine breadcrumbs. Mix in the oil and water, and form the dough into a ball. Place on a wooden board; cover and set aside for 2 to 3 hours.

For the filling, sauté the onion in the oil in a 25 cm (10 inch) frying pan until the onion is limp, about 5 minutes. Add the meat, seasonings, parsley and tomatoes; cook until the meat is thoroughly done and dry, about 25 minutes. Drain off all excess fat. Stir the nuts into the meat mixture and cool.

Divide the dough in half; roll out the first half into a 30 cm (12 inch) square and place on a baking sheet. Spread the filling evenly over the rolled dough. Roll the second half into a square of the same size; place it carefully on top of the filling and press down gently. Brush the top with the egg, sprinkle it with sesame seeds and cut it into 36 squares. Bake in a preheated 180°C (350°F or Mark 4) oven for 30 minutes or until the top is brown.

BARBARA KRAUS (EDITOR)
THE COOKBOOK OF THE UNITED NATIONS

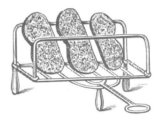

Salvadorian Appetizers

Pupusas

To make 8 pastries

125 g	cooked kidney beans, drained and mashed	4 oz
4	rashers crisply cooked bacon, crumbled	4
1	bay leaf, crushed	1
	fat for shallow frying	
	Cornmeal dough	
350 g	cornmeal	12 oz
1 tsp	salt	1 tsp
45 cl	boiling water	¾ pint

To make the dough, combine the cornmeal and salt. Add the boiling water, stirring constantly. This makes a very stiff dough. Divide it into eight equal portions and cool. When cool, divide each portion in two and flatten into thin cakes about 5 cm (2 inches) in diameter. If the mixture is sticky, dip your hands in cold water.

For the filling, mix the beans, bacon and bay leaf. Place 2 tablespoons of this mixture on each of eight of the cakes. Spread evenly. Cover with the remaining cakes. Press the edges together to seal them. Place the pastries in hot shallow fat and fry over a low heat until each side is golden-brown. Turn the pastries once only.

BARBARA KRAUS (EDITOR)
THE COOKBOOK OF THE UNITED NATIONS

Stuffed Pasties

Samosa

If no ghee is available, vegetable oil may be used for frying and clarified butter may be used in the mixture.

The pastry may be made more flaky by rolling it out and adding another 30 g (1 oz) of *ghee*. Roll up again and knead. *Samosas* are useful for using up small quantities of vegetables, and the stuffing can be varied to suit.

To make 20 to 24 samosas

175 g	flour	6 oz
	salt	
30 g	*ghee*, melted	1 oz
About 5 tbsp	water	About 5 tbsp

Vegetable stuffing

30 g	*ghee*	1 oz
1	small onion, finely chopped	1
2	medium-sized potatoes, boiled and peeled, diced or mashed	2
1 cm	fresh ginger root, finely chopped	$\frac{1}{2}$ inch
175 g	cooked green peas or mixed vegetables, finely chopped	6 oz
1 tsp	salt	1 tsp
1 tsp	ground coriander	1 tsp
$\frac{1}{2}$ tsp	paprika or chili powder	$\frac{1}{2}$ tsp
1 tbsp	chopped coriander leaves	1 tbsp
$\frac{1}{2}$ tsp	*garam masala*	$\frac{1}{2}$ tsp
1 tbsp	lemon juice	1 tbsp

Sieve the flour with a pinch of salt. Rub in the melted *ghee*. Add enough water to make a smooth dough. Knead the dough for 10 minutes, then cover with a damp cloth and allow the dough to stand.

For the stuffing, heat the *ghee* and fry the onion. Stir in the ginger, peas, salt, the coriander and paprika, and fry for 2 minutes. Add the potatoes, coriander leaves, *garam masala* and lemon juice. Fry for a few more minutes and allow to cool. Knead the dough again and divide it into 20 to 24 balls, rolling out each one quite thin. Cut each in half and lay the pieces over each other. Press lightly together and roll as thin as possible to make a semicircle. Put a portion of the filling on one half of the pastry, moisten the edges and fold the other half over. Press the edges well together and deep fry in hot *ghee* until crisp and lightly golden. Serve with a chutney.

JACK SANTA MARIA
INDIAN VEGETARIAN COOKERY

Savoury Pastries with Spicy Potato Filling

Aloo Samosa

The unique feature of these *samosas* is their delicious *khasta*, meaning crispy and flaky pastry crust.

To make savoury meat pastries (*keema samosa*), follow the instructions below, but substitute meat filling for the potato filling. To make the meat filling, heat 2 tablespoons of oil in a large frying pan and fry 150 g (5 oz) of finely chopped onions in it until they are caramel brown. Add 4 teaspoons of finely chopped garlic, $1\frac{1}{2}$ tablespoons of finely chopped ginger root and 2 seeded and minced green chili peppers. Cook for 2 minutes. Add 500 g (1 lb) of lean minced lamb or beef, and cook until the meat begins to brown. Sprinkle $\frac{1}{4}$ teaspoon of turmeric and $1\frac{1}{2}$ teaspoons of coarse salt over the meat, stir for a moment or two, and add 4 tablespoons of hot water. Reduce the heat, cover and let the meat cook thoroughly for about 25 minutes, stirring the mixture often. When all the moisture is absorbed, remove from the heat and stir in 2 teaspoons each of *garam masala* and lemon juice, and 2 tablespoons of chopped fresh coriander leaves. Mash the mixture with a potato masher to break up the lumps of meat.

To make 32 samosas

175 g	flour	6 oz
1 tsp	salt	1 tsp
60 g	*ghee*, vegetable *ghee* or 4 tbsp oil	2 oz
6 to 7 tbsp	cold water	6 to 7 tbsp
	peanut or corn oil for deep frying	

Spicy potato filling

60 g	vegetable *ghee* or 4 tbsp light vegetable oil	2 oz
2 tsp	coriander seeds	2 tsp
125 g	onions, finely chopped	4 oz
$1\frac{1}{2}$ tsp	finely chopped fresh ginger root	$1\frac{1}{2}$ tsp
7	medium-sized potatoes, boiled, peeled and cubed	7
125 g	cooked green peas	4 oz
1 or 2	green chili peppers, seeded and chopped, or $\frac{1}{4}$ tsp cayenne pepper	1 or 2
1 tsp	*garam masala*	1 tsp
2 tsp	ground pomegranate seeds or 1 tbsp lemon juice	2 tsp
2 tsp	salt	2 tsp

Place the flour in a large bowl, add the salt and mix. Make a well in the centre of the flour and add the *ghee* or oil. Pick up some flour and fat in one hand. Place the other hand over the flour and fat mixture. Slide your two hands back and forth from heel to fingertips, rubbing the flour and fat between your palms. This entire motion should be carried out directly over the bowl so that the fat-coated flour may fall back into the bowl. Continue until the entire batch of flour is evenly coated with the fat and no more lumps of fat can be seen. Pour 6 tablespoons of water over the flour and mix. Add the remaining tablespoon in droplets, until all the flour adheres together in a mass that can be kneaded.

Place the dough on a board. Coat your fingers with a little oil and knead the dough for 10 minutes. This will be a firm but pliable dough, not at all sticky. Cover with a towel or plastic film, and let it rest for 30 minutes.

To make the filling, heat the *ghee* or oil over a medium-high heat in a frying pan for 2 minutes. Add the coriander seeds and fry until they turn dark brown, about 15 seconds. Add the onions and ginger root, and continue frying until the onions turn light brown, 4 to 5 minutes. Add the potatoes and peas, stir rapidly and fry until the potatoes begin to turn dry and look fried, about 10 minutes. Turn off the heat. Add the remaining filling ingredients, mix well and set aside.

Knead the dough again for a minute, and divide into two equal portions. Roll each into a 1 cm (½ inch) thick rope and cut into eight equal parts. Roll the small pieces into smooth balls.

Working with one at a time, place a ball on a board, dust it lightly with flour and roll it into a 15 cm (6 inch) circle. Cut the circle in half. Now you have two semicircles. Each semicircle will make a *samosa*.

Form a cone: moisten half of the semicircle's straight edge with water and bring the other half of the straight edge over it, so that the dry side overlaps the moistened portion. Press the overlapped edges securely together to seal.

Place about 1 tablespoon of filling in the cone. Moisten the open end of the cone and quickly pinch the open end shut in a straight line, closing the cone into a triangular shape. Press tightly to seal. Continue with the rest of the dough and filling the same way. (The *samosa* can be rolled and shaped a few hours ahead of time and kept loosely covered with a piece of paper. Do not worry if they dry out slightly. In fact, for best results they *should* be left out to dry for 30 minutes. This makes the crust more crunchy and flaky.)

When ready to fry the *samosas*, heat 7.5 cm (3 inches) of oil in a large pan. When the oil is hot (180°C or 350°F), drop in about eight to 10 *samosas*. The temperature of the oil will drop automatically to around 150°C (300°F). Maintain the temperature at this low point by regulating the heat. This low-temperature cooking is essential for *samosas,* because it enables the pastry dough to brown evenly and become flaky. Fry, stirring and turning the *samosas* until they are light brown, about 12 minutes. Take them out with a slotted spoon or tongs, and drain on paper towels. Continue frying the remaining *samosas* in the same way.

JULIE SAHNI
CLASSIC INDIAN COOKING

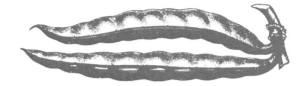

Steamed Dumplings

Serve these dumplings with mustard or with a mixture of soy sauce and vinegar, as preferred.

To make 30 dumplings

500 g	pork, minced	1 lb
250 g	cooked crab meat, shredded	8 oz
1	medium-sized onion, finely chopped	1
1 tbsp	wine	1 tbsp
1 tbsp	soy sauce	1 tbsp
1 tsp	salt	1 tsp
¼ tsp	sugar	¼ tsp
1 tbsp	sesame-seed oil	1 tbsp
1 tbsp	cornflour	1 tbsp

Flower wrappings

175 g	flour, sifted	6 oz
17.5 cl	boiling water	6 fl oz
1 tbsp	cornflour	1 tbsp
1	hard-boiled egg yolk, crumbled	1
1 tbsp	chopped boiled spinach	1 tbsp
1 tbsp	chopped boiled ham	1 tbsp

Mix all the filling ingredients together and let stand while preparing wrappings.

For the wrappings, mix the flour with the boiling water, using chopsticks briskly, until cool enough to handle. Knead well, cover with a damp cloth and let stand for 20 minutes. Roll into a long sausage form and cut into 30 pieces. Flatten each piece with the palm of your hand and roll it into a thin pancake. Sprinkle cornflour on the edges and flatten until the pancake is 8 cm (3½ inches) in diameter.

Place a spoonful of filling in the centre of each pancake; gather up the edges round the filling and pleat them so that the filling is inside a bag of dough, with the top of the filling exposed. Place a pinch each of egg yolk, spinach and ham as a garnish at the mouth of the wrapping.

Lay a layer of cheesecloth in a steamer or brush the steamer rack with oil. Place the dumplings in the steamer, slightly separated, and steam for 15 minutes. After steaming, remove the dumplings at once from the rack to prevent sticking. Serve them hot.

NANCY CHIH MA

Steamed Beef Dumplings

You may substitute minced pork or finely chopped shrimps for the beef in these dumplings.

To make 24 dumplings

250 g	lean beef, minced	8 oz
1 tsp	ground fresh ginger root	1 tsp
1 tbsp	soy sauce	1 tbsp
1 tbsp	dry sherry	1 tbsp
4	water chestnuts, minced	4
1	spring onion, minced	1
2	dried Chinese mushrooms, soaked in warm water for 30 minutes, stems discarded, minced	2
½ tsp	sugar	½ tsp
	lettuce leaves	

Round dumpling skins

125 g	flour	4 oz
¼ tsp	salt	¼ tsp
1	egg, lightly beaten	1
4 to 8 tbsp	water	4 to 8 tbsp

Mix together all the filling ingredients except the lettuce.

For the skins, combine the flour and salt. Add the egg and gradually add enough water to make a pliable dough. Knead for about 10 minutes, until the dough is soft and elastic. Cover with a damp towel and set aside for 15 minutes.

Roll the dough out as thin as you can on a floured board. Cut it into 7.5 cm (3 inch) circles. Flour the skins and stack them until you are ready to use them.

Keeping the rest of the skins covered with a damp cloth while you work, moisten one side of a skin with water. Place 1 tablespoon of filling in the centre of the skin. Gather up the sides into little pleats. (It will have an "hourglass" shape with an open top that shows the meat filling.)

Bring water to the boil in a steamer. Line a steamer rack with lettuce leaves and place the dumplings on the leaves. Steam for 20 minutes.

JOANNE HUSH AND PETER WONG
THE CHINESE MENU COOKBOOK

Sausage Rolls

To make 8 sausage rolls

350 g	cold roast beef, minced	12 oz
125 g	fat cooked ham, minced	4 oz
500 g	rough-puff dough (*page 164*)	1 lb
2	eggs, beaten	2
	salt and pepper	

Roll out the dough 3 mm (⅛ inch) thick; then, with a 12.5 cm (5 inch) square cutter, cut out eight pieces. Wet the edges of the pieces with beaten egg. Mix together the beef and ham and season with salt and pepper. On each square of dough lay 60 g (2 oz) of the meat mixture. Fold the dough in half over the filling and press the edges together to prevent the meat from escaping. Lightly brush the packages with egg. Then bake them in a preheated 220°C (425°F or Mark 7) oven for 15 minutes or until golden-brown.

MRS. LOUISA E. SMITH
BONNES BOUCHES AND RELISHABLE DISHES
FOR BREAKFAST AND LUNCHEON

Liver Knishes

The dough in this recipe may be replaced by the shortcrust or rough-puff dough on page 164. In the filling, the liver, lung and beet may be replaced entirely by poached or sautéed liver.

To make 8 to 10 knishes

250 g	flour	8 oz
1 tsp	baking powder	1 tsp
½ tsp	salt	½ tsp
2 tbsp	water	2 tbsp
1 tbsp	vegetable oil	1 tbsp
2	eggs, well beaten	2
	Liver filling	
250 g	cooked liver	8 oz
1	onion, minced	1
1 tbsp	rendered chicken fat	1 tbsp
125 g	cooked lung	4 oz
250 g	cooked beef	8 oz
1	egg	1
125 g	cooked buckwheat kasha or rice (optional)	4 oz
	salt and pepper	

Sift the flour, baking powder and salt together. Form a well in the centre; add the water, oil and eggs. Mix together and form into a smooth dough.

For the filling, fry the onion in the chicken fat until lightly browned. Mince the liver, lung and beef in a meat grinder. Combine with the onion and the remaining ingredients.

Roll out the dough 3 mm ($\frac{1}{8}$ inch) thick. Leave the sheet of dough whole, or cut it into rounds or squares. If leaving it whole, place the filling in a mound down the middle of the dough. Roll it up to make a cylinder enclosing the filling. Moisten the ends and seal them; if desired, slash the top diagonally at 2.5 cm (1 inch) intervals. If the dough is cut up, place a mound of the filling on each square or round, fold over, and moisten and press the edges to seal.

Bake the knishes on a greased baking sheet in a preheated 180°C (350°F or Mark 4) oven until browned and crisp.

ANNE LONDON AND BERTHA KAHN BISHOV (EDITORS)
THE COMPLETE AMERICAN-JEWISH COOKBOOK

Sausage in Pastry

To make about 20 slices

1	garlic-flavoured poaching sausage, 20 to 25 cm (8 to 10 inches) long and 5 to 6 cm (2 to 2$\frac{1}{2}$ inches) in diameter	1
250 g	shortcrust dough (*page 164*)	8 oz
3 tbsp	Dijon mustard	3 tbsp
1	egg, beaten with 1 tbsp milk or cream	1

Butter a small baking sheet and set it aside. With the tip of a sharp knife, prick the skin of the sausage in eight to 10 places, and put it into a 3 to 4 litre (5$\frac{1}{4}$ to 7 pint) pot with water to cover. Bring the water to the boil over a high heat. Reduce the heat and simmer the sausage, partially covered, for 45 minutes. Drain the sausage and set it aside. When the sausage is cool enough to handle, skin it with a small knife.

Place the dough on a lightly floured surface, dust the top with flour and roll out the dough into an oval 15 by 30 cm (6 by 12 inches) and 3 mm ($\frac{1}{8}$ inch) thick.

Spread the mustard over the sausage. Place the sausage on the long edge of the dough nearest you. Roll up the sausage in the dough, making one complete turn to enclose it. Trim off all but 2.5 cm (1 inch) of the length of the dough. Leave the side flaps of the dough untrimmed.

With a pastry brush dipped in water, dampen the 2.5 cm (1 inch) strip of dough extending beyond the sausage. Fold the dampened strip back on to the dough enclosing the sausage, and press it down. Roll the sausage over the seam to make it adhere better. Turn the sausage parcel so the seam faces you. Trim only the rough edges of the side flaps, fold them inward and press the edges firmly towards the seam. Turn the sausage parcel seam side down on the buttered baking sheet; press the flaps again.

To decorate the top of the sausage parcel, roll out the excess

dough and cut out decorative shapes with a biscuit cutter. Dampen the underside of each shape with water and press it on to the dough. Leave the sausage on the baking sheet and refrigerate it for 15 minutes.

Just before baking, paint a film of the egg mixture on top of the dough. Place the sausage on the middle shelf of the oven and bake it in a preheated 190°C (375°F or Mark 5) oven for 45 minutes, or until the pastry is golden-brown. Transfer the sausage to a warm serving dish. Serve it hot, cut into slices 5 to 10 mm ($\frac{1}{4}$ to $\frac{1}{2}$ inch) thick, with additional mustard.

JOHN CLANCY AND FRANCES FIELD
CLANCY'S OVEN COOKERY

Hot Anchovy Éclairs

Éclairs d'Anchois

These éclairs should have the appearance of miniature sausage rolls. Small cooked sardines may also be prepared in the same manner.

To make 12 éclairs

6	salt anchovies, soaked, filleted, rinsed and dried	6
250 g	rough-puff dough (*page 164*)	8 oz
1	egg white, slightly beaten (optional)	1
30 g	Parmesan cheese, grated	1 oz

Roll out the dough as thinly as possible; cut it into 12 oblong pieces, about 4 by 6 cm (1$\frac{1}{2}$ by 2$\frac{1}{4}$ inches). Lay on each piece an anchovy fillet trimmed slightly shorter than the dough. Fold the edges of the dough together and seal them with a little cold water or the beaten egg white. Sprinkle each éclair with the grated Parmesan cheese; arrange on an ungreased baking sheet and bake in a very hot oven, preheated to 230°C (450°F or Mark 8), for 10 minutes or until nicely browned and glazed. Serve the éclairs at once.

LOUIS P. DE GOUY
THE GOLD COOK BOOK

Pyrenees Barquettes

Barquettes des Pyrénées

*Laruns and Oloron are firm cheeses made from sheep's milk
in south-western France and in the Basque country. A mixture
of Parmesan and Gruyère cheese may be substituted. The
cheese mixture may also be baked in fried bread cases.*

To make 12 barquettes

150 g	Laruns or Oloron cheese, grated or cut into thin strips	5 oz
10 cl	dry white wine	3½ fl oz
1	shallot, chopped	1
3 or 4	eggs, beaten	3 or 4
50 g	butter, diced	2 oz
	salt and pepper	
	ground cinnamon	
350 g	shortcrust dough (*page 164*)	12 oz

Boil the wine in a small saucepan with the shallot until it is
reduced by two-thirds. Strain and leave to cool. Mix together
the cheese, eggs, butter, salt, pepper and cinnamon. Beat in
the reduced white wine.

Line 12 tartlet moulds with the dough. Pour in the cheese
mixture and bake in a preheated 190°C (375°F or Mark 5)
oven for 15 minutes or until the filling is set. Serve hot.

HUGUETTE CASTIGNAC
LA CUISINE OCCITANE

Cheese Tart

Galette au Fromage

To make one 25 cm (10 inch) tart

250 g	Cantal cheese, sliced	8 oz
350 g	flour	12 oz
100 g	butter, softened	3½ oz
5	eggs	5
	salt	

Knead together the flour, butter, eggs and salt to make a firm
dough. Form the dough into a ball and leave it to rest for 2
hours. Roll out and use to line a 25 cm (10 inch) flan tin. Spread
the cheese over the bottom.

Bake in a preheated 180°C (350°F or Mark 4) oven for 45
minutes or until the cheese has melted and browned.

AMICALE DES CUISINIERS ET PÂTISSIERS AUVERGNATS DE PARIS
CUISINE D'AUVERGNE

Roquefort and Walnut Tartlets

Tartelettes au Roquefort

*The author suggests that the tartlets may also be served
without baking the filling. In this case, the egg yolk should be
omitted from the Roquefort cheese mixture. The technique of
baking pastry cases is demonstrated on page 58.*

To make four 8 to 10 cm (3 to 4 inch) tartlets

100 g	Roquefort cheese	3½ oz
30 g	walnuts, 2 halved, the rest finely chopped	1 oz
	cognac	
1	egg yolk	1
1 to 2 tbsp	cream	1 to 2 tbsp
4	baked shortcrust pastry cases (*page 164*)	4
	parsley	

Rub the Roquefort through a sieve. Blend the Roquefort with
the chopped walnuts, a dash of cognac, the egg yolk and
enough cream to form a soft, smooth mixture. Fill the pastry
cases with the cheese mixture and bake them in a preheated
190°C (375°F or Mark 5) oven for 30 minutes, or until they are
golden. Garnish with the walnut halves and parsley.

NANCY EEKHOF-STORK
THE GREAT INTERNATIONAL CHEESE BOARD

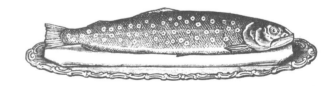

Swiss After-Ski Tarts

To make 24 tarts

250 g	Gruyère cheese, grated	8 oz
60 g	onion, grated	2 oz
30 g	butter	1 oz
3	eggs, beaten	3
½ litre	double cream	16 fl oz
¼ tsp	dry mustard	¼ tsp
1 tsp	salt	1 tsp
⅛ tsp	cayenne pepper	⅛ tsp
500 g	shortcrust dough (*page 164*)	1 lb

Sauté the onion in the butter for 5 minutes. Mix the onion
with the cheese. In a bowl, stir together the eggs, cream,
mustard, salt and cayenne pepper. Combine the egg mixture

with the cheese and onion. Roll out the shortcrust dough 3 mm (⅛ inch) thick on a floured board. Cut 24 rounds of dough to fit 5 cm (2 inch) tartlet tins; press the dough rounds into the tins and pour in the cheese filling. Bake the tarts in a preheated 200°C (400°F or Mark 6) oven for 20 minutes, or until they are puffy and golden-brown.

NANCY FAIR MCINTYRE
COOKING IN CRUST

Potato Pies

To prepare duxelles, *simmer 60 g (2 oz) finely chopped shallots or onions in butter until soft; add 250 g (8 oz) finely chopped mushrooms and cook over a medium heat, stirring, until the mushroom liquid evaporates. Season with salt, pepper and, if you like, Madeira or port.*

	To make twelve 8 cm (3 inch) pies	
2	large potatoes, parboiled for 8 minutes	2
3	large truffles, grated, or 250 g (8 oz) *duxelles* or finely chopped chives	3
¼ litre	double cream	8 fl oz
	salt and pepper	
250 g	shortcrust dough (*page 164*)	8 oz

Roll out the dough and fit it into the cups of a 12-cup tartlet mould or into dariole moulds. Grate the potatoes; they will be slightly gummy. Fill each dough-lined cup half full with potatoes. Add grated truffles or *duxelles* and top with more grated potato. Fill each pastry with seasoned cream. If you use chives, mix them with the cream before filling the moulds. Bake on the lowest rack of a preheated 200°C (400°F or Mark 6) oven for 5 minutes. Then move the mould to the upper middle rack of the oven, and continue baking at 170°C (325°F or Mark 3) until the tops of the pies are golden.

MADELEINE KAMMAN
THE MAKING OF A COOK

Hot Rolled Sandwich

Sanduiche Enrollado

This recipe is sufficient to cover a 37.5 by 50 cm (15 by 20 inch) baking sheet. If a smaller one is used, make half the recipe.

	To make 4 squares	
300 g	butter, softened	10 oz
250 g	cooked ham, thinly sliced	8 oz
100 g	seedless raisins	3½ oz
175 g	*mozzarella* cheese, grated	6 oz
1	egg yolk, beaten	1
	grated Parmesan cheese	
	Yeast dough	
30 g	fresh yeast or 1 tbsp dried yeast	1 oz
¼ litre	milk, lukewarm	8 fl oz
15 g	butter	½ oz
2 tbsp	salt	2 tbsp
1 tbsp	sugar	1 tbsp
4	eggs	4
4	potatoes, boiled and sieved	4
500 g	flour, sieved	1 lb

To make the dough, dissolve the yeast in the warm milk. When it is frothy, add the butter, salt, sugar, eggs and potatoes and mix well. Add half the flour and beat until bubbles form. Let stand for 20 minutes, then stir down, add the rest of the flour and knead until the dough is smooth and no longer sticky. Let stand another 20 minutes to rise.

Roll out the dough as thinly as possible and spread 250 g (8 oz) of the softened butter evenly on top. Fold the dough over into three parts and roll out a second time. Divide the dough into three parts and roll each out to the same size, about 30 by 45 cm (12 by 18 inches). Place one portion on a large buttered baking sheet and spread with the ham and raisins. Cover with a second portion of the dough. Sprinkle evenly with the *mozzarella* cheese. Place the third portion on top. Cover with a towel and let stand until it has doubled in bulk.

Brush the top with egg yolk and dot with the remaining butter. Sprinkle with Parmesan cheese; bake in a preheated 200°C (400°F or Mark 6) oven for 25 minutes, or until golden-brown. Cut into 7.5 cm (3 inch) squares and serve hot.

MARGARETTE DE ANDRADE
BRAZILIAN COOKERY

Cheese Meringues

To make about 12 meringues

75 g	cheese, grated	2½ oz
60 g	fine dry breadcrumbs	2 oz
60 g	flour	2 oz
½ tsp	baking powder	½ tsp
	cayenne pepper	
	grated nutmeg	
	salt and pepper	
30 g	butter	1 oz
1	egg yolk	1
About 4 tbsp	milk	About 4 tbsp
2	egg whites, stiffly beaten	2
	parsley sprigs or stuffed olives	

Place in a basin the breadcrumbs, flour, baking powder, a dash of cayenne pepper, some grated nutmeg, salt and pepper, and 60 g (2 oz) of the cheese. Rub in the butter. Beat the egg yolk and milk together and add them to the breadcrumb mixture to make a stiff paste. Roll out the paste thinly, place in a flat tin and bake in a preheated 180°C (350°F or Mark 4) oven for 20 minutes or until crisp.

Add the remaining cheese, salt and pepper to the egg whites. Spread this meringue on to the pastry and return to the oven for 5 minutes to brown. Cut into fingers using a very sharp knife. Before serving, garnish with parsley or olives.

THE GIRL GUIDES ASSOCIATION, FIJI (EDITORS)
SOUTH SEA ISLANDS RECIPES

Frankish Onion Cake

Fränkischer Zwiebelkuchen

The cracklings that are used in this recipe are crisp pieces of fried pork rind and fat.

To make 12 portions

1 kg	onions, thinly sliced	2 to 2½ lb
50 g	lard or chopped smoked pork fat	2 oz
	salt	
4 tbsp	pork cracklings	4 tbsp

Soft yeast dough

15 g	fresh yeast or 2 tsp dried yeast	½ oz
¼ litre	milk, lukewarm	8 fl oz
375 g	strong plain flour	13 oz
	salt	
50 g	lard	2 oz

To make the dough, dissolve the yeast in half of the milk. Place the flour in a bowl with the salt and lard. Pour in the yeast mixture and the remaining milk. Knead to make a smooth, soft dough. Cover the dough and leave it for about 1 hour, until it has doubled in bulk.

Cook the onions slowly in the lard or smoked fat, with salt and the pork cracklings, until the onions are soft but not brown. Allow to cool.

Roll out the dough into a 25 cm (10 inch) round. Place it on a greased baking sheet and press the edges up slightly to form a rim. Spread the onion mixture over the dough. Leave to rise again for about 15 minutes, then bake in a preheated 200°C (400°F or Mark 6) oven for 30 minutes or until golden. Cut the onion cake into 12 portions and serve it while still warm.

HEDWIG MARIA STUBER
ICH HELF DIR KOCHEN

Meat Cakes

S'fiha

Curdled milk for use in this recipe can be made by stirring 1 tablespoon of lemon juice or vinegar into 60 cl (1 pint) of milk, and letting the mixture rest for 24 hours until the curd separates from the whey. Then strain it through muslin; hang it up for 2 hours to drip.

These cakes may also be made with shortcrust dough (*recipe, page 164*). The curdled milk in the filling may be replaced by 500 g (1 lb) of finely chopped tomatoes. But whether the cakes are made with tomato or curdled milk, they are traditionally served accompanied by curdled milk to pour over.

To make 40 cakes

600 g	lamb, minced	1¼ lb
2	onions, finely chopped	2
1 tsp	salt	1 tsp
¼ tsp	pepper	¼ tsp
15 g	butter, melted	½ oz
10 tbsp	curdled milk or yogurt	10 tbsp
50 g	pine-nuts (optional)	1 oz

Yeast dough		
15 g	fresh yeast or 2 tsp dried yeast	½ oz
20 cl	warm water	7 fl oz
1 tsp	salt	1 tsp
500 g	flour	1 lb

To make the dough, dissolve the yeast in the water, then add the salt and flour, and knead to a smooth dough. Leave the dough to rest for 1 hour.

Mix the lamb with the onions, salt, pepper, melted butter, curdled milk and, if desired, the pinenuts. Divide the dough into pieces the size of an egg, and roll out each piece into a round or oval about 5 mm (¼ inch) thick. Spread a generous tablespoon of the meat mixture on each cake. Place the cakes on baking sheets and bake them in a preheated 200°C (400°F or Mark 6) oven for 15 minutes.

FAYEZ AOUN
280 RECETTES DE CUISINE FAMILIALE LIBANAISE

Roquefort Puffs

To make about 28 puffs

100 g	Roquefort cheese, softened	3½ oz
60 g	cream cheese, softened	2 oz
1	egg, beaten	1

Soured cream dough

90 g	flour	3 oz
125 g	butter	4 oz
60 g	soured cream	2 oz

Place the flour and butter in a medium-sized mixing bowl; cut in the butter until the particles are tiny. Stir in the soured cream until thoroughly blended. Turn out the soft dough on to a piece of plastic film. With a small spatula, shape the dough into a rectangle, then wrap it and chill overnight.

Cut the chilled dough into thirds. Work with one-third at a time, keeping the remaining dough in the refrigerator. Place scraps left after rolling in the freezer for quick chilling before re-rolling them.

Beat the Roquefort and cream cheese together. Cover and chill overnight. On a well-floured pastry cloth, roll out the dough to a thickness of 1.5 mm ($\frac{1}{16}$ inch). Using a round 5 cm (2 inch) biscuit cutter, cut out the dough. With a small metal spatula, place half of the rounds of dough about 2.5 cm (1 inch) apart on a large baking sheet. Put one level teaspoon of the Roquefort mixture in the centre of each round.

Using your finger or a pastry brush, spread the beaten egg round the edges of the filled rounds. Cover the filled rounds with plain rounds of dough. Slip the dull edge of a round 4 cm (1½ inch) biscuit cutter (or use a glass about that size) over the puffs and press to seal; seal again with the floured tines of a fork. (If the puffs are not well sealed, the filling will ooze out of them during baking.) Refrigerate the puffs on the baking sheet while you roll, cut and fill the remaining refrigerated portions of dough.

Bake in a preheated 180°C (350°F or Mark 4) oven until lightly browned—20 to 25 minutes. Drain the puffs on paper towels. Cut off any filling that oozes out. Transfer the puffs immediately to a serving plate and serve hot.

CECILY BROWNSTONE
CECILY BROWNSTONE'S ASSOCIATED PRESS COOK BOOK

Meat Patties

To make about 36 patties

125 g	lean beef	4 oz
125 g	lean pork	4 oz
	salt	
1	rasher bacon	1
1	piece chili pepper	1
1	onion	1
	thyme and marjoram sprigs	
15 g	butter	½ oz
2 tbsp	flour	2 tbsp
12.5 cl	meat stock (*page 165*)	4 fl oz
½ tsp	Worcestershire sauce	½ tsp
750 g	shortcrust dough (*page 164*)	1½ lb
1	egg, beaten	1

Cut the beef and pork into pieces and boil them in lightly salted water until the meat is soft—20 to 30 minutes. Cool the meat and chop it finely with the bacon, chili, onion and herbs. Make a binding sauce by melting the butter in a saucepan, adding the flour gradually, then adding the stock slowly until it is smooth. Add this to the meat mixture and stir in the Worcestershire sauce, making a soft paste.

Roll out the dough and cut it into 5 cm (2 inch) rounds with a pastry cutter; place a teaspoon of the meat mixture on each round. Dampen the edges of each round and cover it with another round of dough. Press the edges together with a fork. With a skewer, make a hole in the top of each patty; brush the top with the beaten egg. Bake the patties on a greased baking sheet in a preheated 230°C (450°F or Mark 8) oven for about 20 minutes, or until very light brown.

RITA G. SPRINGER
CARIBBEAN COOKBOOK

Ham and Pepper Tarts

Romanones

To make 12 tarts

500 g	rough-puff dough (*page 164*)	1 lb
350 g	smoked ham or prosciutto, chopped	12 oz
3	sweet red peppers, grilled, seeded, peeled and chopped	3

Roll out the dough very thinly. Cut out circles with a large glass. Mix the chopped ham, or prosciutto, and sweet red peppers together. Place mounds of the mixture on half of the circles, cover with the remaining circles and press the edges with a fork to seal them. Bake in a preheated 190°C (375°F or Mark 5) oven for 15 minutes or until brown.

ANA MARIA CALERA
COCINA CASTELLANA

Admiral's Cocked Hats

To make about 20 pastries

300 g	cold chicken or other cooked meat, poultry or game, minced	10 oz
60 g	cooked ham, minced	2 oz
60 g	cooked mushrooms, minced	2 oz
15 cl	white sauce (*page 166*)	¼ pint
	salt and pepper	
3	egg yolks, well beaten	3
500 g	rough-puff dough (*page 164*)	1 lb
1	egg white	1
	fat for deep frying	

Stir the minced chicken, ham and mushrooms into the white sauce. Season with salt and pepper, add 2 of the egg yolks and stir the mixture over a low heat until it thickens, but do not let it boil. Spread the mixture 4 cm (1½ inches) thick on a dish. Set aside in the refrigerator to get cold and firm.

Roll out the dough very, very thin—as thin as you can. Cut it into rounds 7.5 cm (3 inches) in diameter. Take some of the meat mixture and make it into as many balls as you want "hats", each the size of a large cherry. Put one of these balls in the middle of each round, and brush the sides of the dough with egg white. Draw up two sides of the round over the top of the ball of savoury meat and pinch the edges together. Doing this will make the other part of the dough project on each side like the points of an admiral's cocked hat. Brush over with the remaining egg yolk and deep fry in fat until brown. Drain on warm, crumpled muslin.

FLORENCE WHITE
GOOD ENGLISH FOOD

Tricornes

Les Corniottes

To make 12 triangles

500 g	shortcrust dough (*page 164*)	1 lb
250 g	*fromage blanc* or curd cheese	8 oz
4	eggs, 1 beaten	4
3 tbsp	double cream	3 tbsp
	salt	
275 g	Gruyère cheese, finely diced	9 oz

Roll out the dough fairly thinly and cut it into 10 cm (4 inch) rounds. Mix together the cheese, three eggs and the cream, and season with salt. Add 250 g (8 oz) of the Gruyère and mix thoroughly. Put a few spoonfuls of the mixture in the centre of each round of dough. Press the edges up on three sides of each round to form a triangle, and pinch the corners. Glaze with the beaten egg and dot with the remaining Gruyère. Place the triangles on a buttered baking sheet and bake in a preheated 200°C (400°F or Mark 6) oven for 20 minutes or until lightly browned. Serve hot or cold.

PIERRE HUGUENIN
LES MEILLEURES RECETTES DE MA PAUVRE MÈRE

Pizza Hors-d'Oeuvre

Pizza Lievitata per Antipasto

Serve this pizza with a variety of salamis and cold meats.

To make 20 squares

2 tbsp	olive oil	2 tbsp
2 tbsp	milk	2 tbsp
2	eggs	2
50 g	butter, softened	2 oz
	salt	
300 g	strong plain flour	10 oz
20 g	fresh yeast or 2 tsp dried yeast	¾ oz
80 g	Parmesan cheese, grated	2½ oz

Pour the oil, milk and eggs into a saucepan, add the butter and salt, and beat with a fork or a small whisk. Set the saucepan over hot water and heat gently until the butter melts. Place the flour on a board, make a well in the centre, and crumble the yeast into the well. Pour in the warmed mixture and knead it into the yeast and flour. Add the cheese and knead until the dough is smooth. Flatten out the dough with your hand and place it on a greased baking sheet. Put the baking sheet in a warm place, sheltered from draughts, for about 1 hour or until the dough has doubled in bulk. Prick the surface of the dough thoroughly with a fork, and bake in a preheated 220°C (425°F or Mark 7) oven for about 20 minutes or until golden. Cut the pizza into squares and serve.

GUGLIELMA CORSI
UN SECOLA DI CUCINA UMBRA

Pizza Neapolitan-Style

Pizza alla Napoletana

The technique of making pizza is shown on page 62. Instead of the canned tomatoes, 5 fl oz (¼ pint) of tomato sauce (recipe, page 166) can be used.

To make 1 pizza		
500 g	basic bread dough made with olive oil (*page 164*)	1 lb
2½ tbsp	olive oil	2½ tbsp
6	canned plum tomatoes, drained and puréed through a food mill	6
125 g	*mozzarella* cheese, coarsely grated	4 oz
6	anchovy fillets	6
1½ tbsp	capers packed in wine vinegar	1½ tbsp
	salt and freshly ground pepper	
	oregano	

Let the dough rest until doubled in size—about 1 hour at room temperature, away from draughts.

When the dough is ready, place on a board a sheet of heavy aluminium foil about 40 by 46 cm (16 by 18 inches). Oil the foil with 1 tablespoon of the olive oil, then place the dough on the foil. Spread the dough (using the tips of your fingers, not a rolling pin) until you have a sheet of dough measuring about 36 by 41 cm (14 by 16½ inches).

Spread the puréed tomatoes over the surface of the dough. Distribute the grated *mozzarella* evenly over the tomatoes, then distribute the anchovy fillets and capers. Add salt, pepper and oregano to taste and pour the remaining 1½ table-spoons of olive oil over everything. Slide the pizza and the foil directly on to the middle shelf of a preheated 230°C (450°F or Mark 8) oven and bake for about 35 minutes, or until crisp. Remove the pizza, slice and serve.

GIULIANO BUGIALLI
THE FINE ART OF ITALIAN COOKING

Genoese Pizza

Pizza Genovese

To make one 20 cm (8 inch) pizza		
500 g	basic bread dough (*page 164*)	1 lb
8 cl	olive oil	3 fl oz
5	eggs, beaten	5
5 tbsp	grated Gruyère cheese	5 tbsp
	salt and pepper	
90 g	basil, chopped	3 oz
100 g	*ricotta* cheese, sieved	3½ oz

After the dough has risen once, knead 4 tablespoons of the olive oil into it. Divide the dough in half, roll out each half into a round and brush the rounds with the remaining olive oil. Line the bottom and sides of a round shallow baking tin with one round of dough. Combine the eggs, Gruyère, salt, pepper, basil and *ricotta*, and pour this filling into the dough case. Cover with the second sheet of dough, seal the edges, and prick the top with a fork. Bake in a preheated 200°C (400°F or Mark 6) oven for 30 minutes or until golden-brown.

FRANCA FESLIKENIAN
CUCINA E VINI DELLA LIGURIA

Pizza with Garlic and Oil

Pizza Aglio e Olio

This is the simplest, most traditional form of pizza.

To make 8 small pizzas		
8	garlic cloves, finely chopped	8
12.5 cl	olive oil	4 fl oz
1.5 kg	basic bread dough (*page 164*)	3 lb
4 tbsp	dried oregano	4 tbsp
	salt	

Let the dough rise once, until it has doubled in bulk. Divide the dough into eight pieces. Roll each piece into a ball, flatten it into a round and press the centre, leaving a thicker, raised edge all round. Pour a little olive oil on to each round, add some finely chopped garlic and oregano, and season with salt. Bake in a preheated 220°C (425°F or Mark 7) oven for 15 to 20 minutes or until browned.

MARIA RIVIECCIO ZANIBONI
CUCINA E VINI DI NAPOLI E DELLA CAMPANIA

Cheese Pastry Ring

La Gougère

The technique of making gougère *is shown on page 48.*

With the exception of the delicious cheese of Époisses, in upper Burgundy, there is no notable Burgundian cheese, but the Burgundians are great cheese eaters for the obvious reason that cheese is one of the best accompaniments for wine. *Gougère*, a kind of cheese pastry made with *choux* paste similar to that used for éclairs, is the great cheese dish of the country. It is rather tricky to make, so if it doesn't come right the first time one just has to persevere.

To make one 20 cm (8 inch) ring		
90 g	Gruyère cheese, finely diced	3 oz
30 cl	milk	½ pint
1 tsp	salt	1 tsp
	freshly ground pepper	
60 g	butter, cut into small pieces	2 oz
125 g	flour, sifted	4 oz
4	eggs	4

The paste is made as follows: bring the milk to the boil and then let it get quite cold. Strain it. Put in the butter, the salt and a little pepper, and bring rapidly to the boil so that the butter and milk amalgamate. Pour in, all at once, the sifted flour. Stir until a thick, smooth paste is obtained; it will come away clean from the sides and bottom of the pan.

Off the heat stir in the eggs one at a time, each egg to be thoroughly incorporated before the next is added. When the paste is shiny and smooth add the cheese, reserving about 1 tablespoon of the little cubes. Leave to cool a little.

Lightly butter a baking sheet. Take tablespoons of the mixture and arrange them, like so many half-eggs, in a circle about 18 cm (7 inches) across, the space in the middle being about 6 cm (2½ inches). When you have made one circle, put the remaining spoonfuls on top of the first, so that you have quite a high wall round the central well. Pat into an even shape with a palette knife. Place the little pieces of reserved cheese on top and all around. Brush with milk. Cook in a preheated 190°C (375°F or Mark 5) oven for about 45 minutes.

Although the *gougère* begins to smell cooked after the first 20 minutes, do not be taken in; it will have swelled up and turned golden-brown, but it is not ready. If you can resist, do not open the oven, because of the risk of the mixture collapsing. If you feel you have to look, open and shut the door of the oven very gently. To test when the *gougère* is done, press the top of the cake lightly with a finger; it should be firm to the touch. If it is too soft, it will fall the instant you take it from the oven into a sad, flat pancake.

If you are going to serve the *gougère* hot, transfer it for 5 minutes to a warm place before transferring it to the serving dish or, if you cook by gas, turn the oven off and leave it 5 more minutes. If to be served cold, ease the cake off the baking sheet on to a wire cake rack so that there is air all round it, but keep it away from sudden draughts.

ELIZABETH DAVID
FRENCH PROVINCIAL COOKING

Cheese Choux Pastry

La Gougère

To make one 20 cm (8 inch) pastry ring		
150 g	Gruyère cheese, finely diced	5 oz
½ litre	milk	16 fl oz
1 tsp	salt	1 tsp
	pepper	
120 g	butter	4 oz
250 g	flour	8 oz
9	eggs, 1 beaten	9
2 tbsp	double cream	2 tbsp

Put the milk, salt, a pinch of pepper and the butter in a pan and bring to the boil. Remove the pan from the heat, place it on the kitchen table and, using a wooden spoon, stir the flour into the liquid. Return the pan to the heat for just 1 minute, stirring constantly, to dry the dough. Return the pan to the table and work the eight eggs into the dough, two by two. Add 125 g (4 oz) of the cheese, and, finally, work in the cream.

Butter a 20 cm (8 inch) flan ring and place it on a baking sheet. Spread the dough out in the ring, brush with the beaten egg, and sprinkle with the remaining diced cheese. Bake in a preheated 220°C (425°F or Mark 7) oven for 40 minutes or until the *gougère* is crisp and golden-brown. Serve warm.

PIERRE HUGUENIN
LES MEILLEURES RECETTES DE MA PAUVRE MÈRE

Anchovy Puffs

"Petourloun" aux Anchois

To make about 8 puffs

5	salt anchovies, soaked, filleted, rinsed, drained and chopped	5
20 cl	milk	7 fl oz
30 g	butter	1 oz
	salt	
100 g	flour	3½ oz
2	eggs	2

Place the milk in a saucepan with 20 g (⅔ oz) of the butter and a pinch of salt. Heat to boiling point, then pour in the flour, stirring with a wooden spoon over a low heat. When the mixture forms a smooth ball of dough that does not stick to the sides of the pan, remove from the heat and allow to cool slightly. Melt four of the anchovies in the remaining butter. Stir one egg, then the other egg, into the dough. Stir in the melted anchovies.

With a spoon, form round or oval mounds of this dough on a greased baking sheet. Place a small piece of the remaining anchovy on each mound. Bake in a preheated 180°C (350°F or Mark 4) oven for 25 minutes or until puffed and browned.

RODOLPHE BRINGER
LES BONS VIEUX PLATS DU TRICASTIN

Olive Loaf

Cake aux Olives

This loaf is served in slices with raw vegetables as a first course or cut into small squares as a cocktail snack.

To make one 1 kg (2 lb) loaf

20 each	black and green olives, stoned	20 each
225 g	flour	7½ oz
4	eggs	4
10 cl	olive oil	3½ fl oz
10 cl	dry white wine	3½ fl oz
1 tsp	baking powder	1 tsp
100 g	Gruyère cheese, finely diced	3½ oz
100 g	cooked ham, finely diced	3½ oz

Place the flour in a bowl and make a well in the centre. Put in the eggs and half of the olive oil. Work with a spatula, gradually adding the rest of the oil and the wine with the baking powder dissolved in it. Mix well, then add the Gruyère cheese, olives and ham.

Butter a loaf tin and line it with greaseproof paper. Pour in the mixture and bake in a preheated 180°C (350°F or Mark 4) oven for 10 minutes. Reduce the heat to 170°C (325°F or Mark 3) and continue to cook for 30 minutes more or until the loaf shrinks from the sides of the pan. Allow the loaf to cool in the pan before unmoulding.

LOUISETTE BERTHOLLE
LA CUISINE DES SAISONS

Pitta Bread

To make about 8 pieces bread

15 g	fresh yeast or 2 tsp dried yeast	½ oz
15 cl	cold water	¼ pint
15 cl	boiling water	¼ pint
¼ tsp	sugar	¼ tsp
2 tbsp	olive oil	2 tbsp
500 g	strong plain flour	1 lb
½ tsp	salt	½ tsp

Put the yeast into a bowl. Mix the cold and boiling water with the sugar and add about a quarter of it to the yeast, creaming the mixture together with a fork. Leave the yeast in a warm place for about 10 minutes until it froths up. Meanwhile, add the oil to the remaining water, and sift the flour and salt into a warmed bowl. Mix the flour to a dough with the yeast mixture, then the water and oil. If necessary, add a fraction more flour to make a firm dough. Turn the dough on to a board and knead it for 10 minutes. Wash, dry and oil the mixing bowl lightly. Return the dough to it and put the bowl into a plastic bag. Fasten tightly. Leave in a warm place for 1½ to 2 hours or until the dough has doubled in size.

Knock down the dough, and divide into lumps, each weighing about 90 g (3 oz). Pat or roll out these lumps into ovals roughly 12 cm (4½ inches) across and 20 to 22 cm (8 to 9 inches) long, and place them to rise on a lightly floured cloth in a warm place for 20 to 30 minutes.

Turn the oven on to 260°C (500°F or Mark 10) and let it heat for at least 15 minutes. For the last 2 minutes, put in two greased baking sheets to heat up. Place as many pitta as you can, without them overlapping, on these very hot sheets, brush the pitta with water and put into the oven. After 3 minutes, lower the heat to 230°C (450°F or Mark 8) and leave for a further 3 minutes, or a little longer, until they are puffed up and lightly spotted with brown. If there are any pitta left, bake them in the same way.

JANE GRIGSON
JANE GRIGSON'S VEGETABLE BOOK

Carrot Pancakes

Porkkanaohukkaat

To make about 12 pancakes

350 g	carrots, grated	12 oz
60 g	fresh breadcrumbs	2 oz
17.5 cl	milk or single cream	6 fl oz
2	eggs, yolks separated from whites, whites stiffly beaten	2
60 g	unbleached white flour	2 oz
1 tbsp	vegetable oil or melted butter	1 tbsp
About 1 tsp	sea salt	About 1 tsp
	butter or oil for frying	

Soak the breadcrumbs in the milk or cream. Mix in the egg yolks, carrots, flour, and vegetable oil or butter. Season to taste with salt. Fold in the beaten egg whites.

Heat a little butter or oil in a pancake pan or a heavy frying pan. With a spoon, drop into the hot pan small patties, about 8 cm (3 inches) in diameter, and fry them on both sides until they are done through.

Alternatively, deep fry the batter in oil by dropping a spoonful of the batter in as if making doughnuts.

ULLA KÄKÖNEN
NATURAL COOKING THE FINNISH WAY

Saint-Lo Pancakes

Galettes de Saint-Lo

To make about 24 pancakes

1 kg	buckwheat flour	2 to 2½ lb
1 tbsp	salt	1 tbsp
About 1.75 litres	water	About 3 pints
300 g	green bacon, diced	10 oz
2 tbsp	oil	2 tbsp
30 g	pork rind	1 oz

Mix the flour and salt. Add enough water to obtain a pancake batter the consistency of double cream. Work with a wooden spoon for 10 minutes.

Fry the bacon in the oil for a few minutes or until it is crisp and golden. Drain the bacon and allow it to cool.

Grease a small frying pan with the pork rind. Heat it over a high heat. Put in a spoonful of the bacon dice, then a large ladle of batter; the pancake should be fairly thick. Cook for 3 minutes on each side. Repeat with the remaining batter.

MARIE BISSON
LA CUISINE NORMANDE

Spring Onion Pancakes

Ts'ung Yu Ping

The technique of rolling and coiling spring onion pancakes is demonstrated on page 46. Sesame-seed oil can be used instead of the softened lard.

To make 4 pancakes

4 tsp	finely chopped spring onions	4 tsp
250 g	flour	8 oz
About 15 cl	water	About ¼ pint
2 tsp	salt·	2 tsp
60 g	lard, softened	2 oz
8 tsp	oil	8 tsp

Put the flour into a large bowl and make a well in the centre of the flour. Gradually add the water, stirring with your fingers to make a soft but not sticky dough (if it is too dry, add more water). Knead the dough until it feels smooth. Put the dough back into the bowl, cover it with a damp cloth and let it rest for about 15 minutes.

Turn the dough out on to a lightly floured surface and knead it again for 2 minutes. Divide the dough into four pieces. Roll out one piece of the dough into a 25 by 15 cm (10 by 6 inch) rectangle about 3 mm (⅛ inch) thick. Sprinkle ½ teaspoon of the salt on the dough and, with a rolling pin, roll the salted dough once. Spread 15 g (½ oz) of the lard on the dough and sprinkle it evenly with 1 teaspoon of the spring onions. From one long side, roll the dough loosely into a 25 cm (10 inch) sausage shape and pinch the dough to seal the open edge. Coil the sausage into a circle and tuck the end underneath. Gently press the circle with your hand ,and roll it into a flat pancake about 5 mm (¼ inch) thick and 15 cm (6 inches) in diameter. Cover the pancake with a dry cloth. Repeat the procedure with the other pieces of dough.

Heat a frying pan. Add 2 teaspoons of the oil and fry the pancakes one at a time over a medium heat, turning them once, for about 5 minutes, or until both sides are browned and crisp. Shake the pan occasionally during the frying. Cut each pancake into four wedges and serve hot.

FLORENCE LIN
FLORENCE LIN'S CHINESE REGIONAL COOKBOOK

Sandwiches and Canapés

Cucumber and Nasturtium Sandwich

To make 3 or 4 sandwiches

2	medium-sized cucumbers, peeled, halved, seeded and finely chopped	2
3 or 4	nasturtium leaves	3 or 4
	onion juice	
	cayenne pepper	
	mayonnaise (*page 167*)	
6 or 8	thin slices brown bread, buttered	6 or 8

To the chopped cucumber, add a little onion juice, a dash of cayenne pepper and enough mayonnaise to spread. For each sandwich, spread one slice of brown bread with the cucumber mixture, lay a nasturtium leaf over it and put another slice of bread on top. Serve at once.

FLORENCE A. COWLES (EDITOR)
1001 SANDWICHES

Cheese and English Walnut Sandwiches

The author of this recipe probably assumed her readers would use a Cheddar cheese. Any firm, flavourful cheese—Edam, Gruyère, Emmenthal or Cantal—is suitable.

To make 4 to 6 sandwiches

125 g	cheese, grated	4 oz
125 g	walnuts, thinly sliced	4 oz
125 g	butter	4 oz
	salt	
	paprika	
8 to 12	slices wholewheat bread	8 to 12

Work the butter to a cream and add the seasonings and the grated cheese gradually; then mix in the nuts. Spread the mixture on the bread and press the slices together in pairs.

JANET MCKENZIE HILL
SALADS, SANDWICHES AND CHAFING-DISH DAINTIES

Cheese and Green Pepper Rings

To make 12 sandwiches

250 g	cream cheese, softened	8 oz
2	medium-sized sweet green peppers	2
2 tbsp	finely chopped chives	2 tbsp
	salt and black pepper	
	soured cream (optional)	
24	thin slices white bread	24
	mayonnaise (*page 167*)	
	butter	

Wash the peppers and cut off the tops, removing the seeds and the ribs. Season the cream cheese with the chives, salt and black pepper. Add soured cream to thin the cheese, if it is needed. Mash the mixture to a smooth consistency. Fill the peppers with the seasoned cream cheese. Chill the peppers thoroughly until the filling is firm—about 2 hours.

When ready to serve, cut the peppers crosswise into thin slices. Cut 12 slices of the bread into rounds slightly larger in diameter than the pepper slices. Spread the rounds with mayonnaise. Lay a pepper slice on each round. Cover the pepper slice with a round of buttered bread cut 1 cm ($\frac{1}{2}$ inch) smaller than the bottom round, so the pepper rings show.

FLORENCE BROBECK
THE LUNCH BOX AND EVERY KIND OF SANDWICH

Goose Sandwiches

Smoked turkey or chicken, which may be more widely available, may be substituted for the goose breast.

To make 4 sandwiches

250 g	smoked goose breast, very thinly sliced	8 oz
8	thin slices bread, buttered	8
2	eggs, hard boiled and thinly sliced	2
1	lemon, juice strained	1
	salt and pepper	
	sprigs parsley	

Lay the slices of goose on four of the bread slices. Cover with the slices of egg, squeeze over the lemon juice, season with salt and pepper and cover with the remaining bread. Cut the sandwiches into fingers, arrange on a folded napkin, and garnish with sprigs of parsley.

OSCAR TSCHIRKY
THE COOK BOOK BY "OSCAR" OF THE WALDORF

Onion Rings

To make 12 sandwiches

12	paper-thin onion slices, each about 4 cm (1½ inches) in diameter	12
6	thin slices firm white bread, or 12 slices plaited egg bread	6
About 125 g	mayonnaise (*page 167*)	About 4 oz
	salt	
About 150 g	parsley, very finely chopped	About 5 oz

With a 4 cm (1½ inch) biscuit cutter, cut four rounds from each slice of white bread or two rounds from each slice of egg bread. Arrange the rounds in 12 pairs. Spread each round with mayonnaise. Put an onion slice on a bread round, salt the onion lightly, then top it with a second bread round.

Spread some mayonnaise on greaseproof paper and put the parsley in a bowl. Take a sandwich and roll the edges in the mayonnaise, then in the chopped parsley. Make sure there are no bare spots; if there are, dab mayonnaise on each spot and dip again in parsley. Place on greaseproof paper on a baking sheet and cover with greaseproof paper. Chill well.

IRMA RHODE
COOL ENTERTAINING

Mushroom Sandwiches

To prepare the scrambled eggs for this recipe, first beat the eggs lightly with 1 teaspoon of water. Melt 15 g (½ oz) of butter in a small frying pan over a medium heat, pour in the eggs and stir them until they begin to form soft curds. Remove the pan from the heat and stir until the eggs are smooth and thick.

This makes a delicious sandwich that tastes like chicken.

To make 2 sandwiches

125 g	fresh mushrooms	4 oz
½ tsp	lemon juice	½ tsp
30 g	butter	1 oz
	salt and pepper	
	cayenne pepper	
2	eggs, lightly scrambled	2
3 tbsp	freshly grated Parmesan cheese	3 tbsp
4	thin slices white bread	4

Cook the mushrooms mixed with the lemon juice in the butter for 8 minutes; remove them from the heat and chop them. Then pound the mushrooms to a paste in a mortar. Season with salt, pepper and a pinch of cayenne. Add the eggs and the cheese and mix well. Pile the mixture on to two bread slices, cover with the other two slices and serve.

ALICE B. TOKLAS
THE ALICE B. TOKLAS COOK BOOK

Clover Sandwich

To make 15 sandwiches

30	clover blossoms	30
1	loaf bread, crust removed	1
250 g	butter	8 oz

Place the bread in a stone jar with the clover blossoms; wrap the butter in cheesecloth and also place in the jar; leave overnight. Cut the bread thin and spread with clover-scented butter; put pairs of slices together and garnish each sandwich with a clover blossom.

EVA GREENE FULLER
THE UP-TO-DATE SANDWICH BOOK

Celery Sandwiches

To make 4 sandwiches

4	sticks celery, finely chopped	4
12.5 cl	double cream, whipped	4 fl oz
30 g	Parmesan cheese, grated	1 oz
	salt and pepper	
8	slices bread, buttered, or milk or water biscuits	8

Mix the celery with the cream, cheese, salt and pepper. Spread on four of the bread slices and top with the remaining slices.

MRS. C. F. LEYEL
SAVOURY COLD MEALS

Roquefort Cheese Sandwich

To make 8 finger sandwiches

60 g	Roquefort cheese	2 oz
30 g	butter	1 oz
	salt and pepper	
4	thin slices sandwich bread, crusts removed	4
	finely chopped parsley (optional)	
	finely chopped chives (optional)	

Work the cheese into a paste with the butter, using a knife, and season to taste with salt and pepper. When it is quite smooth, spread the paste on two slices of the bread, cover the paste with the remaining bread slices, press the halves carefully together and cut the sandwiches into fingers. If desired, parsley or chives, or both, may be mixed with the cheese. The paste may also be spread on crackers in place of bread.

OSCAR TSCHIRKY
THE COOK BOOK BY "OSCAR" OF THE WALDORF

Egyptian Sandwiches

To make 6 sandwiches

175 g	cold boiled ham, minced	6 oz
125 g	butter, creamed	4 oz
¼ tsp each	paprika, mustard and curry powder	¼ tsp each
2	eggs, hard boiled, yolks mashed, whites finely chopped	2
12	thin slices white bread, 6 buttered	12

Mix the butter with the ham, seasonings and eggs. Spread this mixture on the unbuttered slices of bread, cover with the buttered slices, press together and cut into pyramid shapes.

WOMAN'S WORLD MAGAZINE CO. INC.
SALADS AND SANDWICHES

Lamb's Brain Sandwiches

Sandwich à la Cervelle

Ox brain may also be used for the filling: one ox brain will make 10 sandwiches. The sandwich mixture can be served as an hors-d'oeuvre. Simply use slices of bread to make canapés and top with the mixture and a stoned olive.

To make 3 sandwiches

1	lamb's brain, cleaned, soaked, membrane removed	1
	salt and pepper	
½	lemon, juice strained	½
10 cl	oil	3½ fl oz
3	bread rolls or 3 portions (about ¼ loaf each) French bread	3
3	lettuce leaves	3

Cook the brain in salted water for 15 minutes. Drain it, chop it finely and crush with a fork to make a smooth paste. Leave it to cool completely. Season to taste with salt and pepper and add the lemon juice. Beat in the oil gradually as if making mayonnaise, adding very little oil to start. Use a wooden spoon if not using a mixer. The mixture should be firm enough to hold a spoon upright.

Cut the bread or rolls in half and place a lettuce leaf on one half of each. Spread over the brain mixture about 5 mm (¼ inch) thick. Fold the ends of the lettuce leaf over the top and cover with the other half of bread.

DANIELLE NOËL AND MICHEL LEMONNIER
RECETTES DE SANDWICHS

Chicken Giblet Loaf Sandwich

To make 60 to 70 sandwiches

2.5 kg	chicken giblets (gizzards, livers and hearts), finely minced	5 lb
1 kg	sausage-meat	2 to 2½ lb
6	eggs	6
1 kg	water biscuits, finely crumbled	2 to 2½ lb
1 litre	milk	1¾ pints
30 g	salt	1 oz
15 g	pepper	½ oz
3	bay leaves, crushed	3
500 g	bacon, thinly sliced	1 lb
120 to 140	thin slices white or wholewheat bread, buttered	120 to 140
	lettuce leaves	
	stuffed olives or tomato slices	

Mix together well all the ingredients up to and including the bay leaves. Line three loaf tins with the bacon and fill them with the giblet mixture. Bake for 2 hours in a preheated 180°C (350°F or Mark 4) oven. Allow to cool before removing from the tins. Make sandwiches of the giblet loaf on the white or wholewheat bread with lettuce, and garnish with stuffed olives or tomato slices.

EMORY HAWCOCK
SALADS AND SANDWICHES

Western Sandwich

To make 1 sandwich

5	olives, stoned and chopped	5
12	capers, chopped	12
1	gherkin, chopped	1
2 tbsp	mayonnaise (*page 167*)	2 tbsp
3	slices white bread, buttered	3
30 g	cream cheese	1 oz
	salt and pepper	
1	sprig parsley	1

Mix the olives, capers and gherkin with the mayonnaise. Spread a slice of bread with the cream cheese, season with salt and pepper, then put another slice of bread on top of that and spread with the olive mixture. Cover with a third slice, press together, remove the crusts and garnish with the parsley.

EVA GREENE FULLER
THE UP-TO-DATE SANDWICH BOOK

Parisian Rolls

Pagnotte alla Parigina

If you want meatless rolls, substitute fish for the leftover poultry or veal and the tongue.

To make 8 to 10 rolls

8 to 10	small white French rolls, the size of eggs, tops cut off and crumb removed	8 to 10
250 g	leftover stewed or roasted poultry or veal, cut into small slices	8 oz
2 to 3 tbsp	degreased roasting juices or sauce from the meat	2 to 3 tbsp
2 tbsp	olive oil	2 tbsp
1 tsp	mustard	1 tsp
1 tsp	vinegar	1 tsp
	salt and pepper	
1	slice cooked pickled tongue, chopped	1
1	small white truffle, chopped	1
2	pickled onions, chopped	2
1	head chicory, chopped	1

Combine the poultry or veal with all the other ingredients. Stuff the rolls with this mixture and replace the tops.

GIOVANNI VIALARDI
CUCINA BORGHESE

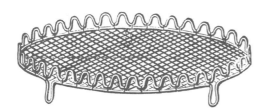

Danish Prince

To make 2 sandwiches

2	eggs, hard boiled and chopped	2
1 tbsp	chopped spring onion	1 tbsp
3	radishes, sliced	3
	salt and pepper	
1 tbsp	grated mature Cheddar cheese	1 tbsp
3 tbsp	mayonnaise *(page 167)*	3 tbsp
2	crusty rolls	2

Add the eggs to the spring onion and radishes, and season to taste. Fold the cheese into the mayonnaise and mix lightly with the egg mixture. Spread the filling on the rolls.

RUTH CHIER ROSEN
JUST BETWEEN US. . .

Black and White Sandwiches

Sandwich Schwarzweiß

To make 6 sandwiches

6	slices white bread	6
6	slices pumpernickel bread	6
6	slices light brown bread	6
90 g	butter	3 oz
250 g	curd cheese	8 oz
1 tsp	mustard	1 tsp
6 to 12	lettuce leaves, thick stalks cut out	6 to 12
125 g	coarse liver sausage	4 oz

Trim all the slices of bread to the same size. Butter the white bread with half the butter and spread a layer of curd cheese on it. Place the slices of pumpernickel on top and press down firmly. Butter the pumpernickel with the remaining butter and spread it thinly with the mustard. Place one or two lettuce leaves on the mustard. Spread the liver sausage on the light brown bread and place on the lettuce, sausage side down. Cut into rectangles or triangles, secure each with a wooden skewer, and place the small sandwiches on a flat dish.

ARNE KRUGER AND ANNETTE WOLTER
KOCHEN HEUTE

Stuffed Salmon Rolls

To make 6 rolls

250 g	salmon, poached in lightly salted water for 10 minutes, drained, skinned, boned, and puréed through a sieve	8 oz
3 to 4 tbsp	mayonnaise *(page 167)*, or stiffly whipped double cream flavoured with a drop each of Worcestershire sauce and tarragon vinegar	3 to 4 tbsp
1	gherkin, finely chopped	1
	salt and pepper	
6	soft rolls or scones	6
	softened butter	
	shredded lettuce	

Mix the salmon with the mayonnaise or the whipped cream mixture. Add the gherkin and salt and pepper.

Cut off the tops of the rolls, remove the soft insides and butter the shells sparingly. Fill the shells with the salmon mixture, place a little shredded lettuce over it and replace the tops together with a thin, buttered slice of the inside.

LADY JEKYLL, D.B.E.
KITCHEN ESSAYS

Boston Club Sandwich

To make 2 sandwiches

250 g	cold boiled or roast mutton, finely chopped	8 oz
	salt and pepper	
2 tbsp	olive oil or melted butter	2 tbsp
2	small crisp lettuce hearts	2
2 tbsp	mayonnaise (*page 167*)	2 tbsp
6	slices brown bread, cut into rounds and lightly buttered	6
2	slices tomato	2

Mix the mutton with a dash of salt and pepper and the oil or melted butter. Dip the lettuce hearts in the mayonnaise. On each bottom round of bread place a lettuce heart. On top of that place a tomato slice, then another slice of bread, then the mutton mixture. Cover with the other round of bread and press the sandwiches down.

EVA GREENE FULLER
THE UP-TO-DATE SANDWICH BOOK

Club Sandwich

This sandwich may also be made in the form of a double-decker, as demonstrated on page 67, by layering the ingredients between three slices of toasted bread.

To make 1 sandwich

2 or 3	slices cooked chicken	2 or 3
2	slices egg bread, toasted and buttered	2
	salt	
	paprika	
1	tomato, sliced	1
1 tbsp	mayonnaise (*page 167*)	1 tbsp
1 or 2	rashers bacon, fried until crisp and drained	1 or 2
	lettuce leaves	

Lay the slices of chicken on one piece of the toasted bread and season lightly with salt and paprika. On top, put the tomato slices, spread the mayonnaise on them, and crumble the bacon over that. Garnish with the lettuce and cover with the second piece of toast.

ALDEN ROBERTSON
THE NO BALONEY SANDWICH BOOK

Liver Patty

To make 8 slices

1	chicken liver	1
1	small onion, chopped	1
	salt and pepper	
30 g	rendered chicken fat or butter	1 oz
1	egg, hard boiled	1
$\frac{1}{2}$ tsp	lemon juice	$\frac{1}{2}$ tsp
1	large slice white bread, cut lengthwise from the loaf, crusts removed	1

Season the liver and onion with salt and pepper, and stew, covered, in the chicken fat or butter over a very low heat for 20 minutes, or until the liver is cooked through. Put the contents of the pan through a meat grinder with the hard-boiled egg—twice, if you wish the mixture to be very smooth. Add the lemon juice. Spread the mixture on the bread slice. Roll up, starting with the long edge, wrap in greaseproof paper and refrigerate for several hours until firm. When ready to use, unwrap the roll, slice and toast.

CORA, ROSE AND BOB BROWN
10,000 SNACKS

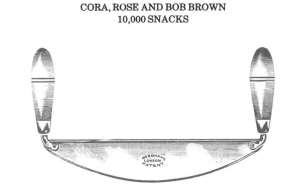

Ribbon Sandwiches

To make 24 small sandwiches

3	slices whole wheat bread, 5 mm ($\frac{1}{4}$ inch) thick	3
4	slices white bread, 5 mm ($\frac{1}{4}$ inch) thick	4
125 g	butter, softened	4 oz

Spread the whole wheat bread and two slices of the white bread on both sides with butter; butter the remaining two pieces of white bread on but one side. Beginning with a white slice buttered on but one side, pile in seven layers of alternating breads, having the second slice of white bread buttered on but one side on top. Wrap in a cheesecloth wrung out of hot water, and place under a light weight. Remove the crusts, cut in 5 mm ($\frac{1}{4}$ inch) slices across the grain; then cut slices in halves crosswise.

MAY E. SOUTHWORTH
THE MOTORIST'S LUNCHEON BOOK

Green Pea Sandwiches

This sandwich filling makes a good alternative to asparagus.

	To make 16 sandwiches	
250 g	shelled peas, cooked	8 oz
	salt and pepper	
17.5 cl	double cream, stiffly whipped	6 fl oz
8	thin slices brown or white bread, crusts removed, buttered and cut into halves	8

Put the cooked peas through a sieve and season well with salt and pepper. When cold, stir the pea purée thoroughly into the whipped cream. Roll small portions of the mixture into cylindrical shapes, then place them on the bread slices and roll the bread round the filling.

NANCY SHAW
FOOD FOR THE GREEDY

Prawns with Pinwheels

Bouquets aux Spirales Pinaudier

	To serve 8	
50	large cooked prawns, tails shelled, heads left on	50
1	sandwich loaf, slightly dry	1
600 g	butter	1¼ lb
	salt and pepper	
	cayenne pepper	
1 tbsp	cooked puréed spinach or *fines herbes*	1 tbsp
1 tsp	mustard	1 tsp
3	hard-boiled egg yolks, sieved	3
50 g	lobster coral or shrimps or prawns, puréed	2 oz
1 tsp	anchovy essence	1 tsp
4	large lemons, halved	4
200 g	sprigs parsley	7 oz

Slice the loaf horizontally to give four slices 14 cm (5½ inches) long and 4 mm (⅙ inch) thick. Remove the crusts and place each slice on a separate sheet of greaseproof paper.

Place a quarter of the butter in each of four bowls. Work until softened, and season with salt, pepper and cayenne. Add the spinach purée to one bowl, the mustard and egg yolks to

the second, the lobster coral to the third and the anchovy essence to the fourth. Mix each butter thoroughly.

Spread each slice of bread with one of the butters, so that each is a different colour. Roll up the slices, wrap them in the greaseproof paper, press them lightly into shape and refrigerate until serving time.

To prepare the prawns, cut off and discard the ends of the legs and feelers. Stick the prawn legs into the rind of the lemon halves, arranging them so that the lemon halves are covered with prawns. Cover a long serving dish with a napkin. Place six of the lemon halves, cut sides down, in a line down the middle, and the other two on either side in the centre, so that the serving dish is divided into four sections.

Unwrap the bread rolls and cut each roll obliquely into slices 5 mm (¼ inch) thick. Arrange these pinwheels on the serving dish, one kind in each section of the dish. Garnish with the parsley sprigs.

ACADÉMIE DES GASTRONOMES
LA HAUTE CUISINE FRANÇAISE

Provençal Sandwich

Pan Bagnat

This is a delicious preparation which is never eaten at table. It forms the essential element of every Provençal picnic, of every Sunday outing.

	To make 4 to 6 sandwiches	
1	round loaf crusty bread, sliced in half horizontally	1
12.5 cl	olive oil	4 fl oz
4 tbsp	wine vinegar	4 tbsp
	salt and pepper	
12	anchovy fillets	12
3	tomatoes, thinly sliced	3
2	onions, thinly sliced	2
1	garlic clove, chopped	1
2 or 3	sweet red or green peppers, grilled, skinned, seeded and cut into thin strips	2 or 3
12	small black olives, stoned	12

Place the halves of the bread crumb side up and sprinkle them with most of the olive oil and all the vinegar. Season with salt and pepper. Arrange on the bottom half of the loaf the anchovy fillets, tomato and onion slices, garlic, pepper strips, and olives. Season lightly with salt and pepper and sprinkle with the remaining oil. Replace the top of the loaf. Wrap the loaf tightly in a clean cloth, and take it with you on your picnic. Unwrap the loaf and cut it into four to six pieces, depending on the number of picnickers.

BENOIT MASCARELLI
LA TABLE EN PROVENCE

Bread and Tomato
Pane e Pomodoro

To make 1 sandwich

2	slices country-style bread	2
1	large tomato, sliced	1
2 tbsp	olive oil	2 tbsp
2 tsp	vinegar or lemon juice	2 tsp
	salt and pepper	
1 tbsp	chopped basil, or mixture of basil, parsley and mint	1 tbsp

Sprinkle the slices of bread with the oil and the vinegar or lemon juice. Season with salt, pepper and the herbs. Arrange the tomato slices on one slice of bread, cover with the other slice of bread and press together lightly.

ELENA SPAGNOL
I PANINI

The Hero

Pepperoncini, *or Tuscan peppers, are whole, pickled, mild-flavoured chili peppers.*

To make 4 portions

1	large loaf Italian bread	1
	olive oil	
1	garlic clove, cut	1
125 g	Gorgonzola cheese, softened	4 oz
500 g	Italian sandwich meats, about 125 g (4 oz) each of 4 or more of the following meats: Genoa salami, prosciutto, mortadella, *cappicola*, and pepperoni	1 lb
125 to 250 g	*provolone* or Taleggio cheese	4 to 8 oz
6	*pepperoncini* (optional)	6
2 or 3	sweet green peppers, roasted, peeled and sliced (optional)	2 or 3
	anchovy fillets	
	small chili peppers (optional)	
	vinegar	

Cut the bread open lengthwise. Brush the cut sides with oil. Rub the garlic clove over the oil. Spread the bottom half of bread with the Gorgonzola. Arrange layers of meat over it. Cover the meat with a layer of *provolone* or Taleggio cheese. Cover the cheese with the *pepperoncini* and/or roasted sweet peppers, a few anchovy fillets and a few chili peppers, if desired. Sprinkle lightly with vinegar. Cover the filling with the top of the bread and wrap the loaf tightly in aluminium foil. At the picnic site, cut the bread into four portions.

ANITA BORGHESE
THE GREAT SANDWICH BOOK

Vegetable-Stuffed Loaf
Patafla

Always make *patafla* the day before it is needed.

To make 1 stuffed loaf

4	tomatoes, skinned	4
60 g	black olives, stoned	2 oz
90 g	green olives, stoned	3 oz
2	sweet green peppers, seeded	2
1	large onion, chopped	1
60 g	capers	2 oz
60 g	gherkins	2 oz
1	long loaf French bread	1
	olive oil	
	paprika	
	salt and black pepper	

Chop the tomatoes, olives and sweet peppers together with the onion, capers and gherkins. Cut the loaf in half lengthwise and, with a sharp knife, remove all the crumb, which you mix with the tomato preparation, kneading it all together with a little olive oil, a pinch of paprika, black pepper and salt.

Now fill the two halves of the loaf with the mixture, press them together and put the loaf into the refrigerator.

To serve, cut into slices about 5 mm (¼ inch) thick and pile them up on a plate.

ELIZABETH DAVID
A BOOK OF MEDITERRANEAN FOOD

Mosaic Bread
Mosaikbrot

To make 12 to 16 small sandwiches

1	loaf French bread, about 250 g (8 oz), halved lengthwise, centre removed	1
50 g	cooked ham, diced	2 oz
50 g	cooked tongue, diced	2 oz
50 g	Swiss or Dutch cheese, diced	2 oz
150 g	gherkins or mixed pickles, diced	5 oz
100 g	butter, beaten until soft	3½ oz
1	egg, hard boiled and chopped	1
1 tbsp	capers, chopped	1 tbsp
1 tsp	mustard	1 tsp
	salt and pepper	
1	salt anchovy, soaked, filleted, rinsed, dried and pounded	1
1 tbsp	very finely chopped parsley	1 tbsp

Add the ham, tongue, cheese and gherkins to the butter. Add the egg and capers. Season with the mustard, salt, pepper and the anchovy. Finally, stir in the parsley. Fill the two halves of the loaf and press them firmly together. Leave for about 2 hours in a cold place or in the refrigerator, then cut into thin slices with a warmed, serrated knife.

EVA EXNER
BROT ZU JEDER ZEIT

Cheeseburger

To make 4 cheeseburgers

500 g	beef, minced	1 lb
	salt and pepper	
4	slices cheese	4
4	soft rolls, toasted and buttered	4

Form your minced beef into eight very thin hamburger cakes. Salt and pepper them and place slices of cheese just smaller than the hamburger cakes on half of the hamburgers. Top with the other hamburger cakes and grill or fry for about 2 minutes on each side. Serve in the toasted rolls.

JAMES BEARD
THE JAMES BEARD COOKBOOK

Bookmaker's Sandwich
Sandwich du Book Maker

This sandwich, popular with those who frequent the race-courses, can take the place of a meal.

To make 1 sandwich

One 175 g	thick rump steak	One 6 oz
	salt and pepper	
2 tsp	grated horseradish	2 tsp
1 tbsp	mustard	1 tbsp
2	slices bread crust cut from the ends of a loaf, buttered	2

Grill the steak to the desired degree of doneness. Season it with salt and pepper, and allow to cool. Sprinkle it with the horseradish and spread with the mustard. Place the steak between the slices of bread and tie it up so that the bread completely encloses the meat. Wrap it in several sheets of blotting paper, place in a copying press or under a heavy weight, and leave for 30 minutes. At the end of this time, the inside of the bread will be saturated with the meat juices, which the crust prevents from escaping. Remove the blotting paper and wrap the sandwich in greaseproof paper.

ALFRED SUZANNE
LA CUISINE ANGLAISE ET LA PÂTISSERIE

A Club Sandwich

To make 1 sandwich

2	slices beef fillet, 1 cm (½ inch) thick	2
90 g	butter, 60 g (2 oz) melted	3 oz
3	slices bread, 1 cm (½ inch) thick	3
	salt and pepper	
30 g	parsley, half chopped, half in sprigs	1 oz
	chutney or relish	

Brush the meat all over with melted butter and thickly butter the bread on both sides. Season the meat with salt and pepper and sprinkle with the chopped parsley. Lay one slice of bread between two of meat, with the other two slices of bread on the outside; fasten together with short wooden skewers. Put this sandwich in a preheated 190°C (375°F or Mark 5) oven and cook for 15 to 20 minutes for rare beef, or 20 to 25 minutes for medium. Baste frequently with the remaining melted butter. The bread should get crisp and brown. Garnish with the sprigs of parsley and serve a little chutney or relish with it.

MAXIME McKENDRY
SEVEN CENTURIES OF ENGLISH COOKING

The Mediator

La Médiatrice

The oyster loaf, popular throughout America in the 19th century, was known in the Vieux Carré of New Orleans as *la médiatrice*, or the mediator. It was the one thing a man felt might effectively stand between his enraged wife and himself when he came home after spending an evening carousing in the saloons of the French Quarter. A man bought his mediators for pennies, just before going home, in the market.

	To make 2 sandwiches	
6	live oysters, shelled	6
2	small French rolls	2
60 g	butter, melted	2 oz
	salt and pepper	
	Tabasco sauce	
2 tbsp	double cream, hot (optional)	2 tbsp

Cut off the tops of the rolls and scoop out most of the centres. Brush the cut side of the tops and the hollowed-out centres of the rolls with some of the melted butter. Place both tops and rolls in a preheated 220°C (425°F or Mark 7) oven until toasted to a very light brown.

Meanwhile, sauté the oysters in the remaining butter until they plump up and the edges curl (this takes 2 to 3 minutes). Add salt, pepper, two or three drops of Tabasco sauce and, if you like, a little hot cream. Fill the hot rolls, allowing three oysters to one roll, and cover with the crusty tops. Serve hot.

THE EDITORS OF AMERICAN HERITAGE
THE AMERICAN HERITAGE COOKBOOK

Miniature Stuffed Rolls

Canapés da Napoli

	To make 36 rolls	
125 g	*mozzarella* cheese, finely chopped	4 oz
60 g	parsley, finely chopped	2 oz
125 g	prosciutto or boiled ham, finely chopped	4 oz
$\frac{1}{4}$ tsp	freshly ground black pepper	$\frac{1}{4}$ tsp
$\frac{1}{4}$ tsp	grated nutmeg	$\frac{1}{4}$ tsp
$\frac{1}{4}$ tsp	oregano	$\frac{1}{4}$ tsp
36	miniature bread rolls	36
	butter	

In a bowl, combine the cheese, parsley, prosciutto or boiled ham, pepper, nutmeg and oregano.

Cut the tops from the miniature rolls; scoop out the bread from the centres, then butter the insides. Spoon 1 tablespoon of filling into each roll and replace the tops. Wrap the rolls in foil and heat them in a 180°C (350°F or Mark 4) oven until the cheese melts, 5 to 10 minutes. Serve hot.

NANCY FAIR McINTYRE
COOKING IN CRUST

Frog's Legs Sandwich

	To make 1 sandwich	
3	pairs small frog's legs or 1 pair large frog's legs	3
15 to 30 g	butter	$\frac{1}{2}$ to 1 oz
	tartare sauce (*page 167*)	
2	thin slices bread, toasted	2
	lettuce leaves	

Sauté the frog's legs in butter for 5 to 10 minutes—depending on size—or until tender and then detach the flesh from the bones. Chop the flesh finely and mix with enough tartare sauce to bind it. Spread it on a thin slice of toast, press on the upper slice, and cut the sandwich into finger shapes. Serve the fingers warm on leaves of lettuce.

ARNOLD SHIRCLIFFE
THE EDGEWATER SANDWICH AND HORS D'OEUVRES BOOK

Codfish Cheeks Sandwich

Cod cheeks are not generally available but you may be able to obtain them by placing a special order with the fishmonger.

To make 4 sandwiches

4	cod cheeks	4
8	slices bread, cut into rounds or squares, toasted and buttered	8
4 tbsp	tartare sauce (*page 167*)	4 tbsp
1	egg yolk, beaten	1
30 g	dry breadcrumbs	1 oz
2 tbsp	oil or 30 g (1 oz) butter	2 tbsp
4	lettuce leaves	4
16	olives	16
4	gherkins, sliced and fanned	4

Spread the buttered toast with tartare sauce and keep it warm. Dip the cod cheeks in the egg yolk, then in the breadcrumbs, and fry until golden in the hot oil or butter. Split the cheeks and arrange them on four slices of the toast.

Add the lettuce leaves and press the other slices of toast on top to make sandwiches. Garnish with the olives and gherkins and serve immediately.

ARNOLD SHIRCLIFFE
THE EDGEWATER SANDWICH AND HORS D'OEUVRES BOOK

Bread and Omelette

Pane e Frittata

Any bread can be eaten with the omelette—white or brown, sliced or rolls, French or country-style. A hollowed-out *baguette* filled with an onion omelette was the working man's traditional mid-morning snack. A plain omelette is delicious as a sandwich with toasted sweet bread. Omelettes for sandwiches should be thoroughly cooked to make them easier to eat. These sandwiches are good hot or cold.

To make 1 sandwich

3	eggs	3
1	large roll, or 2 large slices country-style bread	1
	salt	
2 tbsp	oil	2 tbsp

Beat the eggs with a little salt. Heat the oil in a frying pan over a high heat. Pour in the eggs and cook, pushing the cooked edges towards the centre so that the remaining liquid runs down the sides. When set, turn and cook the other side for a few seconds. Place the omelette in the roll, folding the edges in, or sandwich it between slices of bread.

Onion omelette: Halve a medium-sized onion and slice it thinly. Cook it slowly with 4 tablespoons of oil and a little salt for 20 minutes or until it is soft and golden. Pour in the eggs and finish as above.

Onion and artichoke omelette: Remove the chokes and the outside leaves from two small artichokes; slice the artichokes very thinly. Thinly slice half an onion. Cook the onion and artichokes in 4 tablespoons of oil, with a pinch of salt, for 20 minutes or until soft. Pour in the eggs, beaten with 1 tablespoon of grated Parmesan cheese, and finish as above.

Herb omelette: Add to the eggs, when beating them, 2 to 3 tablespoons of finely chopped herbs (parsley, basil, chives, mint, etc.) and finish as above.

Mushroom omelette: Slice 90 g (3 oz) mushrooms and cook them in 5 tablespoons of oil over a high heat for 6 to 7 minutes. Salt lightly. Beat the eggs with salt and 1 tablespoon of finely chopped parsley, pour into the pan, and finish as above.

ELENA SPAGNOL
I PANINI

Italian Fried Cheese Sandwiches

Mozzarella in Carrozza

The technique of frying egg-coated cheese sandwiches is shown on page 74.

To make 16 or 32 small sandwiches

16	slices bread, 5 mm (¼ inch) thick	16
16	slices whole-milk *mozzarella* cheese, 5 mm (¼ inch) thick	16
2	eggs	2
¼ tsp	salt	¼ tsp
1 tsp	water	1 tsp
About 125 g	fine breadcrumbs	About 4 oz
	oil for deep frying	

Trim the crusts from the bread slices and cut each slice into halves or quarters. Cut the slices of *mozzarella* slightly smaller than the slices of bread and assemble the sandwiches, pressing the edges of the bread together. Beat together the eggs, salt and water. Dip the sandwiches into the beaten egg mixture, coating both sides and all the edges well. Let the sandwiches stand to become well impregnated, then dip the edges in fine breadcrumbs to seal them.

In a small frying pan, fry the sandwiches, a few at a time, to a fine golden colour in hot oil almost 2.5 cm (1 inch) deep, turning them to brown both sides. Drain the sandwiches on absorbent paper and serve immediately on a hot plate.

NARCISSA G. CHAMBERLAIN AND NARCISSE CHAMBERLAIN
THE FLAVOR OF ITALY

Breaded Liver Sandwiches

Liver Hrinky

To make 2 large sandwiches

250 g	thinly sliced calf's liver, sautéed in butter for 5 minutes, drained, and minced in a food processor or grinder	8 oz
2 tsp	grated onion	2 tsp
45 to 60 g	butter	1½ to 2 oz
	salt and pepper	
	milk, stock or white sauce (*pages 165 and 166*) (optional)	
4	slices bread	4
1	egg, lightly beaten	1
5 tbsp	milk	5 tbsp
	dry breadcrumbs	

Cook the onion in 15 g (½ oz) of the butter over a low heat until lightly browned, about 5 minutes. Combine it with the liver and season with salt and pepper to taste. The mixture may be moistened slightly with milk, white sauce or stock. Make two large sandwiches, using the liver mixture as a filling. Cut the sandwiches into triangles or rectangles. Dip each piece in the beaten egg diluted with the milk, then coat with the breadcrumbs. Sauté the pieces in the remaining butter until browned on both sides. Serve at once.

SAVELLA STECHISHIN
TRADITIONAL UKRAINIAN COOKERY

Toast à l'Anglaise

To make 4 sandwiches

4	slices rare roast beef	4
60 g	butter	2 oz
2 tsp	Dijon mustard	2 tsp
	Worcestershire sauce	
	salt and freshly ground pepper	
1 tbsp	vegetable oil	1 tbsp
3	medium-sized onions, thinly sliced	3
8	slices white bread, crusts removed	8
125 g	clarified butter	4 oz
4	dill gherkins, thinly sliced lengthwise	4
4	sprigs parsley	4

Combine half of the butter with the mustard in a small bowl. Add a few drops of Worcestershire sauce and a pinch each of salt and pepper. Mash the mixture with a fork until smooth, then set this mustard butter aside.

Heat the remaining butter and the oil in a heavy frying pan. Add the onions, cover, and cook over a low heat for 30 minutes, or until they are very soft and lightly browned. Drain the onions and set them aside.

Spread the bread slices with the mustard butter. Place a slice of roast beef on half of the bread slices, top the meat with the onions, and cover with the remaining slices of bread.

Heat the clarified butter in a large frying pan, add the sandwiches, and sauté them on both sides until they are nicely browned. Transfer the sandwiches to a serving platter and top each one with a dill gherkin and a sprig of parsley. Serve the sandwiches immediately.

PERLA MEYERS
THE PEASANT KITCHEN

Fried Bread "Cushions"

Cuscinetti di Pandorato

To make 6 bread cases

1	large unsliced loaf sandwich bread	1
500 g	*mozzarella* or Provatura cheese, thinly sliced	1 lb
175 g	prosciutto or other raw ham, thinly sliced, or 6 anchovy fillets, chopped	5 oz
60 g	flour	2 oz
¼ litre	milk	8 fl oz
3	eggs, beaten with a little salt	3
	lard or oil for deep frying	

Slice the loaf into six thick slices, trim off the crusts, and with a sharp knife slit each slice through the middle lengthwise without cutting it completely through, like a cushion cover. Stuff each slice with slices of cheese and the ham or anchovies. Flour each "cushion" lightly, dip it into the milk and arrange it in a deep dish. Pour the eggs over the top. Leave until the eggs are completely absorbed by the bread.

Heat plenty of lard or oil and deep fry the "cushions", two at a time, until they are golden-brown on both sides. Drain them on paper towels. Keep hot in a warm oven until all of the "cushions" are fried. Serve hot.

ADA BONI
ITALIAN REGIONAL COOKING

Fried Cheese and Ham Sandwiches

Les Croque-Monsieur

To make 4 sandwiches

8	thin slices Gruyère cheese	8
4	thin slices ham	4
8	thin slices dry bread	8
1 tbsp	mustard	1 tbsp
60 g	butter or 4 tbsp oil	2 oz

Spread the bread with the mustard. Place a slice of cheese on each of four slices of bread, then a slice of ham, then another slice of cheese. Cover with the remaining bread slices. Heat the butter or oil in a frying pan and fry the sandwiches on both sides. The cheese will melt and hold the sandwiches together. Serve the fried sandwiches hot.

LA CUISINE LYONNAISE

To Make a Nice Whet Before Dinner

To make 4 open sandwiches

4	slices bread, 1 cm (½ inch) thick	4
90 g	butter, melted	3 oz
2	salt anchovies, soaked, filleted, rinsed and dried	2
125 g	Cheshire cheese, grated	4 oz
2 tbsp	chopped parsley	2 tbsp

Fry the bread lightly in 60 g (2 oz) of the butter. Lay an anchovy fillet on each piece of bread. Mix together the cheese and parsley, and sprinkle them over the bread and anchovy. Baste with the remaining butter and brown under the grill; it must be done in the dish in which you send it to table.

ELIZABETH RAFFALD
THE EXPERIENCED ENGLISH HOUSEKEEPER

Parmesan Onion Rounds

To make 48 open sandwiches

60 g	Parmesan cheese, freshly grated	2 oz
175 g	onion, very thinly sliced	6 oz
250 g	mayonnaise (*page 167*)	8 oz
48	5 cm (2 inch) bread rounds	48

Toast the bread rounds on one side. Blend the mayonnaise and the cheese. Put a thin slice of onion on the untoasted side of each round, and top the onion with a generous spoonful of the mayonnaise and cheese mixture. Bake the open sandwiches in a preheated 190°C (375°F or Mark 5) oven for 10 to 12 minutes, until the tops are puffed and golden. Watch carefully, for they burn easily. Serve warm.

THE JUNIOR LEAGUE OF THE CITY OF NEW YORK
NEW YORK ENTERTAINS

Bread and Gorgonzola

Pane e Gorgonzola

To make 1 roll

1	bread roll, about 10 cm (4 inches) in diameter	1
30 g	strong Gorgonzola cheese, diced	1 oz
1 tbsp	double cream	1 tbsp
1 tsp	strong mustard	1 tsp
	salt	

Cut off the top of the roll and remove the inside. Crumble the inside into a bowl with the cream and mash with a fork until the cream is soaked up. Add the mustard and a pinch of salt, and mix. Stir in the Gorgonzola.

Fill the roll with the mixture. Bake in a preheated 220°C (425°F or Mark 7) oven for 10 to 15 minutes or until the roll is golden and crunchy.

ELENA SPAGNOL
I PANINI

Savoury Eggs on Croûtons

To make 5 canapés

3	eggs, yolks separated from whites	3
5	slices bread, cut into rounds	5
30 g	lard	1 oz
60 g	Parmesan cheese, grated	2 oz
2 tbsp	double cream	2 tbsp
	salt and pepper	
	cayenne pepper	
	grated nutmeg	

Fry the bread rounds in the lard, then sprinkle grated Parmesan cheese on top of each, using about half the cheese. Keep these croûtons warm.

Steam two whites of egg and 1 tablespoon of cream with a little pepper and salt very slowly in a buttered dariole mould or small ramekin, for 15 to 20 minutes or until set. Let the mixture cool, then turn it out and slice it into five flat circles.

For the yolk mixture, take the three yolks and the remaining white; beat all with a tablespoon of cream in a saucepan just greased with a little fresh butter; add a small pinch of cayenne and a little grated nutmeg; stir over gentle heat until it thickens, about 5 minutes.

Now put a circular slice of white of egg on each croûton, then put a little yolk mixture on the white slice; next add grated cheese—do not *over* cheese it—and then brown the top under the grill. Serve the eggs on a warmed napkin.

CATHERINE FRANCES FRERE
THE COOKERY BOOK OF LADY CLARK OF TILLYPRONIE

Gloucestershire Cheese and Ale

This is an old farmhouse recipe, still well liked, and usually made with Double or Single Gloucester. The former is a mellow orange cheese the shape and size of a large grindstone. Single Gloucester is a summer cheese excellent for toasting.

To make 6 open sandwiches		
500 g	Gloucester cheese, rind removed, thinly sliced	1 lb
35 cl	strong ale	12 fl oz
2 tbsp	English mustard	2 tbsp
6	thick slices brown bread, toasted	6

Put the cheese into a ovenproof dish, spread the mustard over it and cover it with half of the ale. Cook in a preheated 180°C (350°F or Mark 4) oven for about 20 minutes or until the cheese is tender and melting.

Heat the remaining ale and pour it over the toasted bread to moisten it. Cover with the cheese. Serve immediately very hot, with pickles if liked.

SHEILA HUTCHINS
ENGLISH RECIPES AND OTHERS FROM SCOTLAND, WALES AND IRELAND

Roquefort Croûtons with Walnuts

Tartines de Roquefort aux Noix

To make 4 open sandwiches		
200 g	Roquefort cheese	7 oz
100 g	shelled walnuts, coarsely chopped	3½ oz
75 g	butter, softened	2½ oz
2 tbsp	Armagnac or cognac	2 tbsp
	freshly ground pepper	
2	large thick slices country-style bread, halved	2

Place the butter in a large bowl and, using a wooden spoon, work it into a paste. Then mix in the chopped walnuts. Break up the cheese with a fork and add the crumbs to the bowl. Add the Armagnac or cognac and four or five good turns of the

pepper mill. Mix everything together until all of the ingredients are thoroughly incorporated.

Toast the bread slices. While the croûtons are still hot, spread them with the cheese mixture and serve at once. You can accompany these cheese croûtons with celery hearts and radishes. You can also try grapes, and peeled pear quarters sprinkled with lemon juice to prevent them discolouring.

ROGER VERGÉ
CUISINE OF THE SUN

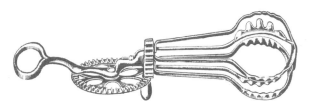

Cheese and Sausage Canapés

Crostini di Ricotta e Salsiccie

To make 24 canapés		
250 g	*ricotta* cheese	8 oz
3	sweet Italian poaching sausages	3
3 tbsp	cold water	3 tbsp
½ tsp	salt	½ tsp
5 tbsp	freshly grated Parmesan cheese	5 tbsp
6 tbsp	olive oil	6 tbsp
60 g	unsalted butter	2 oz
12	slices white bread, crusts removed and slices halved	12
125 g	*fontina* or Gruyère cheese, thinly sliced and cut into rectangles the size of the halved bread slices	4 oz

In a bowl, mix the *ricotta* cheese and cold water. Add the salt and Parmesan cheese and mix until smooth and creamy.

Prick the sausages with a fork and cook in 4 tablespoons of water in a frying pan, over a low heat, until the water evaporates. Continue cooking until the sausages become lightly browned on all sides and thoroughly cooked. Drain the sausages on paper towels, peel them, then chop them finely and stir the sausage-meat into the cheese mixture.

Preheat the oven to 170°C (325°F or Mark 3). Heat the oil and butter in a large, heavy frying pan. Add the bread slices and fry them on one side only. Drain the slices on paper towels. Spread the fried sides of the bread with the cheese and sausage mixture. Place the slices on a well-greased baking sheet and bake them for 5 minutes.

Remove the sandwiches from the oven and top each with the *fontina* or Gruyère cheese. Return them to the oven for about a minute, until the cheese melts.

FRANCESCO GHEDINI
NORTHERN ITALIAN COOKING

Mixed Cheese Toast

Croquetout

This is made with odds and ends from the cheese board. The ham may be replaced by blanched bacon and the pepper by cayenne pepper; you may add a little mustard to the butter used to spread the toast.

To make 8 open sandwiches

200 g	leftover cheese, rinds and dry edges removed, pounded, sieved or grated	7 oz
	double cream or softened butter (optional)	
	pepper	
2	slices ham, quartered	2
8	slices bread, crusts removed, grilled or toasted and buttered	8

Work the cheese to a smooth paste, incorporating a little cream or butter if it is dry. Season with pepper.

Place a piece of ham on each slice of toast. Cover with the cheese. Place in a preheated 220°C (425°F or Mark 7) oven for 15 minutes, or until the melted cheese is bubbling. Serve hot.

PIERRE ANDROUET
LA CUISINE AU FROMAGE

Sassy Carnival Rolls

Panini Rustici

To make 12 rolls

6	hard sesame-seed rolls, cut in half	6
500 g	*ricotta* cheese	1 lb
2	eggs	2
$\frac{1}{2}$ tsp	salt	$\frac{1}{2}$ tsp
250 g	*mozzarella* cheese, diced	8 oz
125 g	salami, chopped	4 oz
125 g	prosciutto, chopped	4 oz
125 g	mortadella, chopped	4 oz
60 g	freshly grated Parmesan cheese	2 oz
	freshly ground black pepper	
60 g	butter, cut into small pieces	2 oz

Preheat the oven to 180°C (350°F or Mark 4). Combine the *ricotta*, eggs, salt, *mozzarella*, salami, prosciutto and mortadella. Using a palette knife, spread the *ricotta* mixture over the halved rolls. Sprinkle the tops with the grated Parmesan cheese, pepper and butter.

Place the rolls on a baking sheet and bake for 10 to 15 minutes. Remove the rolls from the oven and put them under a hot grill long enough to toast the grated cheese—2 to 3 minutes. Serve them hot. If you wish to use the rolls as canapés, cut them into quarters.

ANNA MUFFOLETTO
THE ART OF SICILIAN COOKING

Breton Toast with Herb Butter

Rôties de Bretagne

This recipe was originally composed of plants that grew on the cliffs of Brittany, overlooking the sea. Plants such as samphire, white stonecrop and buckhorn plantain were among the ingredients Menon used in the version of this dish that he published in 1746. This version of his recipe calls for a variety of garden herbs that are commercially available.

To make 4 open sandwiches

60 g	mixed fresh herbs (tarragon, chives, parsley, watercress, etc.), chopped	2 oz
175 g	butter	6 oz
1	lemon, juice strained	1
	coarsely ground pepper	
4	large slices country-style bread	4

Combine the herbs, butter, lemon juice and pepper to taste by mashing all the ingredients together with a fork. Be careful not to soften the butter too much.

Toast the bread on both sides over an open fire or under the oven grill. As soon as the toast is brown and while it is still hot, spread the herb butter on it; serve immediately.

CÉLINE VENCE AND ROBERT COURTINE
THE GRAND MASTERS OF FRENCH CUISINE

Garlic Toast

Bruschetta

To make 4 portions

4	large slices bread, toasted	4
2	garlic cloves	2
4 tbsp	olive oil	4 tbsp
	salt and pepper	

While the toast is still hot, rub it with the garlic cloves. Put it in a dish and sprinkle with olive oil, salt and pepper.

ELENA SPAGNOL
I PANINI

Toasted Bread and Garlic

El Pan de Costra al Ajo (Málaga)

The bitter Seville orange juice may be replaced by 1 tablespoon of lemon juice mixed with 2 tablespoons of sweet orange juice.

To make 1 open sandwich

2 or 3	garlic cloves	2 or 3
1	dried red chili pepper	1
	salt and pepper	
½	Seville orange, juice strained	½
1 tbsp	olive oil	1 tbsp
1	slice white bread	1

Pound the garlic in a mortar with the chili, and salt and pepper to taste. Stir in the orange juice and then the oil. Spread the mixture on the bread and bake in a preheated 180°C (350°F or Mark 4) oven for 5 to 10 minutes.

ELIZABETH CASS
SPANISH COOKING

Black Truffle Canapés

Crostini col Tartufo Nero

To make 6 canapés

1	black truffle, chopped	1
1	salt anchovy, soaked, filleted, rinsed, dried and chopped	1
1	set chicken giblets (liver, heart and gizzard), sautéed in 1 tbsp oil for 5 minutes, chopped	1
	salt and pepper	
6	slices home-made bread, toasted	6
3 tbsp	olive oil	3 tbsp

Pound together in a mortar the truffle, anchovy and chicken giblets, until you obtain a smooth mixture. Season to taste. Sprinkle the toasted bread with olive oil and spread it thinly with the truffle mixture.

LA CUCINA DI FALSTAFF
VINCENZO BUONASSISI

Anchovy Canapés

Roties à la Hollandaise

To make 4 canapés

5	salt anchovies, soaked, filleted, rinsed and dried	5
2 tbsp	chopped parsley	2 tbsp
1	Welsh or spring onion, chopped	1
1	shallot, chopped	1
1	garlic clove, chopped	1
4 tbsp	olive oil	4 tbsp
4	thick slices bread, toasted	4
1 tbsp	orange juice	1 tbsp
	freshly ground pepper	

Chop the fillets of one of the anchovies with the parsley, Welsh or spring onion, shallot and garlic. Stir in enough oil to make the mixture spreadable. Spread this mixture on the hot toast, and arrange the remaining anchovy fillets on top. Mix the rest of the oil with the orange juice and sprinkle over the canapés. Grind on a seasoning of pepper and serve.

LOUIS AUGUSTE DE BOURBON
LE CUISINIER GASCON

Dill Prawns in Caraway Rolls

Dillkrabben in Kümmelstangen

To make 24 small sandwiches

About 125 g	cooked prawns or shrimps, shelled	About 4 oz
2 tbsp	finely chopped dill	2 tbsp
6	caraway finger rolls, each cut into 4 pieces, soft centres removed	6
3 tbsp	mayonnaise (*page 167*)	3 tbsp
½ tsp	curry powder	½ tsp
	salt and pepper	

Mix the prawns or shrimps with the dill and mayonnaise. Season with the curry powder, salt and pepper. Stuff the slices of roll with the mixture. Put them on to a flat ovenproof dish. Warm in a preheated 200°C (400°F or Mark 6) oven for 3 to 4 minutes and serve the rolls immediately.

EVA EXNER
BROT ZU JEDER ZEIT

Mince Croustades Savoury

To make 6 filled bread cases

2	rashers bacon	2
3	pork sausages	3
3 tbsp	tomato sauce (*page 166*)	3 tbsp
6	button mushrooms, coarsely chopped	6
½ tsp	finely chopped parsley	½ tsp
	salt and pepper	
1	loaf stale bread	1
	milk	
1	egg, beaten	1
	dry breadcrumbs	
	butter or lard	
	parsley sprigs	

Fry the bacon until crisp. Prick the sausages and fry them in the bacon fat. When cool, cut both into small dice, first removing the skins of the sausages. Put the mince and the sauce, mushrooms and parsley in a stew-pan, season and reheat.

To make the bread cases, cut six 2.5 cm (1 inch) slices from a stale loaf, stamp out round or oval shapes and scoop out the centres, forming hollows to hold the meat mince. Now dip the cases in milk, let them become moistened without being sodden, then coat them with the egg and breadcrumbs, and fry in 1 cm (½ inch) of butter or lard until nicely browned. Have the mince ready, fill the cases, garnish with parsley sprigs deep fried for a minute or so, and serve.

MRS. ISABELLA BEETON
MRS. BEETON'S HORS D'OEUVRE AND SAVOURIES

Sardine Croustades

To make 10 bread cases

125 g	canned sardines, drained, skinned and boned	4 oz
3 or 4	large slices stale white bread, about 8 mm (¾ in) thick	3 or 4
About 90 g	butter	About 3 oz
1 tbsp	tomato or white sauce (*page 166*)	1 tbsp
	anchovy essence (optional)	
	lemon juice	
2 tsp	freshly grated Parmesan cheese, or 1 tbsp grated Cheddar cheese	2 tsp
	watercress sprigs	

Stamp out of the bread slices eight to 10 rounds or ovals, each about 5 cm (2 inches) in diameter. With a smaller cutter, make a second circle or oval about 1 cm (½ inch) deep and 1 cm inside the edge of each round. Fry these bread cases in hot butter until lightly browned—about 2 to 3 minutes. Drain the bread cases, then with the point of a small knife lift out the inner rings and remove any moist crumbs. If wished, place the bread cases in a 180°C (350°F or Mark 4) oven for a few minutes to crisp the insides. Cool before using.

Mash the sardines and mix in the white sauce or tomato sauce; if using white sauce, add a few drops of anchovy essence. Season, then blend with a few drops of lemon juice and the cheese. Put this sardine filling into the crisp bread cases and garnish them with watercress.

IRENE HIRST (EDITOR)
THE BEETON HOMEBOOKS: HORS D'OEUVRES & SALADS

Mushrooms in Toast Shells

Champignons en Croustade

The technique of hollowing rolls to make toast shells is demonstrated on page 72.

To make 6 filled shells

250 g	mushrooms, finely sliced	8 oz
175 g	unsalted butter	6 oz
6	soft, round rolls	6
2 tbsp	chopped shallots	2 tbsp
1 tbsp	chopped garlic	1 tbsp
1 tsp	salt	1 tsp
¼ tsp	cayenne pepper	¼ tsp
3 or 4 tbsp	lemon juice	3 or 4 tbsp
¼ litre	double cream	8 fl oz
125 g	cooked, smoked ox tongue, finely diced	4 oz
2	egg yolks, beaten	2
1 tsp	Worcestershire sauce	1 tsp

Melt half of the butter. Cut off the top of each roll and remove the soft inside crumb, leaving just the shell. With a pastry brush, paint the inside and outside of the shells with the melted butter. Put the shells into a preheated 230°C (450°F or Mark 8) oven until brown and crisp—about 5 minutes.

Melt the remaining butter in a saucepan. Add the shallots and simmer for 5 minutes; do not brown. Add the garlic and mushrooms, cover the pan and simmer for 3 minutes. Stir in the salt, cayenne pepper, lemon juice, cream and diced tongue. Simmer for 2 minutes. Beat a little of this sauce into the egg yolks so that they will not curdle; blend the egg-yolk mixture into the sauce. Add the Worcestershire sauce. Check the seasoning. Mix well. Spoon the sauce mixture into the shells. Bake the filled shells in a preheated 230°C (450°F or Mark 8) oven for 5 minutes, or until browned.

ANTOINE GILLY AND JACK DENTON SCOTT
ANTOINE GILLY'S FEAST OF FRANCE

Shrimp Toast

A simpler way of making this dish is to warm the shrimps in the cooked butter and flour, flavour with a little cayenne and 5 drops of anchovy essence, and serve on the toast.

To make 1 large open sandwich

750 g	shrimps, shelled, shells and heads bruised and reserved	1½ lb
45 cl	water	¾ pint
90 g	butter	3 oz
½ tsp	flour	½ tsp
	cayenne pepper	
1	thick slice bread crust cut from the bottom of a loaf, slightly hollowed out	1
	lemon juice (optional)	
2	egg yolks, lightly beaten	2

Boil the shells and heads of the shrimps in the water for 30 minutes. Then strain this liquor off through a fine-meshed sieve and reserve it.

Melt half of the butter. Add to it the flour and a little cayenne to your taste. Shake the whole together until the colour darkens, then pour into it gradually and carefully the liquor in which the shells and heads were stewed.

Boil this sauce and, just as it reaches boiling point, put in the shrimps and let them get hot quite through. Fry the bread in the remaining butter.

Add a squeeze of lemon, if you like it, to the shrimps. Off the heat, stir the egg yolks into the mixture. Spread the shrimps on the toast. Serve hot.

MARY JEWRY (EDITOR)
WARNE'S MODEL COOKERY

Toast with Mussels and Bacon

To make 4 open sandwiches

About 30	live mussels, scrubbed and bearded, steamed for 2 minutes and shelled	About 30
4 to 6	rashers bacon, cut into strips	4 to 6
60 g	butter	2 oz
4	slices bread, toasted	4
1 tbsp	chopped parsley	1 tbsp

Fry the mussels in the butter for 2 to 3 minutes. Remove from the heat and keep hot. Fry the bacon strips until crisp. Drain the bacon. Put the mussels on the toast and top with the bacon. Sprinkle with the parsley and serve.

BENGT PETERSEN
DELICIOUS FISH DISHES

Mussel Canapés

Canapés Gallegos

For instructions on steaming mussels, see the recipe, page 167.

These canapés are most authentic when made with cornbread. They may also be made as large open sandwiches, using one slice of bread per serving.

To make 12 canapés

36	live mussels, steamed and shelled	36
4 tbsp	olive oil	4 tbsp
½ tsp	cayenne pepper, or ¼ tsp each cayenne pepper and paprika	½ tsp
	salt	
½ tsp	vinegar	½ tsp
3	slices bread, cut into quarters	3
12	onion rings	12

Beat together the oil, cayenne pepper (or cayenne and paprika), salt and vinegar. Using a pastry brush, brush the bread with half of this mixture. Place an onion ring in the centre of each piece of bread, and fill the onion rings with the mussels. Spread the tops with the remaining oil mixture.

GLORIA ROSSI CALLIZO
LAS MEJORES TAPAS, CENAS FRÍAS Y PLATOS COMBINADOS

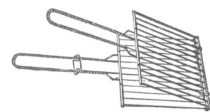

Oysters on Toast

Huîtres Tartinettes

To make 12 canapés

12	live oysters, shelled, liquor strained and reserved	12
12	thin bread rounds, cut from a sandwich loaf and toasted	12
3	egg yolks	3
60 g	butter, softened	2 oz
	lemon juice	

Place the oysters in an ovenproof dish and sprinkle them with their liquor. Place in a preheated 180°C (350°F or Mark 4) oven. As soon as the liquid begins to bubble a little, remove the dish from the oven. Immediately spread each round of toast with a mixture of the egg yolks and the butter. Place a poached oyster on each toast round. Sprinkle the oysters with drops of lemon juice and serve.

LA CUISINE LYONNAISE

Crayfish on Toast

If you cannot get crayfish (*écrevisses*), Dublin Bay prawns (*langoustines*) can be used instead.

	To make 12 portions	
12	crayfish, boiled for 2 minutes and shelled	12
1	lemon, juice strained	1
2 tbsp	*fines herbes*	2 tbsp
12	thin rashers streaky bacon	12
12	oblongs of toast, buttered	12

Sprinkle the crayfish with the lemon juice and herbs. Roll each crayfish in a rasher of bacon. Bake them on a baking sheet in a preheated 200°C (400°F or Mark 6) oven—turning them once or twice—for 7 to 10 minutes, until the bacon begins to brown. Serve on the buttered toast.

AMBROSE HEATH
GOOD SAVOURIES

Smoked Haddock Canapés Albemarle

Croûtes de Findon Haddock Albemarle

	To make 12 canapés	
½	smoked haddock, skinned, boned, crushed and sieved	½
2	egg yolks	2
3 to 4 tbsp	double cream	3 to 4 tbsp
	salt and pepper	
12	slices bread, toasted	12
60 g	dry breadcrumbs	2 oz
60 g	butter, melted	2 oz
	parsley sprigs	

Mix the haddock with the egg yolks and cream. Season with salt and pepper to taste. Spread the mixture on the toast and sprinkle with the breadcrumbs and melted butter. Place on a baking sheet and cook in a preheated 170°C (325°F or Mark 3) oven for 7 to 8 minutes, just the time to poach them. When a little crust has formed on the top, cover with buttered paper and cook for 5 minutes more. Serve on a napkin with parsley.

A. BAUTTE
MODERN FRENCH AND ENGLISH COOKERY

Kipper Toastie

	To make 16 toast fingers	
1	kipper	1
30 g	butter	1 oz
	pepper	
4	slices bread, toasted and buttered	4

Put the kipper in a pan with just enough boiling water to cover it. Simmer for 3 minutes. Drain, remove the bones carefully and put the pieces of fish into a small basin. Beat with the butter and pepper.

Cut the toast into fingers, spread each piece with the fish mixture, put into a preheated 200°C (400°F or Mark 6) oven for a few moments and serve quite hot.

MRS. ARTHUR WEBB
FARMHOUSE COOKERY

Tuna as a Cocktail Spread

	To make about 500 g (1 lb) spread	
200 g	canned tuna, drained and mashed	7 oz
100 g	capers, rinsed and drained	3½ oz
2 tbsp	mayonnaise (*page 167*)	2 tbsp
1 tsp	paprika	1 tsp
2 tbsp	onion juice	2 tbsp
3	egg whites, stiffly beaten	3
	toast fingers	

Blend all of the ingredients except the toast. Spread the mixture on fingers of toast and place them under the grill until lightly browned and puffy, about 5 minutes.

JAMES BEARD
JAMES BEARD'S NEW FISH COOKERY

Herring Roe on Toast

	To make 4 open sandwiches	
125 g	herring roe	4 oz
60 g	butter	2 oz
	salt and pepper	
	milk	
4	slices bread	4
2 tbsp	double cream	2 tbsp

Melt half the butter in a saucepan and put in the roe. Cook well, mashing the roe with a wooden spoon; while it is cooking add salt and pepper to taste and a little drop of milk, but on no account let the roe get too liquid. It should be cooked in about 5 minutes. Meanwhile, toast the bread and spread it with the remaining butter. Beat the cream into the cooked roe and pile it on the hot buttered toast. Serve very hot.

NANCY SHAW
FOOD FOR THE GREEDY

Bull's Eye

To make 4 open sandwiches

4	salt anchovies, soaked, filleted, rinsed and dried	4
4	slices bread, trimmed into rounds and buttered	4
4	onion rings	4
4	egg yolks	4
2 tsp	capers	2 tsp
	watercress sprigs	

Drape the anchovy fillets round the edges of the bread; place a ring of onion inside and an egg yolk in the middle, with capers sprinkled round it. Serve garnished with watercress.

ELISE SVERDRUP
NORWAY'S DELIGHT

Hot Mushroom Sandwich

To make 1 open sandwich

6 to 8	small mushrooms	6 to 8
30 g	butter	1 oz
¼ tsp	lemon juice	¼ tsp
	pepper	
½ tsp	chopped parsley	½ tsp
1	slice wholewheat bread, toasted	1

Stem the mushrooms; chop the stems and sauté them in 10 g (⅓ oz) of the butter. Combine half of the remaining butter with the lemon juice, a pinch of pepper and the parsley. Spread the slice of toast with the butter mixture. Sprinkle the sautéed mushroom stems on the toast; top with the raw mushroom caps, gill sides down.

Melt the remaining butter, brush it over the mushroom caps and set the toast slice in a covered dish. Bake in a preheated 180°C (350°F or Mark 4) oven for 12 to 15 minutes, until the mushroom caps are tender.

JANICE MURRAY GILL
NOVA SCOTIA DOWN-HOME COOKING

Leek Toast

Rôties au Blanc de Poireaux

To make 6 open sandwiches

12	leeks, thinly sliced	12
45 g	butter	1½ oz
	salt and pepper	
100 g	bacon, diced	3½ oz
¼ litre	double cream	8 fl oz
30 g	fresh white goat cheese, grated	1 oz
	freshly ground pepper	
6	slices dry French bread	6
1	garlic clove	1
45 g	clarified butter	1½ oz
	chopped parsley	

Heat the butter in a large frying pan; add the leeks and toss them in the butter. Salt and pepper lightly and cover. Let steam over a low heat for about 10 minutes.

Meanwhile, fry the bacon until it is crisp. Drain. Add the bacon to the leeks. Increase the heat and cook, uncovered, until all moisture has evaporated. Add the cream and reduce until it coats the leeks. Add the cheese and pepper; mix well.

Rub the slices of bread with the garlic and brown them in the clarified butter. Top with the leeks and a dash of chopped parsley. Serve very hot.

MADELEINE M. KAMMAN
WHEN FRENCH WOMEN COOK

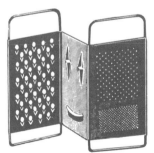

Hamburg Rolls

Hamburger Rundstück

To make 8 open sandwiches

4	rolls, halved	4
8	thick slices roast veal or pork	8
4	pickled cucumbers, halved lengthwise	4
4 to 6 tbsp	very hot meat roasting juices	4 to 6 tbsp

Top each half roll with a slice of meat and half a cucumber. Pour over the hot roasting juices.

DOROTHEE V. HELLERMANN
DAS KOCHBUCH AUS HAMBURG

Tartare Rolls

Brötchen à la Tatare

To make 8 open sandwiches

150 g	beef fillet, finely minced	5 oz
1	egg yolk	1
2	gherkins, finely chopped	2
1 tsp	capers	1 tsp
1 tsp	chopped onion	1 tsp
	dry mustard	
	salt and pepper	
	paprika	
4	crisp rolls, halved, some of crumb removed if desired	4
4	anchovy fillets	4
1 tbsp	grated horseradish	1 tbsp
4	slices lemon, halved	4

Mix the beef with the egg yolk, gherkins, capers and onion. Season with a pinch of mustard, salt, pepper and paprika.

Spread the seasoned meat evenly over the eight roll halves. Place one anchovy fillet on four halves, and put a little horseradish on the other four. Top each half with half a lemon slice.

GRETE WILLINSKY
KOCHBUCH DER BÜCHERGILDE

Almond Soufflé Sandwiches

To make 4 open sandwiches

60 g	almonds, blanched and chopped	2 oz
2	eggs, yolks separated from whites	2
½ tsp	Worcestershire sauce	½ tsp
100 g	Cheddar cheese, grated	3½ oz
1 tbsp	mayonnaise (*page 167*)	1 tbsp
1 tbsp	chopped parsley	1 tbsp
½ tsp	salt	½ tsp
4	slices toast	4

Beat the egg yolks until they are thick. Add the almonds, Worcestershire sauce, cheese, mayonnaise and parsley. Beat the egg whites with the salt until they are stiff and fold them into the yolk mixture. Pile the mixture lightly on the toast. Heat the sandwiches under the grill until they are puffy and lightly browned, about 5 minutes.

WOMAN'S DAY COLLECTOR'S COOK BOOK

St. Paul Sandwich

To make 1 open sandwich

1	slice ham, finely chopped	1
1	slice onion, finely chopped	1
1	slice sweet green pepper, finely chopped	1
1	small sweet pickle, finely chopped	1
1	egg, beaten	1
30 g	butter	1 oz
1	slice bread, toasted	1
	lettuce leaves	
	olives	

Stir the ham, onion, sweet pepper and pickle into the beaten egg. Fry in the butter until brown on both sides. Serve on toast with lettuce leaves and olives.

EMORY HAWCOCK
SALADS AND SANDWICHES

Marrow Crusts

To make 8 open sandwiches

2	beef marrow bones, each about 10 cm (4 inches) long	2
8	slices bread, toasted and buttered	8
	finely chopped parsley	
	salt	
	black pepper	

Remove the marrow carefully from the bones and soak it in lukewarm water for 1 hour. Shortly before serving time, cut the marrow into 2.5 cm (1 inch) slices; place the slices in cold water, bring the water to the boil and pour it off immediately. Spread the marrow on very hot toast, sprinkle with a little parsley, lots of salt and a little black pepper. Pass under the grill. Serve immediately.

SIGRID SCHULTZ (EDITOR)
OVERSEAS PRESS CLUB COOKBOOK

Boiled Beef and Bacon Sandwiches

Sandwich Boeuf Bouilli et Lard

To make 4 open sandwiches

125 g	boiled or braised beef leftovers, cut into small cubes	4 oz
4	thin rashers smoked lean bacon	4
2 tsp	finely chopped gherkins	2 tsp
1 tsp	capers	1 tsp
2 tbsp	mayonnaise (*page 167*)	2 tbsp
4	slices country-style bread, or 2 bread rolls or portions of French bread, halved	4

Scald the bacon in boiling water for 2 minutes, then dry it thoroughly. Fry it, turning often, until it is crisp but not burnt, then cut it into small pieces. Add the gherkins and capers to the mayonnaise and mix with the beef and bacon. Spread the mixture over the pieces of bread or rolls.

DANIELLE NOËL AND MICHEL LEMONNIER
RECETTES DE SANDWICHS

Woodcock Loaf Spread

To make 6 open sandwiches

3	woodcocks, boned	3
125 g	calf's liver	4 oz
1 tsp	chopped parsley	1 tsp
2 tbsp	breadcrumbs	2 tbsp
30 g	butter	1 oz
1	anchovy fillet	1
$\frac{1}{2}$ tsp	salt	$\frac{1}{2}$ tsp
$\frac{1}{8}$ tsp	pepper	$\frac{1}{8}$ tsp
$\frac{1}{8}$ tsp	thyme	$\frac{1}{8}$ tsp
2	egg yolks	2
6	slices bread, buttered	6
90 g	cheese, grated	3 oz

Put through a grinder together twice, until very finely minced, the woodcock, liver, parsley, breadcrumbs, butter, anchovy and seasonings. Add the egg yolks and mix well.

Spread this mixture on the slices of buttered bread. Sprinkle with the cheese. Brown in a preheated 220°C (425°F or Mark 7) oven for 5 minutes. Serve.

MARTIN RYWELL (EDITOR)
WILD GAME WILD FOWL COOK BOOK

Game on Toast

Crostini di Caccia

To make 6 open sandwiches

250 g	cold cooked game (preferably pheasant breast), sliced	8 oz
6	thin slices bread, toasted	6
100 g	butter	$3\frac{1}{2}$ oz
	salt and white pepper	
1	sweet green pepper, grilled, seeded, peeled and cut into strips	1

Work together the butter, salt and pepper. Spread the toast with this mixture. Arrange the slices of game on the toast and garnish with the strips of grilled sweet pepper.

GIOVANNI RIGHI PARENTI
LA CUCINA DEGLI ETRUSCHI

Radish Canapés

Crostini di Rafano

To make 6 canapés

250 g	radishes, scraped, soaked in cold water for 30 minutes and cut into fine *julienne*	8 oz
	salt and pepper	
1 tsp	sugar	1 tsp
1 tsp	wine vinegar	1 tsp
1 tsp	lemon juice	1 tsp
6	thick slices black bread	6

Combine the radishes with a generous seasoning of salt and pepper, the sugar, vinegar and lemon juice. Leave to soften for a few minutes, then spread on the bread and serve. It is important that the mixture remains cold at all times.

VINCENZO BUONASSISI
LA CUCINA DI FALSTAFF

Caviare Canapés

Canapés au Caviar

The caviare may be replaced by very thinly sliced veal, ham, tongue, game or chicken.

	To make 16 canapés	
125 g	caviare	4 oz
16	small rounds or squares of bread, lightly buttered	16
4	spring onions, very finely chopped	4

Spread the caviare on the buttered bread and sprinkle the spring onions on top.

A. PETIT
LA GASTRONOMIE EN RUSSIE

Celeriac Canapés

Kanapki z Pasta Selerowa

Watercress canapés can be made in the same way by replacing the celeriac with 4 tablespoons of finely chopped watercress.

	To make 20 canapés	
100 g	celeriac, finely grated	3½ oz
2 to 3 tbsp	mayonnaise (page 167)	2 to 3 tbsp
5	slices wholemeal bread, buttered and cut into quarters	5
1 tbsp	finely cut chives	1 tbsp

Mix the celeriac with the mayonnaise. Spread the mixture on the prepared slices of bread and sprinkle with the chives.

HELENA HAWLICZKOWA
KUCHNIA POLSKA

Tomato Cream Sandwich

	To make 12 open sandwiches	
250 g	tomatoes, skinned and seeded	8 oz
2 tbsp	whipped cream	2 tbsp
6	salt anchovies, soaked, filleted, rinsed, dried and chopped	6
	pepper	
	cayenne pepper	
6	finger rolls, halved and buttered	6
	mustard and cress	

Pound the tomatoes with the anchovies, season with pepper and cayenne and stir in the cream. Spread the rolls with this mixture and decorate them with mustard and cress.

MRS. C. F. LEYEL AND MISS OLGA HARTLEY
THE GENTLE ART OF COOKERY

Fresh Tomato and Chive Appetizers

Croûtons aux Tomates et à la Ciboulette

	To make 8 canapés	
2	ripe tomatoes, skinned, seeded and coarsely chopped	2
2 tbsp	finely chopped chives	2 tbsp
8	slices bread, 5 mm (¼ inch) thick, cut from a small French loaf; or 8 rounds, 6 cm (2½ inches) in diameter, cut from slices of sandwich bread	8
30 g	butter, softened	1 oz
	salt and pepper	
2 tbsp	crème fraîche or double cream	2 tbsp
1 tbsp	finely chopped shallots	1 tbsp
1 tsp	lemon juice	1 tsp
About ½ tsp	Tabasco sauce	About ½ tsp

Butter the pieces of bread on both sides and toast them on both sides under the grill, or fry them in the butter as you would croûtons. Season the tomatoes and mix them with all the other ingredients (except the toast) in a bowl, then place the bowl in the refrigerator for at least 1 hour to chill thoroughly. Spread the tomato and chive mixture evenly over the eight pieces of toast. Serve cold.

MICHEL GUÉRARD
MICHEL GUÉRARD'S CUISINE GOURMANDE

Swedish Buckling Snacks

Swedish bucklings (böckling) are smoked herring, always eaten raw. Smoked sprats may be substituted.

	To make about 16 canapés	
1	large buckling, skinned and filleted	1
60 g	butter, or 30 g (1 oz) butter and 2 tbsp double cream	2 oz
¼ tsp	mustard	¼ tsp
	vinegar	
4	thin slices white bread, crust removed	4

Stir the buckling with half of the butter or with the cream to obtain a smooth paste. Pass through a sieve.

Mix the remaining butter with the mustard and a few drops of vinegar. Spread the slices of bread with this butter and cut them into small squares or oblongs. Pipe the buckling paste in strips across diagonally.

INGA NORBERG (EDITOR)
GOOD FOOD FROM SWEDEN

Nasturtium Savoury

To make 12 canapés

12	small nasturtium flowers	12
12	thin slices cucumber	12
12	slices brown bread, trimmed into small rounds and buttered	12
12.5 cl	double cream, whipped until thick	4 fl oz
30 g	Parmesan cheese, grated	1 oz
	salt and cayenne pepper	
1 tsp	grated horseradish (optional)	1 tsp

Lay a slice of cucumber on each round of bread. Mix the cream and Parmesan, and season with salt and cayenne pepper to taste. A little grated horseradish may also be added. Pile this mixture on top of the cucumber in the form of a dome, or it may be put through a forcing bag, and on the top put a small nasturtium flower. Serve arranged on a lace-edged paper.

FLORENCE B. JACK
COOKERY FOR EVERY HOUSEHOLD

Herring Salad

Sillsalad

When this salad is served as a topping for smørrebrød, *one of the herring fillets may be sliced and placed on top.*

To make 6 portions

2	salt herring fillets, soaked overnight in cold water and drained	2
4 or 5	potatoes, boiled and peeled	4 or 5
2 or 3	pickled beetroots	2 or 3
1	dill pickle	1
1 or 2	apples	1 or 2
1 to 2 tbsp	chopped onion	1 to 2 tbsp
	salt and white pepper	
	beetroot juice (optional)	
7 tbsp	double cream, whipped (optional)	7 tbsp

Cut the herring, potatoes, beetroots, pickle and apples into small, uniform cubes and mix them carefully. Add the onion and seasoning to taste, including juice from the beetroots, if desired. For a richer salad, add the whipped cream. Put the salad into a bowl or pack it into a mould. Chill the salad for at least 3 hours before serving.

J. AUDREY ELLISON (TRANSLATOR AND EDITOR)
THE GREAT SCANDINAVIAN COOK BOOK

Red Cabbage with Apples

Rödkal med Äpplen

This braised cabbage is traditionally used as a topping for smørrebrød *(pages 76-79).*

To make about 1.5 kg (3 lb) braised cabbage

1	large head red cabbage, halved, cored and cut into thin shreds	1
4	cooking apples, peeled, cored and sliced	4
1	small onion, finely chopped	1
3 tbsp	wine vinegar	3 tbsp
3 tbsp	water	3 tbsp
1 tsp	salt	1 tsp
½ tsp	pepper	½ tsp
1 tbsp	sugar	1 tbsp
60 g	butter	2 oz
3 to 4 tbsp	red wine	3 to 4 tbsp

Put the cabbage in a heavy enamelled, stainless-steel or tin-lined pot with the onion, vinegar, water, salt and pepper. Cover the pot tightly and cook over a low heat for 2½ to 3 hours.

At the end of the first hour of cooking, add the apples and the sugar. Cover the pot again and continue the slow cooking. No more water or vinegar should be required if the cabbage is a fresh, moist head; it will cook in its own juices. A few minutes before serving, add the butter and wine.

FLORENCE BROBECK AND MONIKA B. KJELLBERG
SMÖRGÅSBORD AND SCANDINAVIAN COOKERY

Swedish Marinated Salmon

Gravlax

To make 850 g (1¾ lb) marinated salmon

1 kg	fresh salmon, filleted, skin left on	2 lb
1 tbsp	salt	1 tbsp
24	white peppercorns, crushed	24
3 tbsp	sugar	3 tbsp
125 g	dill sprigs	4 oz

Mix the salt, peppercorns and sugar together. Rub the fish with this mixture and place it in a bowl between thick layers of the dill. Put a weighted plate on top of the fish. Refrigerate for at least 24 hours, turning the fish occasionally. Scrape off the seasoning before serving.

E. DONALD ASSELIN, M.D.
SCANDINAVIAN COOKBOOK

Standard Preparations

Shortcrust and Rough-Puff Dough

One simple formula produces dough for both plain shortcrust and for rough-puff dough. Shortcrust dough may be made with as little as half the weight of butter to flour, but up to equal quantities may be used for superior results. Rough-puff dough, using equal quantities of butter and flour, may be used in any recipe calling for puff dough. The quantity of dough given here will line a 20 cm (8 inch) flan tin or six small tins.

To make 250 g (8 oz) dough

125 g	flour	4 oz
¼ tsp	salt	¼ tsp
60 to 125 g	cold unsalted butter, cut into small pieces	2 to 4 oz
3 to 4 tbsp	cold water	3 to 4 tbsp

Mix the flour and salt in a mixing bowl. Add the butter and cut it into the flour rapidly, using two table knives, until the butter is in tiny pieces. Do not work for more than a few minutes. Add half the water and, with a fork, quickly stir it into the flour and butter mixture. Add just enough of the rest of the water to allow you to gather the dough together with your hands into a firm ball. Wrap the dough in plastic film or waxed paper and refrigerate it for at least 1 hour, or, alternatively, put it into the freezer for about 20 minutes until the surface is slightly frozen.

To roll out shortcrust dough: Remove the ball of dough from the refrigerator or freezer and put it on to a cool floured surface (a marble slab is ideal). Press the dough out partially with your hand, then give it a few gentle smacks with the rolling pin to flatten and render it more supple. Roll out the dough from the centre, until it forms a circle about 1 cm (½ inch) thick. Turn the dough over so that both sides are floured and continue rolling until the circle is about 3 mm (⅛ inch) thick. For small open pastries, cut out small rounds with a biscuit cutter to fit your baking tins. For barquettes, lay the sheet of dough over the tins and trim the excess from each tin.

To roll out rough-puff dough: Place the dough on a cool floured surface and smack it flat with the rolling pin. Turn the dough over to make sure that both sides are well floured, and roll out rapidly into a rectangle about 30 cm (1 foot) long and 12 to 15 cm (5 to 6 inches) wide. Fold the two short ends to meet each other in the centre, then fold the dough in half to align the folded edges with each other. Following the direction of the fold lines, roll the dough into a rectangle again, fold again in the same way, wrap in plastic film and refrigerate for 1 to 2 hours or for 15 to 20 minutes in the freezer. Repeat this process two or three more times before using the dough. Always refrigerate the dough between rollings.

Basic Bread

To make 2.5 kg (5 lb) bread dough or two loaves

1.5 kg	strong plain flour	3 lb
1 tbsp	salt	1 tbsp
30 g	fresh yeast or 1 tbsp dried yeast	1 oz
90 cl	tepid water	1½ pints

Sift the flour and salt into a bowl. Mix the yeast with a little of the water; if you are using dried yeast, leave it to soften for about 15 minutes. When the yeast mixture is frothy, pour it into the flour with the rest of the water. Mix the flour and liquid together into a stiff, sticky dough. Put the dough on to a floured board and knead it thoroughly until it is elastic and glossy, about 15 minutes.

Shape the dough into a ball and place it in an oiled bowl. Cover the bowl with plastic film and leave the dough to rise until doubled in bulk, 1½ to 2½ hours. The dough is ready when a finger pressed into it leaves a dent that does not immediately smooth itself out.

Put the dough on to a working surface and divide it in half. Knead each half briefly, then shape into a ball. Cover the balls with a damp cloth and leave them to rest for 10 to 15 minutes. Flatten each ball into a circle less than 2.5 cm (1 inch) thick. Roll up the circle into a cylinder, then flatten and stretch the cylinder until it is twice its original length. Fold in both ends so that they meet in the middle. Press the long sides of the dough outwards to form a rectangle and roll up the rectangle to produce a compact cylinder that will keep its shape during baking. Place each cylinder in a greased bread tin. Leave until doubled in bulk, 45 minutes to 1 hour.

Place in a preheated 230°C (450°F or Mark 8) oven. After 40 minutes, when the tops of the loaves are well browned, remove the tins from the oven and tip each loaf on to a cloth held in one hand. Rap the base of the loaf with your knuckles; if the bread sounds hollow, it is cooked; if not, reduce the oven heat to 200°C (400°F or Mark 6), return the loaves to the oven for 10 to 15 minutes, and test again.

Cool the loaves on wire racks. Do not slice them until they are cold, preferably the next day.

Pizza dough: Add 1 to 2 tablespoons of olive oil when mixing the liquid with the flour and salt.

Choux Dough

75 g	flour	2½ oz
½ tsp	salt	½ tsp
12.5 cl	water	4 fl oz
60 g	unsalted butter, diced	2 oz
2	eggs	2

Sift the flour and salt together. Put the water and the diced butter into a heavy pan; set the pan over a high heat and bring the water to the boil. When the butter has completely melted, reduce the heat to medium and pour the flour and salt into the water. Stir the mixture with a wooden spoon until thoroughly combined, then beat until the mixture forms a solid mass that comes away cleanly from the sides of the pan. Remove the pan from the heat and cool the mixture for a few minutes.

Break one egg into a bowl and add it to the contents of the pan, beating with a spoon to incorporate the egg thoroughly. Repeat with the other egg. Continue beating until the ingredients are smoothly blended.

For choux balls, place teaspoonfuls of this dough on an ungreased baking sheet, or fill a piping bag with the dough and pipe it on to the sheet in small mounds. The uncooked balls should be about 1 cm (½ inch) in diameter. Bake in a preheated 190°C (375°F or Mark 5) oven for 15 to 20 minutes or until the pastry is puffed and lightly browned. Cool on a rack. Slice the tops off the balls to fill them.

Fish Stock

To make about 2 litres (3½ pints) stock

1 kg	fish trimmings (bones, heads, skin), rinsed and cut into pieces	2 to 2½ lb
About 2 litres	water	About 3½ pints
1 each	carrot and onion, sliced	1 each
2	sticks celery, sliced	2
2	garlic cloves, crushed	2
30 g	parsley stalks	1 oz
1	large sprig thyme	1
3 or 4	fennel branches, fresh or dried	3 or 4
1	bay leaf	1
	salt	
½ litre	dry white wine	16 fl oz
4	peppercorns (optional)	4

Put the fish trimmings into a large pan. Add the water to cover. Bring to a simmer over a low heat. With a large, shallow spoon, skim off the scum that rises to the surface. Skim until no more scum rises, then add the vegetables, herbs and salt. Simmer, partially covered, for 15 minutes. Add the wine, return the liquid to the boil and simmer for 10 to 15 minutes more. If you are using the peppercorns, add them 5 minutes before the end of cooking. Strain through a colander lined with two layers of dampened muslin.

Meat Stock

This stock will set to a firm aspic jelly. It will keep for up to a week if refrigerated and brought to the boil every two days.

To make about 3 litres (5 pints)

1 kg	shin of veal, including meaty veal knuckle	2 to 2½ lb
2	calf's feet, halved lengthwise and blanched	2
1 kg	chicken backs, necks, feet and wing tips	2 to 2½ lb
250 g	pork rinds	8 oz
1	bouquet garni, including leek and celery	1
1	garlic head	1
2	onions, 1 stuck with 2 cloves	2
4	large carrots	4
	salt	

Place a round metal grill in the bottom of a large stock-pot to prevent the ingredients from sticking. Fit all the meat, bones and chicken pieces on to the grill and add water to cover by about 5 cm (2 inches). Bring slowly to the boil and skim off the scum that rises. Keep skimming, occasionally adding a glass of cold water, until no more scum rises. Add the bouquet garni, garlic, onions, carrots and salt, and skim once more as the liquid returns to the boil. Reduce the heat to very low, cover the pot with the lid ajar and simmer for 8 hours.

Ladle the stock into a colander lined with dampened muslin placed over a large bowl. Leave the strained stock to cool completely, then refrigerate. When the stock has set, spoon off the solidified fat.

Vinaigrette

To make about 15 cl (¼ pint) vinaigrette

1 tsp	salt	1 tsp
¼ tsp	freshly ground pepper	¼ tsp
2 tbsp	wine vinegar or lemon juice	2 tbsp
10 cl	olive oil	4 fl oz

Put the salt and pepper in a bowl. Add the vinegar or lemon juice, and stir until the salt is dissolved. Then stir in the oil.

A Wine or Vinegar Court-Bouillon

This court-bouillon is a general-purpose poaching liquid. A couple of stalks of dill or fennel should be included if you are poaching fish or shellfish; otherwise, use thyme.

To make about 2 litres (3½ pints) court-bouillon

½ litre	white or red wine or 20 cl (7 fl oz) wine vinegar	16 fl oz
1 each	large onion and carrot, sliced	1 each
2	garlic cloves, crushed	2
1	stick celery, diced	1
60 g	parsley, including stalks	2 oz
2	sprigs thyme, dill or fennel	2
1	bay leaf	1
1.5 litres	water	2½ pints
	salt	
5 or 6	peppercorns	5 or 6

Put the vegetables, herbs and water into a large pan and season with a pinch of salt. Bring to the boil, then reduce the heat, cover and simmer for 15 minutes. Pour in the wine or vinegar and simmer for a further 15 minutes, adding the peppercorns just before the end of cooking.

White Sauce

This recipe can be used whenever béchamel sauce is required.

To make about 45 cl (¾ pint) sauce

30 g	butter	1 oz
2 tbsp	flour	2 tbsp
60 cl	milk	1 pint
	salt and pepper	
	freshly grated nutmeg (optional)	
	double cream (optional)	

Melt the butter in a heavy saucepan. Stir in the flour and cook, stirring, over a low heat for 2 to 5 minutes. Pour in all the milk, whisking constantly to blend the mixture smoothly. Increase the heat and continue whisking while the sauce comes to the boil. Season with a very little salt. Reduce the heat and simmer for about 40 minutes, stirring every so often to prevent the sauce from sticking to the bottom of the pan. Add pepper and a pinch of nutmeg if desired; taste for seasoning. Whisk again until the sauce is perfectly smooth and add cream if you prefer a richer, whiter sauce.

Thick white sauce for fillings: Make as above, but double the amounts of butter and flour. Cook until it is almost too thick to pour—about 10 minutes—stirring constantly.

Velouté Sauce

If a fish velouté is required, replace the meat stock by fish stock (*recipe, page 165*).

To make about 45 cl (¾ pint) sauce

30 g	butter	1 oz
2 tbsp	flour	2 tbsp
60 cl	meat stock (*page 165*)	1 pint
	salt and pepper	

Melt the butter in a heavy saucepan. Stir in the flour and cook, stirring, over a low heat for 3 to 4 minutes. Pour in all of the stock, whisking constantly to blend the mixture smoothly. Increase the heat and continue whisking while the sauce comes to the boil. Reduce the heat to very low, move the pan so that one side of it is off the heat, and simmer the sauce for about 40 minutes, occasionally skimming off the scum that appears on the cooler side of the liquid. Correct the seasoning before using the sauce.

Chaud-froid sauce: When the velouté sauce is finished, stir in ¼ litre (8 fl oz) of gelatinous meat stock, a spoonful at a time. Cook, stirring, until the sauce reduces again. Gradually stir in 12.5 cl (4 fl oz) of double cream and reduce again. Stir over ice until the sauce cools and starts to thicken.

Tomato Sauce

When fresh ripe tomatoes are not available, use canned Italian plum tomatoes. The sauce can be flavoured with herbs other than those given below; parsley, basil, oregano and marjoram are all suitable substitutes.

To make about 30 cl (½ pint) sauce

750 g	very ripe tomatoes, chopped or one 500 g (1 lb) can tomatoes	1½ lb
1	onion, finely chopped	1
1 tbsp	olive oil	1 tbsp
2	garlic cloves, chopped	2
1 tsp	thyme	1 tsp
1	bay leaf, chopped	1
1 to 2 tsp	sugar (optional)	1 to 2 tsp
	salt and freshly ground pepper	

In a large enamelled or stainless steel saucepan, gently fry the onion in the oil until soft but not brown. Add the other ingredients and simmer for 20 to 30 minutes or until the tomatoes have been reduced to a thick pulp. Sieve the mixture using a wooden pestle or spoon.

Return the sauce to the heat, to warm through. If a thicker consistency is required, simmer the sauce, uncovered, for 20 to 30 minutes, stirring frequently to prevent sticking. Adjust the seasoning, if necessary, just before serving.

Flavoured Butter

To make 300 g (10 oz) spread

250 g	unsalted butter	8 oz

Soften the butter to room temperature, or beat it to make it pliable. Using a wooden spoon or an electric beater, work in the flavouring of your choice. If desired, sieve the mixture. Use immediately, or cover and refrigerate.

Anchovy butter: Soak and fillet 100 g (3½ oz) of salt anchovies. Rinse, drain and pound the fillets, and mix with the softened butter.

Green butter: Blanch 60 g (2 oz) of mixed fresh herbs for 1 minute. Drain the herbs and pound them to a purée. Mix with the softened butter.

Red butter: Skin, seed and purée a large tomato. Cook the purée until all excess liquid has evaporated and about 60 g (2 oz) of purée remains. Cool and mix with the softened butter.

Yellow butter: Dissolve ¼ teaspoon of powdered saffron in 1 tablespoon of hot water. Allow to cool, then mix with the softened butter.

Tapenade butter: Place 60 g (2 oz) of anchovy fillets and 100 g (3½ oz) of stoned black olives in a food processor with 1 tablespoon of capers, 1 teaspoon each of mustard and lemon juice, 1 tablespoon of brandy and ¼ teaspoon of pepper. Process to a smooth purée. Blend in 2 to 3 tablespoons of olive oil. Work half of this mixture into the softened butter; add more *tapenade* for a stronger flavour. Sieve the mixture.

Montpellier butter: Blanch 30 g (1 oz) each of spinach, watercress and parsley, and a few leaves of tarragon. Squeeze them dry. Finely chop two shallots, blanch, then squeeze them dry. Place two anchovy fillets, 1 teaspoon each of capers and chopped gherkins, one garlic clove, 1 teaspoon of coarse salt and a small pinch of cayenne pepper in a mortar; add the shallots and pound. Add the spinach, watercress and herbs, and pound again. Add two hard-boiled egg yolks and pound again. Pound in the softened butter. Sieve the mixture and whisk in 4 tablespoons of olive oil.

Crayfish butter: Shell the tails of 250 g (8 oz) of cooked crayfish, reserving the tail meat for garnish. Purée the heads and bodies of the crayfish in a food processor, or pass them through the coarse disc of a food mill. Pass the purée through a very fine sieve to remove the shell debris. Season the purée with a little lemon juice, salt, pepper and cayenne. Mix the purée with a little lemon juice, salt, pepper and cayenne. Mix the purée with the softened butter.

Blue cheese butter: Pound together equal quantities of softened butter and softened well-flavoured blue cheese such as Roquefort or Stilton. Sieve, then whisk until fluffy.

Red pepper butter: Roast two sweet red peppers in a 220°C (425°F or Mark 7) oven, or grill them, until the skins blister. Cover the peppers with a damp towel until cool enough to handle, then skin and seed them. Sieve the flesh and put it in a sieve lined with damp muslin to drain off excess liquid. Mix the purée with the softened butter and sieve again.

Mayonnaise

To prevent curdling, the egg yolks and oil should be at room temperature and the oil should be added very gradually at first. Mayonnaise will keep for several days in a covered container in a larder or refrigerator. Stir it well before use.

To make about ½ litre (16 fl oz) mayonnaise

3	egg yolks	3
	salt and white pepper	
1 tbsp	wine vinegar or lemon juice	1 tbsp
1 to 2 tsp	Dijon mustard (optional)	1 to 2 tsp
½ litre	olive oil	16 fl oz

Put the egg yolks in a bowl. Season with salt and pepper and whisk until smooth. Add the vinegar or lemon juice, and the mustard if using. Mix thoroughly. Whisking constantly, add the oil, drop by drop to begin with. When the sauce starts to thicken, pour the remaining oil in a thin, steady stream, whisking rhythmically. If the mayonnaise becomes too thick, thin with a little more vinegar or lemon juice.

Red mayonnaise: Whisk in 2 to 3 tablespoons of drained, puréed sweet red pepper or reduced puréed tomato.

Green mayonnaise: Whisk in 1 to 2 tablespoons of juice squeezed out of pounded raw spinach. Or blanch separately one bunch of watercress and 2 tablespoons each of parsley, chives and tarragon. Chop finely and add to the mayonnaise.

Tartare sauce: Stir into the mayonnaise a mixture of finely chopped sour gherkins, capers and *fines herbes;* vary the proportions according to taste.

Steamed Mussels

Moules à la Marinière

This recipe may be adapted to prepare other bivalves.

To make about 1 litre (1¾ pints) shelled mussels and broth

4 litres	live mussels, scrubbed	7 pints
1	onion, chopped, or 2 or 3 shallots, chopped	1
2	garlic cloves, crushed (optional)	2
4 tbsp	finely chopped parsley	4 tbsp
	freshly ground pepper	
60 g	butter (optional)	2 oz
¼ litre	dry white wine	8 fl oz

Place all the ingredients in a saucepan, cover and cook for a few minutes over a high heat, shaking the pan several times to ensure even cooking. When all the mussels have opened, remove the pan from the heat. Discard any unopened mussels. For use in other dishes, shell the mussels and strain the broth over them.

Recipe Index

English recipe titles are listed by categories such as "Anchovies", "Butter", "Dips", "Filling", "Potted Meats and Fish", "Sandwiches" and "Tartlets", and within those categories alphabetically. Foreign recipe titles are listed alphabetically without regard to category.

General Index/Glossary

Included in this index are definitions of many of the culinary terms used in this book: definitions are in italics. The recipes in the Anthology are listed in the Recipe Index on page 168.

Allspice: *the dried berry—used whole or ground—of a member of the myrtle family. Called allspice because it has something of the aroma of clove, cinnamon and nutmeg combined.*
Almond oil, 12
Almonds, 19, 82; roasting and salting, 12-13
Amuse-gueule, 5
Anchovies, 16, 17, 29, 30, 31, 34, 35, 68, 69; in compound butters, 6, 7; filleting, 6; paste, 73; sauce, 74, 75; in tapenade, 6, 29, 37, 38
Apples, 77
Asparagus, 56, 57, 83
Aspic, 65, 76, 77
Bacon, 34, 56, 57; in club sandwiches, 66, 67
Baking, choux puffs, 48; gougère, 48, 49; omelettes, 29, 32, 33; pastry cases, 57; pastry wrappers, 50, 51; phyllo pastries, 60, 61; pies, 53, 54, 55; pizza, 62, 63; sandwiches, 72; see also Pre-baking
Basil, 62
Bay leaves, 24
Béchamel sauce, 72
Beef, chopping, 16-17; in Cornish pasty, 52; raw, 16-17, 29, 34, 35, 68; roast, 34, 76, 78
Beetroot, 76, 78
Biscuit cutters, 52, 54, 65, 74, 79, 80, 82, 83, 84, 86
Blanch: *to plunge food into boiling water for a short period. Done for a number of reasons: to remove strong flavours, such as the excess saltiness of some bacon; to soften vegetables before further cooking; to facilitate the removal of skins or shells. Another meaning is "to whiten"; nuts, 12; vegetable leaves, 7*
Bouquet garni: *bunch of mixed herbs—the classic three being parsley, thyme and bay leaf—used for flavouring sauces and stews;* 24, 26
Brandy, 6, 11, 16, 18, 24, 27
Brazil nuts, 12
Bread, 65, 66, 70, 72, 73, 74, 76; baps, 72; dough, 41, 42-43, 62; French, 65, 73; Italian, 65; potato, 73; pumpernickel, 76; rolls, 65, 72; rye, 21, 65, 66, 70, 71, 73, 76, 78; sandwich, 65, 66, 67, 70, 71, 73, 76, 77, 86; slicing, 66, 67, 70, 71, 73, 76, 80; toasted, 19, 20, 21, 65, 66, 67, 72, 73, 76, 77, 78, 80, 81, 82, 83, 84, 86; wholemeal, 65, 66
Breadcrumbs, 37, 50, 74, 75
Brie, 18
Broccoli, 56
Buckwheat: *a variety of grain much used in Russian cooking.*
Burghul: *cracked wheat that has first been partially cooked and dried.*
Butter, 6, 30, 34, 60, 61, 72, 76; anchovy, 6, 7; clarified, 20, 21, 42, 43; clarifying, 20; compound, 6-7, 29, 30, 36, 65, 70, 80; crayfish, 82; flavouring and colouring, 6-7; herb, 6, 30, 67, 70, 71; Montpellier, 6, 7, 36; parsley, 66, 67; in pastry dough, 44; red pepper, 6, 7, 30, 70, 82; Roquefort, 6, 7; saffron, 6, 81, 83; spinach, 6, 58, 59, 70, 81, 86; watercress, 6; see also Dips, Sandwiches, Spreads
Cabbage, red, 76, 77
Camembert, 18
Canapés, 6, 16, 42, 65; preparation, 80-86
Cantal, 18
Capers, 16, 17, 30, 31; in compound butters, 6, 7; tapenade, 6, 29, 37, 38
Caraway seeds, 18
Carrots, 19
Cashew nuts, 12
Cauliflower, 56
Caviare, 58, 59, 76
Celery, 19, 29, 37, 38; in court-bouillon, 22
Chard, 34
Cheddar, 18, 73, 74
Cheese, 11, 29, 33, 37, 38, 41; in compound butters, 6, 7; dips, 11, 18-19; in fillings for pastries, 60, 61; in fillings for sandwiches, 65, 68, 74-75; grilled, 65, 73; in gougère, 48-49;

leftover, 11, 18, 73; mound, 11, 18-19; for pizza, 62; spreads, 11, 18-19; see also individual cheeses
Chervil, 19, 24, 27, 30, 58, 59
Cheshire cheese, 73
Chicken, 32, 66, 67; in béchamel sauce, 72; liver spread, 11, 20-21; in mayonnaise, 48; wings, 24, 26
Chiles serranos: *pickled chili peppers (q.v.), available in cans from delicatessens and speciality foodstores.*
Chili peppers: *numerous varieties of small, finger-shaped hot peppers, native to tropical America and the West Indies.*
Chives, 19, 27, 34, 80
Choux dough, 41, 44-45; gougère, 48-49; puffs, 48
Clarified butter: *butter from which the water, milk solids and salt have been removed.*
Cleansing, see Degreasing, Skimming
Colander, 25
Cornish pasties, 52-53
Courgettes, 22, 32, 56, 57
Court-bouillon, 22, 78
Crayfish, butter, 82; canapés, 65, 82; dip, 11, 22-23; purée, 22-23, 37, 56; shelling, 22, 23, 46-47; shells as containers, 37
Cream, in custards, 56; in dips, 11, 18, 22; in fillings, 50; in sauces, 24, 26, 27, 84, 85; soured, 78
Cream cheese, 18
Crème fraîche: *slightly ripened, sharp-tasting double cream widely available in France. The nearest equivalent is fresh double cream which can be substituted in most recipes where crème fraîche is required.*
Crispbread, 76, 79
Crisps, 11, 14-15, 18
Croûtons: *small cubes of bread fried in butter and used as garnish.*
Cucumbers, 19, 22, 23, 34; as containers, 29, 37, 38; sandwiches, 66-67
Curd cheese, 18, 50
Custards, 41, 56-57
Dates, 34
Deep frying, crisps, 14, 15; pastries, 46, 52, 55, 60, 61; sandwiches, 65, 74, 75
Deglaze: *to pour a liquid—such as wine, stock, water or cream—into a pan in which meat or vegetables have been fried or roasted, in order to incorporate the particles remaining on the bottom of the pan in a sauce or soup;* 24, 26, 27
Degrease: *to remove fat from cooking juices, stock and broths;* 24, 26, 85
Dill, 34, 37, 76, 77, 78, 79, 82
Dips, 8-9, 11; cheese, 18-19; shellfish, 22-23
Doughs, 41; bread, 41, 42-43; choux, 41, 44-45; flour and water, 41, 46-47, 60-61; kneading, 41, 42, 43, 46, 62; pastry, for frying, 46-47; phyllo, 41, 60-61; pizza, 41, 62-63; rough-puff, 41, 44-45, 52-55; samosa, 41, 42-43, 55; shortcrust, 41, 44-45, 50-51, 52, 56-59
Egg whites, 50, 51; as containers, 29, 30, 31; as garnish, 58, 59, 84, 85; see also Eggs
Egg yolks, 17, 50, 51; in fillings, 29, 30, 31, 72; as garnish, 58, 59; in mayonnaise, 8, 78; in Montpellier butter, 6, 7; in open sandwiches, 76, 79; see also Eggs
Eggs, beaten, 29, 32-33, 60, 74, 75; boiling, 30; in choux paste, 44, 45; in custards, 56-57; glaze, 48, 49, 51, 52, 53, 54, 55; in liver, egg and onion filling, 55; in open sandwiches, 65, 76, 78, 79; quail's, 65, 80, 83; see also Egg whites, Egg yolks
Electric food processor, 16, 18, 20, 21, 56, 73
Emmenthal, 18
Emulsions, 8-9, 29
Fennel, 22
Feta: *a Greek curd cheese made from sheep's milk;* 41
Fillings, 6-9, 29, 34-39, 41; for choux pastries, 41, 48; for flour and water pastries, 46, 60-61; for hard-boiled eggs, 29, 30-31; for omelettes, 29, 32-33; for pastry cases, 41, 56-59; for phyllo pastries, 41, 60-61; for rough-puff pastries, 41, 52-55; for samosa pastries, 55; for sandwiches, 16, 65-79; for shortcrust pastries, 41, 50-59
Fines herbes: *mixture of finely chopped fresh herbs that always incorporates parsley plus one or more other herbs, such as chives, tarragon and chervil.*
Fish, 11, 20, 29, 41, 66, 72, 76, 80, 84; see also Seafood, Shellfish, individual fish.
Food mill, 22
Frying, 46, 47, 67, 74, 78; see also Deep frying, Sautéing

Funnel, for sausage-making, 16, 17; for filling pastry, 53
Game, 20, 72
Garam masala: *mixture of ground spices, usually equal parts of cinnamon, cloves, cardamoms, black cumin seeds, nutmeg and mace, and sometimes also coriander seeds and bay leaves. Available from Indian grocers.*
Garlic, 12, 24, 25, 26, 68; in Montpellier butter, 6, 7; in potato and garlic sauce, 8-9, 37, 39; steeped in olive oil, 7
Ghee: *Indian cooking fat; either clarified butter or made from vegetable fats. It can be bought from Indian grocers and will keep for up to one year if refrigerated.*
Gherkins, 16, 17, 21, 39, 80; in Montpellier butter, 6, 7
Glazing, 11, 24; canapés, 65, 84, 86; chicken wings, 24, 26; monkfish, 24, 27; pastries, 48, 49, 50, 51, 52, 53, 54, 55; prawns, 24, 26; squid, 24, 27; veal, 24-25
Gouda, 73, 74
Gougère, 48-49
Green bacon: *unsmoked bacon; see Bacon*
Green sauce, 8-9
Groundnut oil, 48, 56, 57, 73, 74
Gruyère, 48, 56, 57, 73, 74
Ham, 46, 74; raw, 29, 34, 35; see also Parma ham, Prosciutto
Hazelnuts, 12, 19
Herbs, 8, 16, 22, 25; in butters, 6, 30, 67, 70, 71; on canapés, 65, 80; in cheese dip, 18-19; as colouring, 84; in glaze, 26; in sauces, 8; see also individual herbs
Herring, 76, 78
Julienne: *the French term for vegetables or other food cut into thin strips.*
Kneading, doughs, 41, 42, 43, 46, 62
Lamb, minced, 16; roast, 34; sausage casings, 16
Leeks, 54; in bouquet garni, 24
Leftovers, 11; cheese, 11, 18, 73; meats, 50; vegetables, 50
Lemon, juice, 22, 34, 37, 78; in anchovy sauce, 75; in mayonnaise, 8; in potato and garlic sauce, 8, 9; rind, 24, 25, 54; slices, as garnish, 58, 59, 76, 77; in tapenade, 6
Lettuce, 35; in club sandwiches, 66, 67; in open sandwiches, 77, 78, 79
Liver, 55; loaf, 76, 77
Lumpfish roe, 76, 79
Mace, 21
Mandoline, 14
Marinate, chicken livers, 21; cucumbers, 34; salmon, 79
Mayonnaise, 8-9, 30, 31, 37, 39, 48; herbs, 8, 78, 79; in sandwiches, 66, 67, 76, 77
Meat, 11, 24, 29, 34, 41, 50; in canapés, 80, 84; chopping, 16-17; leftover, 50; in sandwiches, 65, 66; spreads, 20-21
Meat grinder, 16, 17, 22, 23
Melon, 29, 34, 35
Meze, 5
Mincing, crayfish, 22, 23; meat, 16-17
Monkfish, 24, 27
Montpellier butter, 6, 7, 36; see also Herb butter
Mortar and pestle, 6, 7, 8-9, 21, 22, 75
Mozzarella: *soft, kneaded cheese from southern Italy, traditionally made from buffalo's milk, but now also made from cow's milk;* 62, 74
Mushrooms, 50, 52, 56, 58, 62, 80; in fillings, 60, 61, 72; omelettes, 32, 33
Mussels, 29, 34, 37, 39; preparation, 36
Mustard and cress, 66
Nutmeg, 32, 56
Nuts, 11, 18, 50; cooking and salting, 12-13; see also individual nuts
Olive oil, 12, 30, 31, 32, 46, 68, 73; in anchovy sauce, 75; in emulsions, 8-9; in Montpellier butter, 6, 7; in tapenade, 6
Olives, 56, 57, 68, 69, 80, 82; in fillings, 30, 31, 32, 34, 35; in tapenade, 6, 37, 38
Omelettes, 29, 32-33
Onions, 24, 25, 26, 27, 32, 36, 58; in sandwiches, 68, 76, 78, 79
Orange rind, 24
Oregano, 24, 27, 62
Oysters, 34, 54
Paprika, 18, 30
Parboil, asparagus, 56; bacon, 56; to blanch almonds, 12; shallots, 7; spinach, 32, 36
Parma ham, 35, 65
Parmesan, 33, 50, 57, 62, 73
Parsley, 17, 18, 19, 24, 78, 82; butter, 66, 67; in custard, 56,

Recipe Credits

The sources for the recipes in this volume are shown below. Page references in brackets indicate where the recipes appear in the Anthology.

Académie des Gastronomes, Académie Culinaire de France, La Haute Cuisine Française. © Jean-Pierre Delarge, le Bélier Prisme, 1975. Published by Jean-Pierre Delarge, Éditeur, Paris. Translated by permission of Éditions Universitaires, Jean-Pierre Delarge, Éditeur (*pages 102, 146*).
Acton, Eliza, Modern Cookery. Published by Longman, Green, Longman, and Roberts, London 1860 (*pages 99, 100, 101 and 102*).
Adams, Charlotte, The Four Seasons Cookbook. Copyright 1971 in all countries of the International Copyright Union by the Ridge Press, Inc. By permission of The Ridge Press, Inc., and Crown Publishers, Inc., New York (*page 111*).
Allen, Ida Bailey, Best Loved Recipes of the American People. Copyright © 1973 by Ruth Allen Castelli. Published by Doubleday & Company, Inc. New York. By permission of Doubleday & Company (*page 96*).
American Heritage, The Editors of, The American Heritage Cookbook. Copyright © 1964 by American Heritage Publishing Co., Inc. Published by American Heritage Publishing Co.,

Inc. New York. By permission of American Heritage Publishing Co., Inc. (*page 149*).
Amicale des Cuisiniers et Pâtissiers Auvergnats de Paris, Cuisine d'Auvergne. (Cuisines du Terroir). © 1979 Denoël-Paris. Published by Éditions Denoël, Paris. Translated by permission of Éditions Denoël (*page 132*).
Andrade, Margarette de, Brazilian Cookery. Copyright in Japan, 1965, by the Charles E. Tuttle Company, Inc. Published by the Charles E. Tuttle Company, Inc., Tokyo. By permission of the Charles E. Tuttle Company, Inc. (*pages 90, 106, 133*).
Andreis, Florence de, La Cuisine Provençale d'Aujourd'Hui. © Rivages 1980. Published by Éditions Rivages, Marseille. Translated by permission of Éditions Rivages (*pages 94, 102, 106 and 120*).
Androuet, Pierre, La Cuisine au Fromage. ©1978, Éditions Stock, Paris. Published by Éditions Stock, Paris. Translated by permission of Éditions Stock (*page 154*).
Aoun, Fayez, 280 Recettes de Cuisine Familiale Libanaise. © 1980, Jacques Grancher, Éditeur. Published by Jacques Grancher, Éditeur, Paris. Translated by permission of Jacques Grancher, Éditeur (*pages 89, 91 and 134*).
Asselin, M.D., E. Donald, Scandinavian Cookbook. Copyright in Japan, 1970, by the Charles E. Tuttle Company, Inc. Published by the Charles E. Tuttle Company, Inc., Tokyo. By permission of the Charles E. Tuttle Company Inc., (*page 163*).
Bautte, A., Modern French and English Cookery (for Private

Families, Hotels, Restaurants, and Clubs). Published by Malcolmson and Co. Limited, London, 1901 (*page 158*).
Beard, James, Hors d'Oeuvre and Canapés. Copyright © 1940, 1963 by James Beard. Published by M. Barrows & Company Incorporated, New York. By permission of John Schaffner Associated, Inc., Literary Agents, New York (*pages 99, 100*).
Beard, James, James Beard's New Fish Cookery. Copyright 1954, © 1976 by James A. Beard. Published by Little, Brown and Company, Boston. By permission of Little, Brown and Company (*page 158*).
Beard, James, The James Beard Cookbook. © Copyright, 1959, by James Beard. Published by Dell Publishing Co., Inc., New York. By permission of John Schaffner Associates, Inc., Literary Agents, New York (*page 148*).
Beeton, Mrs. Isabella, Mrs. Beeton's Hors d'Oeuvre and Savouries. © Ward Lock & Co., Limited. Published by Ward, Lock & Co., Limited, London. By permission of Ward, Lock & Co., Limited (*page 156*).
Benell, Julie, Kitchen Magic. Copyright © 1973 by Julie Benell. Published by Shoal Creek Publishers, Inc., Austin, Texas. By permission of the author (*page 115*).
Berjane, J., French Dishes for English Tables. Copyright Frederick Warne & Co. Ltd., London 1931. Published by Frederick Warne & Co. Ltd., London. By permission of Frederick Warne (Publishers) Ltd. (*page 114*).

Bertholle, Louisette, *La Cuisine des Saisons.* © Opera Mundi, Paris, 1980. Jointly published by Éditions Albin Michel and Opera Mundi, Paris. Translated by permission of Éditions Albin Michel (*page 139*).

Bisson, Marie, *La Cuisine Normande.* © Solar, 1978. Published by Solar, Paris. Translated by permission of Solar (*page 140*).

Boni, Ada, *The Talisman Italian Cook Book.* Translated and augmented by Matilde La Rosa. Copyright 1950, 1977 by Crown Publishers, Inc. Published by Crown Publishers, Inc., New York. By permission of Crown Publishers, Inc. (*page 151*).

Borghese, Anita, *The Great Sandwich Book.* Copyright © 1978 by Anita Borghese. Published by Rawson Associates Publishers, Inc., New York. By permission of Rawson, Wade Publishers, Inc. New York (*page 147*).

Bouché, Daniel, *Invitation à la Cuisine Buissonnière.* © Atelier Marcel Jullian, 1979. Published by Atelier Marcel Jullian. Translated by permission of Librairie Hachette, Paris (*page 96*).

Bourbon, Louis Auguste de, *Le Cuisinier Gascon.* Published by Éditions Daniel Morcrette, Luzarches, 1976. Translated by permission of Éditions Daniel Morcrette (*page 155*).

Bozzi, Ottorina Perna, *Vecchia Milano in Cucina.* © 1975 by Aldo Martello-Giunti Editore S.p.A. Published by Aldo Martello-Giunti Editore S.p.A., Florence. Translated by permission of Giunti Publishing Group, Florence (*pages 99, 104*).

Bringer, Rodolphe, *Les Bons Vieux Plats du Tricastin.* Published by Les Amis du Tricastin. Reprinted by Éditions Daniel Morcrette, Luzarches. Translated by permission of Éditions Daniel Morcrette (*page 139*).

Brobeck, Florence, *The Lunch Box and Every Kind of Sandwich.* Copyright 1946 by Florence Brobeck. Published by M. Barrows & Company, Inc., Publishers, New York, 1970. By permission of William Morrow and Company, Inc., New York (*pages 91, 141*).

Brobeck, Florence and Kjellberg, Monika B., *Smörgåsbord and Scandinavian Cookery.* Copyright 1948, by Little, Brown and Company. Published by Grosset & Dunlap, Publishers, New York, 1970 (*page 163*).

Brown, Cora, Rose and Bob, *10,000 Snacks.* Copyright, 1937, by Garden City Publishing Co., Inc. Published by Halcyon House, 1948. By permission of Laura P. Brown, Massachusetts (*page 145*).

Brownstone, Cecily, *Cecily Brownstone's Associated Press Cook Book.* © Copyright 1972 by The Associated Press. Published by David McKay Company, Inc., New York. By permission of David McKay Company, Inc. (*page 135*).

Bugialli, Giuliano, *The Fine Art of Italian Cooking.* Copyright © 1977 by Giuliano Bugialli. Published by Times Books, a Division of Quadrangle/The New York Times Book Co., Inc., New York. By permission of Times Books, a Division of Quadrangle/The New York Times Book Co., Inc. (*page 137*).

Buonassisi, Vincenzo, *La Cucina di Falstaff.* © 1964 Edizioni Milano Nuova S.p.A. Published by Edizioni Milano Nuova, Milan. Translated by permission of Ferro Edizioni s.a.s., Milan (*pages 155, 161*).

Burros, Marian Fox and Levine, Lois, *The Elegant but Easy Cookbook.* Copyright © 1960, 1963, 1967 by Marian F. Burros and Lois L. Levine. Published by Collier Books, a Division of Macmillan Publishing Co., Inc., New York. By permission of Macmillan Publishing Co., Inc. (*page 111*).

Calera, Ana Maria, *Cocina Castellana.* © Ana Maria Calera, 1974. Published by Editorial Bruguera, S.A., Barcelona. Translated by permission of Editorial Bruguera S.A. (*pages 109, 136*).

Carrier, Robert, *Robert Carrier's Entertaining.* Copyright © 1978, 1977, by Robert Carrier. Published by A & W Publishers, Inc., New York. By permission of Sidgwick & Jackson, London (*pages 93, 116*).

Cass, Elizabeth, *Spanish Cooking.* Copyright © Elizabeth Cass 1957. First published by André Deutsch Ltd., London 1957. Also published by Mayflower Books Ltd., St. Albans, Herts., 1970. By permission of André Deutsch Ltd. (*page 155*).

Castignac, Huguette, *La Cuisine Occitane.* © Solar, 1973. Published by Solar, Paris. Translated by permission of Solar (*page 132*).

Ceccaldi, Marie, *Cuisine de Corse. (Cuisines du Terroir).* © 1980, by Éditions Denoël, Paris. Published by Éditions Denoël, Paris. Translated by permission of Éditions Denoël (*page 110*).

Chamberlain, Narcissa, *French Menus for Parties.* Copyright © 1968 by Hastings House, Publishers, Inc. Published by Hastings House, Publishers, New York. By permission of Hastings House, Publishers, Inc. (*page 119*).

Chamberlain, Narcissa G. and Chamberlain, Narcisse, *The Flavor of Italy.* Copyright © 1965 by Hastings House, Publishers, Inc. Published by Hastings House, Publishers, New York. By permission of Hastings House, Publishers, Inc. (*page 150*).

Clancy, John and Field, Frances, *Clancy's Oven Cookery.* Copyright © 1976 by John Clancy and Frances Field. Published by Delacorte Press/Eleanor Friede, New York. By permission of Delacorte Press/Eleanor Friede (*page 131*).

Correnti, Pino, *Il Libro d'Oro della Cucina e dei Vini di Sicilia.* Copyright © 1976 Ugo Mursia Editore, Milano. Published by Ugo Mursia Editore S.p.A., Milan. Translated by permission of Ugo Mursia Editore S.p.A. (*page 121*).

Corsi, Guglielma, *Un Secolo di Cucina Umbra.* Published by Tipografia Porziuncola, Assisi, 1968. Translated by permission of Tipografia Porziuncola (*page 136*).

Cowles, Florence. A. (Editor), *1001 Sandwiches.* Copyright, 1928, 1936, by Florence A. Cowles. Published by Little, Brown and Company, Boston, 1936. By permission of Hartford National Bank & Trust Co., for the Estate of Florence A. Cowles, Connecticut (*pages 100, 141*).

Cuisine Lyonnaise, La. Published by Éditions Gutenberg, Lyon 1947 (*pages 105, 152 and 157*).

Dannenbaum, Julie, *Julie Dannenbaum's Creative Cooking School.* Copyright © 1971 by Julie Dannenbaum. Published by The McCall Publishing Company, New York. By permission of John Schaffner Associates, Inc., Literary Agents, New York (*pages 93, 117*).

Darden, Norma Jean and Carole, *Spoonbread and Strawberry Wine.* Copyright © 1978 by Norma Jean Darden and Carole Darden. Published by Anchor Press/Doubleday, New York. By permission of Doubleday & Company, Inc. (*page 113*).

David, Elizabeth, *A Book of Mediterranean Food.* Published in 1980 under the title "Elizabeth David Classics", comprising "A Book of Mediterranean Food", "French Country Cooking" and "Summer Cooking", by Jill Norman Ltd., London. © Elizabeth David, 1950, 1951, 1955, 1958, 1965, 1980. By permission of Jill Norman Ltd. (*page 147*).

David, Elizabeth, *English Potted Meats and Fish Pastes.* Copyright Elizabeth David 1968. Published in London by the author, 1968. By permission of the author (*page 98*).

David, Elizabeth, *French Provincial Cooking.* Copyright © Elizabeth David, 1960, 1962, 1967, 1969. Published by Penguin Books Ltd., in association with Michael Joseph, London. By permission of the author (*page 138*).

David, Elizabeth, *Spices, Salt and Aromatics in the English Kitchen.* Copyright © Elizabeth David, 1970. Published by Penguin Books Ltd., London. By permission of Penguin Books Ltd. (*page 105*).

Davidson, Alan, *Fish and Fish Dishes of Laos.* © Alan Davidson 1975. Published by Charles E. Tuttle Co., Inc., Tokyo, 1975. By permission of the author (*page 103*).

Davidson, Alan, *Seafood of South-East Asia.* © Alan Davidson 1976. First published 1977 by Federal Publications (S) Pte Ltd., Singapore. Published 1978 by Macmillan London Limited, London and Basingstoke. By permission of the author (*pages 101, 107*).

Drysdale, Julia (Editor), *The Game Cookery Book.* © 1975 The Game Conservancy. Published by William Collins Sons and Company Limited, Glasgow and London. By permission of Collins Publishers, London (*page 98*).

Eekhof-Stork, Nancy, *The Great International Cheese Board.* Edited by Adrian Bailey. © 1979 Paddington Press Ltd. Published by Paddington Press Ltd., New York and London. Based on selections from the "Spectrum Kaasatlas". © 1976, 1979 by Het Spectrum B.V., Utrecht. By permission of Het Spectrum B.V. (*page 132*).

Ellison, J. Audrey (Translator and Editor), *The Great Scandinavian Cook Book.* Published by George Allen & Unwin (Publishers) Ltd., London. © J. Audrey Ellison, 1966. Newly revised original Swedish edition "Moderna Stora Kokboken" (Editor-in-Chief: Karin Fredrikson) published by Wezäta Förlag, Göteborg. © Wezäta Förlag 1974. By permission of George Allen & Unwin (Publishers) Ltd. (*pages 102, 163*).

Exner, Eva, *Brot zu Jeder Zeit.* Copyright © Kochbuchverlag Heimeran Munich 1975. Published by Kochbuchverlag Heimeran. Translated by permission of BLV Verlagsgesellschaft mbH, Munich (*pages 148, 155*).

Feslikenian, Franca, *Cucina e Vini della Liguria.* © Copyright 1972 U. Mursia & C. Published by U. Mursia & C., Milan. Translated by permission of Ugo Mursia Editore (*page 137*).

Frere, Catherine Frances (Editor), *The Cookery Book of Lady Clark of Tillypronie.* Published by Constable & Company Ltd., London 1909 (*page 152*).

Fuller, Eva Greene, *The Up-To-Date Sandwich Book.* Copyright A. C. McClurg & Co., 1909-1927. Published by A. C. McClurg & Co., Chicago 1929 (*pages 142, 143 and 145*).

Ghedini, Francesco, *Northern Italian Cooking.* Copyright © 1973 by Paola Schiavina Ghedini, Gabriella Martelli Ghedini, and Anita Ghedini Gardini. Published by Hawthorn Books, Inc., New York. By permission of Hawthorn Properties (Elsevier-Dutton Publishing Co., Inc.) New York (*page 153*).

Gill, Janice Murray, *Nova Scotia Down-Home Cooking.* Copyright © Janice Murray Gill, 1978. Published by McGraw-Hill Ryerson Limited, Scarborough, Ontario. By permission of McGraw-Hill Ryerson Limited (*page 159*).

Gilly, Antoine and Scott, Jack Denton, *Antoine Gilly's Feas of France.* Copyright © 1971 by Antoine Gilly and Jack Scott Published by Thomas Y. Crowell Company, New York. By permission of Raines & Raines, authors' representatives, New York (*page 156*).

Girl Guides' Association, Fiji (Editors), The, *South Sea Islands Recipes.* Published by The Girl Guides' Association, Fiji 1958. By permission of Fiji Girl Guides' Association (*page 134*).

Gouy, Louis P. de, *The Gold Cook Book.* Copyright © 1947 1948, 1964 by Louis P. de Gouy. Published by Chilton Book Company, Radnor, Pennsylvania. By permission of Chilton Book Company (*page 131*).

Great Cooks' Guide to Omelets from Around the World The. Copyright © 1977, Laura Sloate. Published by Bearc Glaser Wolf Ltd. By permission of Carol Cutler (*page 118*).

Grigson, Jane, *Good Things.* Copyright © Jane Grigsor 1971. First published by Michael Joseph 1971. Published b Penguin Books Ltd., 1973. By permission of David Higham Associates Ltd., for the author (*page 123*).

Grigson, Jane, *Jane Grigson's Vegetable Book.* © 1978 by Jane Grigson. Published by Michael Joseph Limited, London By permission of David Higham Associates Ltd., for the autho (*page 139*).

Grigson, Jane, *The Mushroom Feast.* © 1975 by Jane Grigson. Published by Michael Joseph, London. By permission o David Higham Associates Ltd., for the author (*page 91*).

Grossouvre, Renée de, *Les Recettes d'une Grand'Mère e Ses Conseils.* © Hachette 1978. Published by Librairie Hachette, Paris. Translated by permission of Librairie Hachett (*page 98*).

Guérard, Michel, *Michel Guérard's Cuisine Gourmande.* © Macmillan London Ltd., 1977, 1978. Published by Macmilla London Ltd. Originally published in French as "La Cuisin Gourmande", © Éditions Robert Laffont S.A., Paris, 1978. B permission of Macmillan, London and Basingstoke (*pag 162*).

Harrington, Geri, *The Salad Book.* Copyright © 1977 by Ge Harrington. Published by Atheneum Publishers, Inc., Nev York 1977. By permission of Atheneum Publishers, Inc. (*pag 96*).

Hawcock, Emory, *Salads and Sandwiches.* Copyright, 192 by Harper & Brothers. Copyright renewed 1956 by Emor Hawcock. Published by Harper & Brothers Publishers, Nev York and London, 1928. By permission of Harper & Row Publishers, Inc. (*pages 143, 160*).

Hawliczkowa, Helena, *Kuchnia Polska.* Copyright by Helen Hawliczkowa. Published by Panstwowe Wydawnictwo Ekonomiczne, Warsaw, 1979. Translated by permission c Agencja Autorska, Warsaw, for the author (*page 162*).

Hazelton, Nika, *The Picnic Book.* Copyright © 1969 by Nik Hazelton. Published by Atheneum, New York 1969. By permission of Curtis Brown, Ltd., New York (*page 118*).

Heath, Ambrose, *Good Savouries.* Copyright Ambros Heath 1934. Published by Faber and Faber Limited, London By permission of Faber and Faber Limited (*page 158*).

Hellermann, Dorothee v., *Das Kochbuch aus Hamburg.* Copyright 1975 by Verlagsteam Wolfgang Hölker. Publishe by Verlag Wolfgang Hölker, Münster. Translated by permis

sion of Verlag Wolfgang Hölker (*page 159*).
Herisko, Clarence, *Drinks and Snacks for all Occasions.* Copyright 1960 by Imperial Publishing Co. Published by Imperial Books Publishing Co., New York (*page 111*).
Hewitt, Jean, *The New York Times Large Type Cookbook.* © Copyright 1968 by The New York Times Company. Published by Golden Press, New York, a division of Western Publishing Company, Inc. By permission of Times Books, a division of Quadrangle/The New York Times Book Co., Inc., New York (*page 119*).
Hill, Janet McKenzie, *Salads, Sandwiches and Chafing-Dish Dainties.* Copyright 1899, 1903, 1914 by Janet M. Hill. Published by Little, Brown and Company, Boston, 1925 (*page 141*).
Hirst, Irene (Editor), *The Beeton Homebooks: Hors d'Oeuvres and Salads (Volume 6).* © Ward Lock & Co. Limited 1964. Published by Ward Lock & Co. Limited, London. By permission of Ward Lock Limited (*page 156*).
Horváth, Ilona, *Szakácskönyv.* © The legal successors of Ilona Horváth, 1980. Originally published in Hungarian by Magyar Nők Országos Tanácsa, Kossuth, Budapest, 1979. Translated by permission of Artisjus, Agence Littéraire Théâtrale et de Musique, Budapest, on behalf of the legal successors of Ilona Horváth (*pages 97, 100*).
Huguenin, Pierre, *Les Meilleures Recettes de Ma Pauvre Mère.* Published by Comité de la Foire Gastronomique de Dijon, Dijon, 1936. Translated by permission of Maître Patrice Huguenin, heir to the author, Beaune (*pages 136, 138*).
Hush, Joanne and Wong, Peter, *The Chinese Menu Cookbook.* Copyright © 1976 by Joanne Hush and Peter Wong. Published by Holt, Rinehart and Winston, New York 1976. By permission of Holt, Rinehart and Winston and The Lescher Agency, authors' representatives, New York (*page 130*).
Hutchins, Sheila, *English Recipes and Others from Scotland, Wales and Ireland.* © 1967 by Sheila Hutchins. First published by Methuen & Co., Ltd., 1967. Published by The Cookery Book Club. By permission of the author (*page 153*).
Jack, Florence B., *Cookery for Every Household.* Published by Thomas Nelson & Sons Limited, London and Edinburgh, 1934. By permission of Thomas Nelson & Sons Limited, Walton-on-Thames, Surrey (*page 163*).
Jekyll, D.B.E., Lady, *Kitchen Essays.* © Lady Freyberg. Published by Collins Publishers, London, 1969. By permission of Collins Publishers (*page 144*).
Jen, Eva Lee, *Chinese Cooking in the American Kitchen.* Copyright © 1978 by Kodansha International Ltd. Published by Kodansha International Ltd., Tokyo. By permission of Kodansha International Ltd. (*pages 108, 114*).
Jewry, Mary (Editor), *Warne's Model Cookery.* © Copyright F. Warne (Publishers) Limited, London. Published by Frederick Warne and Company, London 1869. By permission of Frederick Warne (Publishers) Ltd. (*page 157*).
Junior League of the City of New York, The, *New York Entertains.* Copyright © 1974 by The Junior League of the City of New York Inc. Published by Doubleday & Company, Inc., New York. By permission of Doubleday & Company, Inc. (*page 152*).
Käkönen, Ulla, *Natural Cooking the Finnish Way.* Copyright © 1974 by Ulla Käkönen. Published by Quadrangle/The New York Times Book Company, New York. By permission of Quadrangle/The New York Times Book Company, Inc. (*page 140*).
Kamman, Madeleine, *The Making of a Cook.* Copyright © 1971 by Madeleine Kamman. By permission of Atheneum Publishers, Inc. (*page 133*).
Kamman, Madeleine M., *When French Women Cook.* Copyright © 1976 by Madeleine M. Kamman. Published by Atheneum Publishers, Inc., New York. By permission of Atheneum Publishers, Inc. (*pages 96, 159*).
Kennedy, Diana, *Recipes from the Regional Cooks of Mexico.* Copyright © 1978 by Diana Kennedy. Published by Harper & Row, Publishers, Inc., New York. By permission of Harper & Row, Publishers, Inc. (*page 88*).
Kenney-Herbert, A., (Wyvern), *Common-Sense Cookery for English Households.* Second Edition published by Edward Arnold, London, 1894 (*page 93*).
Kraus, Barbara (Editor), *The Cookbook of the United Nations.* Copyright © 1964 by United Nations Association of the United States of America Inc., New York 11, N.Y. Copyright © 1967 new material to this edition by Barbara Kraus. Published by The Cookery Book Club, London 1969. By permission of John R. Fernbach, Attorney for the author's estate, New York (*page 127*).
Kruger, Arne and Wolter, Annette, *Kochen Heute.* © by Grafe und Unzer GmbH, München. Published by Grafe und Unzer GmbH, Munich. Translated by permission of Grafe und Unzer GmbH (*page 144*).
Lang, George, *The Cuisine of Hungary.* Copyright © 1971 by George Lang. Published by Atheneum Publishers, Inc., New York. By permission of Atheneum Publishers, Inc. (*page 94*).
Langseth-Christensen, Lillian, *Cold Foods for Summer and Winter.* Copyright © 1974 by Lillian Langseth-Christensen. Published by Doubleday & Company, Inc., New York, 1974. By permission of Doubleday & Company, Inc. (*pages 114, 115 and 120*).
Levy, Faye, *La Varenne Tour Book.* © 1979 La Varenne U.S.A., Inc. Published by Peanut Butter Publishing, Seattle, Washington. By permission of Latoque International Ltd., Pennsylvania (*page 101*).
Leyel, Mrs. C. F., *Savoury Cold Meals.* Published by George Routledge & Sons Ltd., London. By permission of Routledge & Kegan Paul Ltd., London (*page 142*).
Leyel, Mrs. C. F., and Hartley, Miss Olga, *The Gentle Art of Cookery.* Copyright The Executors of the Estate of Mrs. C. F. Leyel 1925. Published by Chatto & Windus Ltd., London, 1925. By permission of Chatto & Windus Ltd. (*page 162*).
Lin, Florence, *Florence Lin's Chinese Regional Cookbook.* Copyright © 1975 by Florence Lin. Published by Hawthorn Books, Inc., Publishers, New York. By permission of John Schaffner Associates, Inc., Literary Agents, New York (*pages 125, 140*).
London, Anne and Bishov, Bertha Kahn (Editors), *The Complete American-Jewish Cookbook.* Copyright 1952 by The Homemakers Research Institute. Revised edition copyright © 1971 by The Homemakers Research Institute. Published by The World Publishing Company, Cleveland and New York. By permission of W. H. Allen & Co. Ltd., London (*page 130*).
Ma, Nancy Chih, *Cook Chinese.* Copyright © 1964 by Kodansha International Ltd. Published by Kodansha International Ltd., Publishers, Tokyo. By permission of Kodansha International Ltd. (*page 129*).
MacMillan, Diane, *The Portable Feast.* Copyright 1973 by Diane MacMillan. Published by 101 Productions, San Francisco. By permission of 101 Productions (*page 103*).
Mallos, Tess, *Greek Cookbook.* © Copyright Tess Mallos 1976. First published by Paul Hamlyn Pty Limited, Dee Why West, N.S.W., Australia. Published by The Hamlyn Publishing Group Limited, London. By permission of Lansdowne Press, Dee Why and the author (*page 89*).
Marcus, Melanie, *Cooking with a Harvard Accent.* Copyright © 1979 by Melanie Marcus. Published by Houghton Mifflin Company, Boston. By permission of Houghton Mifflin Company (*page 104*).
Maria, Jack Santa, *Indian Vegetarian Cookery.* © Jack Santa Maria 1973. Published by Rider and Company, London. By permission of Hutchinson Publishing Group Ltd., London (*page 128*).
Marty, Albin, *Fourmiguetto: Souvenirs, Contes et Recettes du Languedoc.* Published by Éditions CREER, F63340 Nonette, 1978. Translated by permission of Éditions CREER (*page 95*).
Mascarelli, Benoit, *La Table en Provence & sur la Côte d'Azur.* Copyright 1946, by Jacques Haumont, Paris. Published by Jacques Haumont, 1947 (*page 146*).
McIntyre, Nancy Fair, *Cooking in Crust.* © Copyright 1974 by Gala Books. Published by Gala Books, Laguna Beach, California. By permission of Gala Books and the author (*pages 122, 125, 132 and 149*).
McKendry, Maxime, *Seven Centuries of English Cooking.* Copyright © by Maxime McKendry 1973. Published by Weidenfeld and Nicolson, London. By permission of George Weidenfeld & Nicolson Ltd. (*page 148*).
70 Médecins de France, *Le Trésor de la Cuisine du Bassin Méditerranéen.* Published by Les Laboratoires du Dr. Zizine (*page 103*).
Meighn, Moira, *Simplified Cooking and Invalid Diet.* Published by Faber and Faber Limited, London 1939. By permission of Faber and Faber Limited (*page 100*).
Meyers, Perla, *The Peasant Kitchen.* Copyright © 1975 by Perla Meyers. Published by Harper & Row, Publishers, Inc., New York. By permission of McIntosh & Otis, Inc., New York and the author (*pages 118, 151*).
Muffoletto, Anna, *The Art of Sicilian Cooking.* Copyright © 1971 by Anna Muffoletto. Published by Doubleday & Company, Inc., New York. By permission of Doubleday & Company, Inc. (*page 154*).
Nilson, Bee (Editor), *The WI Diamond Jubilee Cookbook.* © A. R. Nilson and National Federation of Women's Institutes 1975. Published by William Heinemann Ltd., London. By permission of William Heinemann Ltd. (*page 94*).
Noël, Danielle and Lemonnier, Michel, *Recettes de Sandwichs.* Published by Centre d'Information des Farines et du Pain, Paris. Translated by permission of Centre d'Information des Farines et du Pain (*pages 143, 161*).
Norberg, Inga (Editor), *Good Food from Sweden.* Published by Chatto & Windus, London 1935. By permission of Curtis Brown Ltd., London, agents for the editor (*page 162*).
Ojakangas, Beatrice A., *The Finnish Cookbook.* © 1964 by Beatrice A. Ojakangas. Published by Crown Publishers, Inc., New York. By permission of Crown Publishers, Inc. (*page 97*).
Ortega, Simone, *Mil Ochenta Recetas de Cocina.* © Simone K. de Ortega, 1972. © Alianza Editorial, S.A., Madrid, 1972. Published by Alianza Editorial, S.A. Translated by permission of Alianza Editorial, S.A. (*page 112*).
Owen, Sri, *Indonesian Food and Cookery.* © Sri Owen, 1976, 1980. Published by Prospect Books, London and Washington D.C., 1980. By permission of Prospect Books and the author (*pages 105, 109 and 115*).
Parenti, Giovanni Righi, *La Cucina degli Etruschi.* Copyright © Sugar Editore & C., Milano. Published by Sugar Editore & C. Translated by permission of SugarCo Edizioni (*pages 91, 112 and 161*).
Pascoe, Ann, *Cornish Recipes Old and New.* Copyright © by Tor Mark Press. Published by Tor Mark Press, Truro, Cornwall. By permission of Tor Mark Press (*page 122*).
Pearl, Anita May, *Completely Cheese: The Cheeselover's Companion.* Co-authors: Constance Cuttle and Barbara B. Deskins. Edited by David Kolatch. Copyright © 1978 by Jonathan David Publishers, Inc. Published by Warner Books by arrangement with Jonathan David Publishers, Inc., New York. By permission of Jonathan David Publishers, Inc. (*page 94*).
Pellaprat, Henri Paul, *The Great Book of French Cuisine.* Copyright © 1966, 1971 by René Kramer, Publisher, Castagnola/Lugano, Switzerland. Published in U.K. by William Collins & Co. Ltd., London and in U.S.A. by Thomas Y. Crowell Company, New York. First published as "Modern French Culinary Art", 1966. Originally published in French as "L'Art Culinaire Moderne". By permission of William Collins & Co. Ltd. (*page 92*).
Petersen, Bengt, *Delicious Fish Dishes.* © Bengt Petersen/Wezäta Förlag 1976. Published by Wezäta Förlag, Göteborg, Sweden. By permission of Wezäta Förlag (*page 157*).
Petit, A., *La Gastronomie en Russie.* Published by the author and Émile Mellier, Libraire-Éditeur, Paris 1860 (*page 162*).
Petits Propos Culinaires VIII, July 1981. © Prospect Books 1981. Published by Prospect Books, London and Washington D.C. By permission of the publisher (*page 117*).
Pilar, Maria, *Tu Cocina.* © Maria Pilar Jerez, 1976. Published by Ediciones 29, Barcelona. Translated by permission of Ediciones 29 (*page 124*).
Poulson, Joan, *Old Lancashire Recipes.* © Joan Poulson 1973. Published by Hendon Publishing Co. Ltd., Hendon Mill, Nelson, Lancashire. By permission of Hendon Publishing Co. Ltd., (*page 123*).
Raffald, Elizabeth, *The Experienced English Housekeeper.* A facsimile of the 1782 edition. Published by Paul Minet Reprints, Bucks. By permission of Paul Minet Reprints, London (*page 152*).
Ranhofer, Charles, *The Epicurean.* Originally published by R. Ranhofer, New York 1893. Republished by Dover Publications, Inc., New York 1971 (*pages 111, 112*).
Rao, Nguyen Ngoc, *La Cuisine Chinoise à l'Usage des Français.* © 1980, by Éditions Denoël, Paris. Published by Éditions Denoël, Paris. Translated by permission of Éditions Denoël (*pages 107, 108, 113 and 116*).
Rhode, Irma, *Cool Entertaining.* Copyright © 1976 by Irma Rhode. Published by Atheneum Publishers, Inc., New York. By permission of John Schaffner Associates, Inc., Literary Agents, New York (*page 142*).

Robbins, Ann Roe, *Treadway Inns Cook Book.* Copyright © 1958 by Ann Roe Robbins. Published by Little, Brown & Company, Boston. By permission of Little, Brown & Company (*page 120*).

Robertson, Alden. *The No Baloney Sandwich Book.* Copyright © 1978 by Alden Robertson. Published by Doubleday & Company, Inc., New York. By permission of Doubleday & Company, Inc. (*page 145*).

Roden, Claudia, *A Book of Middle Eastern Food.* Copyright © Claudia Roden, 1968. Published by Penguin Books, London, 1970. By permission of the author, London (*pages 90, 110*).

Rosen, Ruth Chier, *Just Betwen Us. . . .* Copyright 1956 Richards Rosen Associates, Inc., New York. Published by Richards Rosen Associates, Inc. By permission of Richards Rosen Press Inc., New York (*page 144*).

Rossi Callizo, Gloria, *Las Mejores Tapas, Cenas Frías y Platos Combinados.* © Editorial De Vecchi S.A., Barcelona, 1978. Published by Editorial De Vecchi S.A. Translated by permission of Editorial De Vecchi S.A. (*pages 108, 109, 113 and 157*).

Rywell, Martin (Editor), *Wild Game Wild Fowl Cook Book.* Copyright 1952, 1955, 1960, 1963, 1964, 1965 by Martin Rywell. Published by Pioneer Press, Harriman, Tennessee (*page 161*).

Sahni, Julie, *Classic Indian Cooking.* Copyright © 1980 by Julie Sahni. Published by William Morrow and Company, Inc., New York. By permission of Jill Norman and Hobhouse Ltd., London (*pages 110, 128*).

Schryver, Alice and Wallace, Francille, *The Complete Hors d'Oeuvres Cookbook.* Copyright © 1957, 1958 by Alice Schryver and Francille Wallace. Published by Coward McCann, Inc., New York. By permission of Curtis Brown Ltd., New York (*page 121*).

Schultz, Sigrid (Editor), *Overseas Press Club Cookbook.* Copyright © 1962 by Overseas Press Club of America, Inc. Published by Doubleday & Company, Inc., New York. By permission of Doubleday & Company, Inc. (*pages 106, 160*).

Shaw, Nancy, *Food for the Greedy.* Published by Cobden-Sanderson, London 1936 (*pages 146, 158*).

Shircliffe, Arnold, *The Edgewater Sandwich and Hors d'Oeuvres Book.* First published in 1930 by the Hotel Monthly Press under the title "The Edgewater Sandwich Book." Published by Dover Publications Inc., New York 1975. By permission of Dover Publications Inc. (*pages 92, 149 and 150*).

Shulman, Martha Rose, *The Vegetarian Feast.* Copyright © 1979 by Martha Rose Shulman. Published by Harper & Row, Publishers Inc., New York. By permission of Harper & Row, Publishers, Inc. (*pages 90, 95*).

Smith, Mrs. Louisa E., *Bonnes Bouches and Relishable Dishes for Breakfast and Luncheon.* © Ward Lock Ltd. Published by Ward, Lock, Bowden and Co., London 1892. By permission of Ward, Lock Ltd. (*page 130*).

Southworth, May E., *The Motorist's Luncheon Book.* Copyright 1923 by Harper & Brothers. Published by Harper & Brothers, Publishers, New York (*page 145*).

Spagnol, Elena, *I Panini.* © 1976 Rizzoli Editore Milano. Published by Rizzoli Editore. Translated by permission of Rizzoli Editore (*pages 147, 150, 152 and 154*).

Springer, Rita G., *Caribbean Cookbook.* © Rita G. Springer 1968. Published by Evans Brothers Limited, London. By permission of Evans Brothers Limited (*page 135*).

Spry, Constance and Hume, Rosemary, *The Constance Spry Cookery Book.* First published 1956 by J. M. Dent & Sons Ltd., London. Published by Pan Books Ltd., London 1972. By permission of J. M. Dent & Sons Ltd. (*page 112*).

St. Paul's Greek Orthodox Church, The Women of, *The Art of Greek Cookery.* Copyright © 1961, 1963 by St. Paul's Greek Orthodox Church of Hempstead, New York. Published by Doubleday & Company, Inc., New York. By permission of Doubleday & Company, Inc. (*pages 89, 104*).

St. Stephen's Episcopal Church, *Bayou Cuisine: Its Tradition and Transition.* Copyright 1970 St. Stephen's Episcopal Church. Published by St. Stephen's Episcopal Church, Indianola, Mississippi. By permission of St. Stephen's Episcopal Church (*page 113*).

Stechishin, Savella, *Traditional Ukrainian Cookery.* Copyright, 1957, 1959 by Savella Stechishin. Published by Trident Press Ltd., Winnipeg, Canada 1979. By permission of Trident Press Ltd. (*page 151*).

Stuber, Hedwig Maria, *Ich Helf Dir Kochen.* © BLV Verlagsgesellschaft mbH, München, 1976. Published by BLV Verlagsgesellschaft mbH, Munich. Translated by permission of BLV Verlagsgesellschaft mbH (*pages 121, 134*).

Suzanne, Alfred, *La Cuisine Anglaise et la Pâtisserie.* Privately published by the author, 1894 (*page 148*).

Sverdrup, Elise, *Norway's Delight.* © Elise Sverdrup 1957. Published by Johan Grundt Tanum Forlag, Oslo, 1968. By permission of Forlaget Tanum/Norli A/S (*page 159*).

Theoharous, Anne, *Cooking the Greek Way.* Copyright © 1977 by Anne Theoharous. Published in Great Britain by Methuen Paperbacks Ltd., London. First published as "Cooking and Baking the Greek Way" by Holt, Rinehart and Winston, Inc., New York. By permission of Eyre Methuen Ltd. (*pages 89, 126*).

Toklas, Alice B., *The Alice B. Toklas Cook Book.* Copyright 1954 by Alice B. Toklas. By permission of Harper & Row, Publishers, Inc., New York (*page 142*).

Tschirky, Oscar, *The Cook Book by "Oscar" of the Waldorf.* Copyright 1896 by Oscar Tschirky. Published by The Werner Company, New York (*pages 141, 142*).

Uvezian, Sonia, *The Book of Yogurt.* Copyright © 1978 Sonia Uvezian. Published by 101 Productions, San Francisco. By permission of 101 Productions (*page 95*).

Vaughan, Beatrice, *Yankee Hill-Country Cooking.* Copyright © 1963 by Beatrice Vaughan. Published by The Stephen Greene Press, Brattleboro, Vermont. By permission of The Stephen Greene Press (*page 124*).

Vence, Céline and Courtine, Robert, *The Grand Masters of French Cuisine.* Copyright © 1978 by G. P. Putnam's Sons. Published by G. P. Putnam's Sons, New York. Originally published in France as "Les Grands Maîtres de la Cuisine Française", copyright © 1972 by Bordas. By permission of G.

P. Putnam's Sons (*page 154*).

Verdon, René, *The White House Chef Cookbook.* Copyright © 1967 by René Verdon. Published by Doubleday & Company, Inc., New York. By permission of Doubleday & Company, Inc. (*page 120*).

Vergé, Roger, *Cuisine of the Sun.* © Macmillan London 1979. Published by Macmillan London Ltd. Originally published in France as "Ma Cuisine du Soleil". © Éditions Robert Laffon S.A., 1978. By permission of Macmillan, London and Basingstoke (*page 153*).

Vialardi, Giovanni, *Cucina Borghese.* Published by Roux E Frassati and Co., Turin 1897 (*Page 144*).

Waldo, Myra, *The Complete Round-The-World Cookbook.* Copyright 1954 by Myra Waldo Schwartz. Published by Doubleday & Company, Inc., New York. By permission of Doubleday & Company, Inc. (*page 88*).

Webb, Mrs. Arthur, *Farmhouse Cookery.* Published by George Newnes Ltd., London c.1930. By permission of Miss Gwynneth Webb, heiress to the author (*page 158*).

White, Florence, *Good English Food.* Published by Jonathan Cape Ltd., London 1952. By permission of Jonathan Cape Ltd. (*page 136*).

Willinsky, Grete, *Kochbuch der Büchergilde.* © Büchergilde Gutenberg, Frankfurt am Main 1958. Published by Büchergilde Gutenberg, 1967. Translated by permission of Büchergilde Gutenberg (*pages 125, 160*).

Willinsky, Grete, *Kulinarische Weltreise.* © 1961 by Mary Hahns Kochbuchverlag, Berlin W. Published by Büchergilde Gutenberg, Frankfurt/Main. Translated by permission of Mary Hahn's Kochbuchverlag (*page 92*).

Witty, Helen and Colchie, Elizabeth Schneider, *Better than Store-Bought.* Copyright © 1979 by Helen Witty and Elizabeth Schneider Colchie. Published by Harper & Row, Publishers Inc., New York. By permission of Harper & Row, Publishers Inc. (*page 92*).

Wolfert, Paula, *Mediterranean Cooking.* Copyright © 197 by Paula Wolfert. Published by Quadrangle/The New York Times Book Co., Inc., New York. By permission of the author (*page 126*).

Wolf Trap Associates, *Wolf Trap Picnic Cookbook.* © 197 by the Wolf Trap Associates. Published by the Wolf Trap Associates, Vienna, Virginia. By permission of the Wolf Trap Associates (*page 126*).

Woman's Day Collector's Cook Book. Revised and enlarged. Prepared and edited by the Editors of Woman's Day. Copyright © 1970, 1973 by Fawcett Publications, Inc. Published by Simon & Schuster, New York. By permission of Simon & Schuster, a Division of Gulf & Western Corporation (*page 160*).

Woman's World Book of Salads and Sandwiches. Copyright 1927, Woman's World Magazine Co., Inc. Published by Woman's World Magazine Co., Inc., Chicago (*page 143*).

Zaniboni, Maria Rivieccio, *Cucina e Vini di Napoli e della Campania.* © Copyright 1975 Ugo Mursia, Milan. Published by Ugo Mursia Editore S.p.A. Translated by permission of Ugo Mursia Editore S.p.A. (*pages 119, 124 and 137*).

Acknowledgements and Picture Credits

The Editors of this book are particularly indebted to François Dionot, Maryland, U.S.A.; Gail Duff, Maidstone, Kent; Pierre Olaf Fahlman, chef for the Embassy of Sweden, Washington, U.S.A.; Ann O'Sullivan, Deya, Mallorca; Dr. R. H. Smith, Aberdeen; Stary Zacharias, Virginia, U.S.A.

They also wish to thank the following: Bruce Bolton, New York, U.S.A.; Katherine Boulukos, St. Paul's Greek Orthodox Church, Hempstead, New York, U.S.A.; The British Information Service, New York, U.S.A.; Lesley Coates, Ilford, Essex; Emma Codrington, London; Mimi Errington, London; David Glover, London; Annie Hall, London; Maggi Heinz, London; Pippa Millard, London; Sonya Mills, Oxford; Wendy Morris, London; Dilys Naylor, Kingston-upon-Thames, Surrey; Winona O'Connor, London; Joan Reynolds, The Wheat Flour Institute, Washington, U.S.A.; Robert Rodriguez, American Institute of Baking, Manhattan, Kansas, U.S.A.; Dr. Malcolm Ross, U.S. Geological Survey, Reston, Virginia, U.S.A.; Ann Seranne, Newton, New Jersey, U.S.A.; Tina Walker, London; Donald Bruce White, New York, U.S.A.

Photographers (alphabetically): Tom Belshaw: 4, 16—top, 17, 18—top, 19—top, 32—top, 33—top, 64. John Cook: 7—bottom right (box), 12, 13, 16—bottom, 28, 32—bottom, 33—bottom, 34 to 36, 42—bottom, 43—bottom, 56, 57, 68—bottom, 69—bottom. John Elliott: Cover, 6, 7—top, centre and bottom left (box), 8 to 10, 14, 15, 18—bottom, 19—bottom, 20 to 27, 30, 31—top, 37 to 39, 58, 59, 66, 67, 68—top, 69—top, 70—bottom, 71—bottom, 80 to 86. Louis Klein 2. Aldo Tutino: 31—bottom, 40, 42—top, 43—top, 44 to 55, 60 to 63, 70—top, 71—top, 72 to 79.

All line cuts from Mary Evans Picture Library and private sources.

Colour separations by Gilchrist Ltd.—Leeds, England; and Scan Studios Ltd.—Dublin, Ireland
Typesetting by Camden Typesetters—London, England
Printed and bound by Brepols S.A.—Turnhout, Belgium.